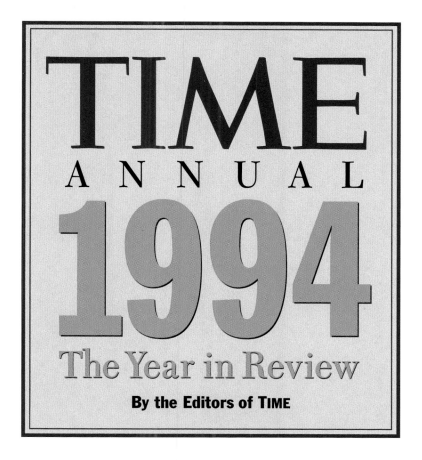

TIME
ANNUAL
1994
The Year in Review
By the Editors of TIME

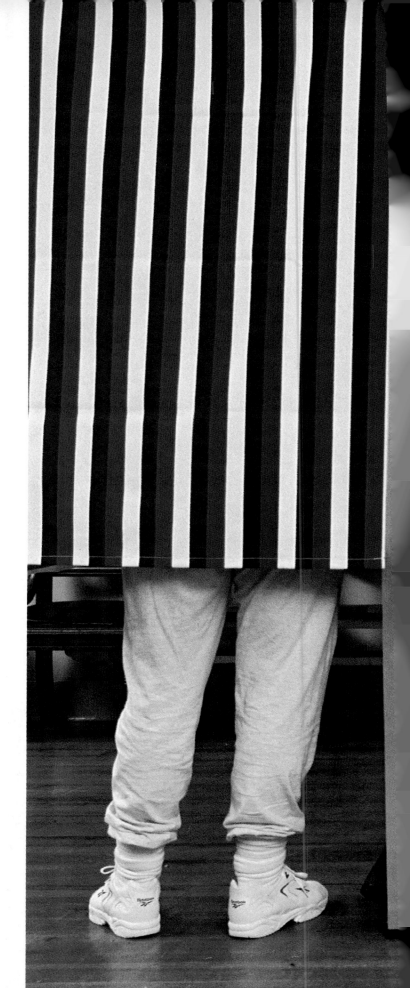

NOVEMBER 8, 1994:
Voters—and spectators—go to the polls
in Muscatine, Iowa.

Copyright 1995 Time Inc. Home Entertainment

Published by TIME Books
Time Inc.
1271 Avenue of the Americas
New York, NY 10020

ISBN #1-883013-05-4
Printed in the United States of America
First edition

TIME ANNUAL

1 9 9 4 : T H E   Y E A R   I N   R E V I E W

SOCIETY

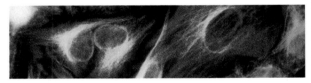

SCIENCE

THE ARTS & MEDIA

PEOPLE

MILESTONES

EDITOR-IN-CHIEF: Norman Pearlstine
EDITORIAL DIRECTOR: Henry Muller
EDITOR OF NEW MEDIA: Walter Isaacson

TIME INC.
CHAIRMAN: Reginald K. Brack Jr.
PRESIDENT, CEO: Don Logan

TIME

Founders: Briton Hadden 1898-1929   Henry R. Luce 1898-1967

MANAGING EDITOR: James R. Gaines
DEPUTY MANAGING EDITOR: John F. Stacks
EXECUTIVE EDITORS: Richard Duncan, James Kelly
ASSISTANT MANAGING EDITORS: Joelle Attinger, Stephen Koepp, Christopher Porterfield
DIRECTOR OF OPERATIONS: Andrew Blau
SENIOR EDITORS: Lee Aitken, Charles P. Alexander, Howard Chua-Eoan, James Collins, Philip Elmer-DeWitt, Marta Fitzgerald Dorion (Operations), Nancy Gibbs, Bruce Handy, Johanna McGeary, Priscilla Painton, Barrett Seaman (Special Projects)
ART DIRECTOR: Arthur Hochstein
CHIEF OF RESEARCH: Betty Satterwhite Sutter
PICTURE EDITOR: Michele Stephenson
ADMINISTRATIVE EDITOR: Suzanne Davis
COPY CHIEF: Susan L. Blair   **PRODUCTION MANAGER:** Gail Music
SENIOR WRITERS: Margaret Carlson, George J. Church, Richard Corliss, Martha Duffy, Elizabeth Gleick, Paul Gray, John Greenwald, Robert Hughes, Richard Lacayo, Michael D. Lemonick, Lance Morrow, Bruce W. Nelan, Jill Smolowe, David Van Biema, Steve Wulf, Richard Zoglin
ASSOCIATE EDITORS: Richard Behar, Janice Castro, Christine Gorman, Sophfronia Scott Gregory, Thomas McCarroll, Anastasia Toufexis **STAFF WRITERS:** Ginia Bellafante, Christopher John Farley, Kevin Fedarko
CONTRIBUTORS: Bonnie Angelo, Laurence I. Barrett, Jesse Birnbaum, Nina Burleigh, Jay Cocks, Barbara Ehrenreich, John Elson, Pico Iyer, Edward L. Jamieson (Consulting Editor), Leon Jaroff, Gregory Jaynes, Michael Kinsley, Charles Krauthammer, Eugene Linden, John Rothchild, Richard Schickel, Walter Shapiro, R.Z. Sheppard, John Skow, Martha Smilgis, Mark Alan Stamaty, Richard Stengel, Andrew Tobias, Claudia Wallis, Michael Walsh, Robert Wright
ASSISTANT EDITORS: Ursula Nadasdy de Gallo, Andrea Dorfman, Brigid O'Hara-Forster, William Tynan, Sidney Urquhart, Jane Van Tassel (Department Heads); Bernard Baumohl, David Bjerklie, Val Castronovo, Georgia Harbison, Ratu Kamlani, Sue Raffety, Susan M. Reed, Elizabeth Rudulph, Susanne Washburn, Linda Young
REPORTERS: Elizabeth L. Bland, Hannah Bloch, Barbara Burke, Tresa Chambers, Tom Curry, Kathryn Jackson Fallon, Janice M. Horowitz, Jeanette Isaac, Daniel S. Levy, Lina Lofaro, Lisa McLaughlin, Lawrence Mondi, Alice Park, Michael Quinn, Jeffery C. Rubin, Andrea Sachs, Alain L. Sanders, David Seideman, Sribala Subramanian, David E. Thigpen
COPY DESK: Barbara Dudley Davis, Judith Anne Paul, Shirley Barden Zimmerman (Deputies); Dora Fairchild, Evelyn Hannon, Jill Ward (Copy Coordinators); Minda Bikman, Doug Bradley, Robert Braine, Bruce Christopher Carr, Barbara Collier, Julia Van Buren Dickey, Irene Gashurov, Judith Kales, Sharon Kapnick, Claire Knopf, Jeannine Laverty, Ellin Martens, Peter J. McGullam, M.M. Merwin, Maria A. Paul, Jane Rigney, Elyse Segelken, Terry Stoller, Amelia Weiss (Copy Editors)
CORRESPONDENTS: Joelle Attinger (Chief), Richard Hornik (Deputy, Foreign), Janice C. Simpson (Deputy, Domestic) **Chief Political Correspondent:** Michael Kramer **Washington Contributing Editor:** Hugh Sidey **Senior Correspondents:** David Aikman, Jonathan Beaty, Sandra Burton, Douglas Frantz, J. Madeleine Nash, Richard N. Ostling **National Correspondents:** Margot Hornblower, Jon D. Hull, Jack E. White **Diplomatic Correspondent:** J.F.O. McAllister **Washington:** Dan Goodgame, Ann Blackman, James Carney, John F. Dickerson, Michael Duffy, Jay Peterzell, Suneel Ratan, Elaine Shannon, Ann M. Simmons, Dick Thompson, Mark Thompson, Karen Tumulty, Douglas Waller, Adam Zagorin, Melissa August **New York:** John Moody, Edward Barnes, Massimo Calabresi, Adam Cohen, Marguerite Michaels, Sharon Epperson, Jenifer Mattos **Boston:** Sam Allis **Chicago:** Elizabeth Taylor, Wendy Cole **Detroit:** William McWhirter **Atlanta:** Michael Riley **Austin:** S.C. Gwynne **Miami:** Cathy Booth, Tammerlin Drummond **Los Angeles:** Jordan Bonfante, Patrick E. Cole, Elaine Lafferty, Jeanne McDowell, Sylvester Monroe, Jeffrey Ressner, James Willwerth **San Francisco:** David S. Jackson **Denver:** Richard Woodbury
Europe: James O. Jackson **London:** Barry Hillenbrand **Paris:** Thomas Sancton **Brussels:** Jay Branegan **Bonn:** Bruce van Voorst **Central Europe:** James L. Graff **Moscow:** John Kohan, Sally B. Donnelly **Rome:** Greg Burke **Istanbul:** James Wilde **Jerusalem:** Lisa Beyer **Cairo:** Dean Fischer **Beirut:** Lara Marlowe **Nairobi:** Andrew Purvis **Johannesburg:** Scott MacLeod **New Delhi:** Jefferson Penberthy **Beijing:** Jaime A. FlorCruz **Hong Kong:** William Dowell **Southeast Asia:** Frank Gibney Jr. **Tokyo:** Edward W. Desmond **Ottawa:** Gavin Scott **Latin America:** Laura López
Administration: Susan Lynd, Sheila Charney, Donald N. Collins, Corliss M. Duncan, Ann V. King, Anne D. Moffett, Sharon Roberts, Judith R. Stoler **News Desks:** Pamela H. Thompson, Brian Doyle, Anderson Fils-Aime, Eileen Harkin, Waits L. May III, Susanna Schrobsdorff, Alexander Smith, Diana Tollerson, Ann Drury Wellford, Mary Wormley
ART: Janet Waegel (Deputy Art Director); Linda Louise Freeman (Covers); Steve Conley, Jamie Elsis, Paul Lussier, Thomas M. Miller, Sharon Okamoto (Associate Art Directors); Joseph Aslaender, Kenneth B. Smith (Assistant Art Directors); Ron Plyman, Leah M. Purcell (Designers) **Maps and Charts:** Joe Lertola (Associate Graphics Director); Paul J. Pugliese (Chief of Cartography); Steven D. Hart, Deborah L. Wells **Administration:** Carrie A. Zimmerman
PHOTOGRAPHY: Richard L. Booth, MaryAnne Golon, Hillary Raskin (Deputy Picture Editors); Robert B. Stevens (Associate Picture Editor); Kevin J. McVea (Operations); Sarah Buffum, Gary Roberts, Cristina T. Scalet, Nancy Smith-Alam, Marie Tobias, Mary Worrell-Bousquette (Assistant Editors) **Bureaus:** Martha Bardach, Paul Durrant, Leny Heinen, Stanley Kayne, Barbara Nagelsmith, Mark Rykoff, Anni Rubinger, Mary Thompson, Simonetta Toraldo **Photographers:** Forrest Anderson, Terry Ashe, P.F. Bentley, William Campbell, Greg Davis, Dirck Halstead, Barry Iverson, Kenneth Jarecke, Cynthia Johnson, Shelly Katz, Steve Liss, Peter Magubane, Christopher Morris, Robin Moyer, Carl Mydans, James Nachtwey, Robert Nickelsberg, David Rubinger, Anthony Suau, Ted Thai, Diana Walker
MAKEUP: Robyn M. Mathews (Chief)
TECHNOLOGY: Ken Baierlein, Hope Almash, David Richardson (Managers); Nora Jupiter, Kevin Kelly, George Mendel, Peter K. Niceberg, Michael M. Sheehan, Lamarr Tsufura
IMAGING: Mark Stelzner (Manager); Gerard Abrahamsen, Raphael Joa, Lois Rubenstein (Supervisors); Steven Cadicamo, Charlotte Coco, Michael Dohne, John Dragonetti, Paul Gettinger, Carl Leidig, Linda Parker, Mark P. Polomski, Richard Shaffer, David Spatz, Lorri Stenton, Paul White
PRODUCTION: Trang Ba Chuong, Theresa Kelliher, L. Rufino-Armstrong (Supervisors); Silvia Castañeda Contreras, Osmar Escalona, Garry Hearne, Sandra Maupin, Michael Skinner
ADMINISTRATION: Alan J. Abrams, Catherine M. Barnes, Denise Brown, Breena Clarke, Anne M. Considine, Tosca LaBoy, Marilyn V.S. McClenahan, Ann Morrell, Teresa D. Sedlak, Marianne Sussman, Raymond Violini
EDITORIAL FINANCE: Nancy Krauter (Manager); Carl Harmon, Morgan Krug (Domestic); Camille Sanabria (News Service); Linda D. Vartoogian, Wayne Chun (Pictures)
LETTERS: Amy Musher (Chief); Gloria J. Hammond (Deputy); Marian Powers (Administration)

TIME INC. EDITORIAL OPERATIONS
Director: Sheldon Czapnik **Editorial Services:** Claude Boral (General Manager); Thomas E. Hubbard (Photo Lab); Larry Walden McDonald (Library); Beth Bencini Zarcone (Picture Collection); Thomas Smith (Technology); **Editorial Technology:** Dennis Chesnel
TIME INTERNATIONAL
Managing Editor: Karsten Prager
Assistant Managing Editor: José M. Ferrer III
Regional Editors: Donald Morrison (Asia), Christopher Redman (Europe), George Russell (The Americas), John Saar (Middle East), Jacob Young (South Pacific)
Senior Writers: Michael S. Serrill, James Walsh
Associate Editor: Barbara Rudolph
Staff Writer: Emily Mitchell
Contributors: Robert Ball, Christopher Ogden, Frederick Painton, Anthony Spaeth, George M. Taber, Rod Usher
Assistant Editors: Tam Martinides Gray (Research Chief), Ariadna Victoria Rainert (Administration), Oscar Chiang, Mary McC. Fernandez, Lois Gilman, Valerie Johanna Marchant, Adrianne Jucius Navon
Reporters: Julie K.L. Dam, Leslie Dickstein, Tamala M. Edwards, Margaret Emery, Sinting Lai, Stacy Perman, Megan Rutherford
Art: Jane Frey (Senior Associate Director); Billy Powers (Associate Director); Victoria Nightingale (Designer)
Photography: Julia Richer (Associate Editor); Eleanor Taylor, Karen Zakrison (Assistant Editors)
Makeup: Alison E. Ruffley (Chief)
Administration: Helga Halaki, Barbara Milberg

PRESIDENT: Elizabeth Valk Long
PUBLISHER: John E. Haire
FINANCIAL DIRECTOR: Daniel M. Rubin
CONSUMER MARKETING DIRECTOR: Kenneth Godshall
ASSOCIATE PUBLISHER: Richard A. Raskopf
REGIONAL SALES DIRECTOR: Thomas M. Ott
MARKETING DIRECTOR: Linda McCutcheon Connealy
PUBLIC AFFAIRS DIRECTOR: Robert Pondiscio

TIME ANNUAL
1994: THE YEAR IN REVIEW

Editor
Edward L. Jamieson

Managing Editor
Kelly Knauer

Design Direction
Walter Bernard, Milton Glaser

Art Director
Nancy Eising

Research Director
Leah Gordon

Picture Editor
Rose Quinn Keyser

Design Associates
Chalkley Calderwood, Linda Root

Information Design
Joe Lertola, Steve Hart, Paul Pugliese

Research Associates
Valerie Marchant, Sue Raffety

Editorial Production
Michael Skinner

Copy Desk
Doug Bradley, Ellin Martens

NEW BUSINESS DEVELOPMENT

Director
David Gitow

Senior Development Manager
Peter Shapiro

Fulfillment Director
Mary Warner McGrade

Operations Director
David Rivchin

Production Director
John Calvano

Associate Development Manager
Rebecca Bradshaw

Development Assistant
Dawn Weland

The work of the following TIME writers, editors and contributors is included in this volume:

Laurence I. Barrett, Lisa Beyer, Margaret Carlson, George J. Church, Howard Chua-Eoan, Richard Corliss, Philip Elmer-DeWitt, Martha Duffy, Michael Duffy, John Elson, Christopher John Farley, Kevin Fedarko, Nancy Gibbs, Paul Gray, John Greenwald, Sophronia Scott Gregory, Bruce Handy, William A. Henry III, Barry Hillenbrand, Margot Hornblower, Robert Hughes, John Kohan, Michael Kramer, Richard Lacayo, Michael D. Lemonick, Eugene Linden, Lara Marlowe, J.F.O. McAllister, J. Madeleine Nash, Bruce W. Nelan, Richard N. Ostling, Andrew Purvis, James Reston Jr., Richard Shickel, Hugh Sidey, John Skow, Jill Smolowe, John F. Stacks, Anastasia Toufexis, David Van Biema, Michael Walsh, Jack E. White, Paul A. Witteman, Richard Zoglin.

Thanks to:

Ken Baierlein, Robin Bierstedt, Susan L. Blair, Andrew Blau, Jay Colton, Richard Duncan, Linda Louise Freeman, Arthur Hochstein, Nora Jupiter, Kevin Kelly, Nancy Krauter, Morgan Krug, Michael D. Lemonick, Bob Marshall, Robyn Mathews, Gail Music, Peter Niceberg, Lamarr Tsufura, Michael M. Sheehan, Michele Stephenson, Betty Satterwhite Sutter, Linda Vartoogian, Janet Waegel. Special thanks to Mark Stelzner and the TIME Imaging Staff.

IN THE EASY ILLUMINATION OF HINDSIGHT, YEARS CAN TAKE on a character uniquely their own. Like all years, 1994 saw revelations, discoveries that ranged in scale from the fleeting

THE YEAR IN REVIEW

glimpse of a long-sought quark to a vast collision in outer space. It brought tidings from the past in the form of fossil teeth 4.4 million years old; it heralded the future, as U.S. voters swept Republicans to control of the U.S. Congress and South Africans inaugurated Nelson Mandela as their President.

Yet more than most, 1994 was a year devoted to anniversaries and remembering. As aging veterans returned to Normandy, and music and mud returned to Woodstock, Americans paused to reflect on the passing of an era, a pause accentuated by the loss of two figures of near mythic dimension—Jacqueline Kennedy Onassis and Richard Nixon. This book records not simply a memorable year, but a year of memory.

1994

IMAGES

POLITICAL UPHEAVAL. OLYMPIC heroism—and villainy. Incomprehensible acts of violence, sometimes engulfing whole countries. Tabloid spectacle. 1994 proved to be a memorable, if occasionally frightening, year for photojournalists. On the following pages are some of the year's most compelling photos—and the stories behind them.

MAJORITY RULERS When an exultant Senator Bob Dole and Speaker-to-be Newt Gingrich held a postelection photo opportunity on "Dole's Beach," the sun porch outside the Senator's office, Terry Ashe bolted from the pack of photographers and shot this unusual perspective through a window inside the building.

**It's more than I thought it would be.** —NEWT GINGRICH ON HIS NEW POSITION

CITIZEN MANDELA

Much to its delight (for the most part), South Africa underwent what may have been the most orderly revolution in history. "There were such immense crowds, there was such a crush, often you couldn't get a shot," says photographer Louise Gubb, who followed Nelson Mandela on the campaign trail. "Blacks, whites— everyone wanted to see him." Here Mandela was arriving at a Johannesburg hospital to visit the victims of a right-wing bombing. Gubb got the picture by climbing onto the hospital's entrance.

IMAGES

WOODSTOCK LIVES

About 350,000 fans showed up in Saugerties, New York, to mark the 25th anniversary of Woodstock I (as it must now be known) with three more days of peace, music, mud and corporate sponsorship. Michael Lawton took this shot of Woodstock II with a panoramic camera mounted on a 10-foot pole.

BASEBALL DIES

Stee-rike! A labor squabble succeeded in doing what the Depression, two World Wars and an earthquake hadn't: it snuffed out the World Series. The strike, whose results are seen here at Mile High Stadium in Denver, killed a season of white-hot pennant races and superlatives on the diamond, a season when two players were making credible runs at Roger Maris's home run record. It also showed that—despite their claims otherwise— baseball's wealthy owners and players cared about only one stat: the bottom line.

"SAY IT AIN'T SO." —A fan's sign at Yankee Stadium

SARAJEVO

Though the U.N. and NATO made a lot of noise, they ultimately managed to do precious little to protect Bosnian civilians, who were targets in their nation's civil war. Photographer Christopher Morris: "This street is where the Serbs were sniping on civilians. The kids were safe because they were behind a building. They were waiting to run across the street when they saw me. The kid had a toy gun, and he started mimicking shooting it. People everywhere send their kids out to play, but in Sarajevo, it's like you're sending them out to play on a superhighway."

RWANDAN REFUGEE CAMP

Rwanda was convulsed by some of the most horrific genocidal violence ever seen, with hundreds of thousands, mainly Tutsi, slaughtered by the Hutu-led army and militias. James Nachtwey took this photo at one of the refugee camps in Zaire that quickly filled with desperate Rwandans. At the time, cholera was sweeping the camps; thousands were ultimately killed by the disease. Here the dead are being gathered up by bulldozers for mass burial.

OLYMPIC FINALS **Seconds into her long program at the Olympic finals in Lillehammer, Norway, Tonya Harding asked the judges for permission to fix a broken lace and restart her routine. Having been at an earlier competition where Harding had had a problem with a clasp on her costume, photographer Jack Smith had a premonition: "I wanted to be close to the judges in case something happened." He positioned himself accordingly and got this shot. Harding finished eighth and won a role in a B movie.**

OLYMPIC TRIALS In Detroit, skater Nancy Kerrigan's knee was clubbed by a man later linked to Harding. Kerrigan ultimately won a silver medal and became America's sweetheart, until she proved cranky at Disney World.

"Why me?" —NANCY KERRIGAN

IMAGES

NO REMORSE Paul Hill, shortly after his arrest in Pensacola, Florida, for killing the head of an abortion clinic and his escort.

MOTHER'S PRAYERS The nation gawked in anger and disbelief when Susan Smith of Union, South Carolina, confessed to killing her two young sons, ages 3 years and 14 months, after earlier claiming the boys had been abducted in a carjacking. Shortly after her arrest, Jonathan Tedder took this photograph through a window of the York County Detention Center as Smith was being led from a holding cell. "She had no idea that I was taking her picture."

" Cry if you will, but make up your mind that you will never let your life end like this. **"** —THE REV. WILLIE JAMES CAMPBELL, ADMONISHING MOURNERS

YUMMY'S FUNERAL The story only got worse: three days after killing a 14-year-old girl in a botched revenge shooting, Chicago gang member Robert ("Yummy") Sandifer, 11, was executed by two teenage confederates. Steve Liss photographed the funeral and found the experience deeply disturbing: "It was embarrassing, to be perfectly blunt. Photographers sticking cameras in the coffin—the whole thing should have been closed to the press. I stayed to the side, but I still felt like I didn't belong there."

IN THE SPOTLIGHT:

MIDDLE EAST NOBELISTS
After decades of hatred and terror, they embarked on a gutsy journey toward peace.

MICKEY MOUSE
A stone wall of historians and residents turned back Disney's march to Manassas.

KING HUSSEIN
A Johnny-come-lately to the peace process, but welcomed all the same.

ALAN GREENSPAN
The Fed boss and former saxman kept interest up with his high notes.

JIMMY CARTER
Born again as a free-lance diplomat, he toasted peace from Seoul to Serbia.

GERRY ADAMS
Sinn Fein's main man: from apologist for terrorism to advocate of peace.

LORENA BOBBITT
Found innocent. But that didn't end the argument: was it justice—or victim chic?

MARION BARRY
Lazarus-like, the crack politician came back from prison to run Washington again.

BOBBY RAY INMAN
He said no to running the Pentagon in a spectacular televised self-immolation.

WEBSTER HUBBELL
Fishy tax dealings hooked the
Clintons' man at Justice.

JESSE HELMS
Now running the Senate Foreign Relations
Committee; still running off at the mouth.

HAFEZ AL-ASSAD
The terrorists' favorite banker welcomed
peace pilgrim Bill Clinton to Damascus.

PAULA JONES
Her accusations against the President
were both tawdry—and tardy.

NEWT GINGRICH
Tom fell down and broke his crown,
and Newt came, rumbling laughter.

LEON PANETTA
Could the new chief of staff stand up to
the White House's chief problem?

DAVID KESSLER
Where there's smoke, there's ire: the FDA's
first hand choked on second-hand fumes.

PRINCESS DIANA
Was she had by a cad? Major James Hewitt
claimed Di was his mistress for 5 years.

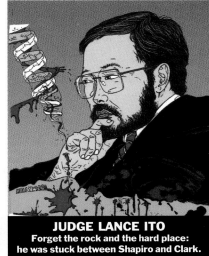

JUDGE LANCE ITO
Forget the rock and the hard place:
he was stuck between Shapiro and Clark.

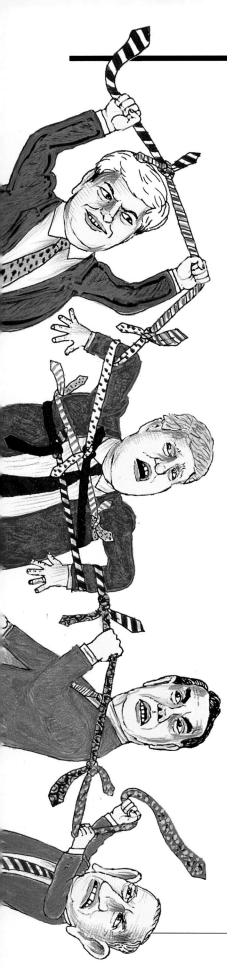

"MAYBE IT'S THE BOY IN ME."

DR. JACK KEVORKIAN, explaining his passion for research into death

"What the President lacks in skill, talent, imagination, technique and swing, he more than makes up for with desire and hustle."

WYNTON MARSALIS, on Clinton's sax playing

"Only fruits wear earrings."

MARGE SCHOTT, Cincinatti Reds owner, objecting to players with pierced ears

"I can't really remember the names of the clubs we went to."

SHAQUILLE O'NEAL, on being asked if he visited the Parthenon on a trip to Greece

"Shaking hands with Bill Clinton is a fullbody sexual experience."

Author JUDITH KRANTZ

"I'm not an expert on

"PRESIDENT CLINTON HAD A BILL, E-I-E-I-O. AND IN THAT BILL WAS LOTS OF PORK, E-I-E-I-O."

SEN. AL D'AMATO, singing to the tune of "Old MacDonald" on the Senate floor during the crime-bill debate

"YOU MAY NOT KNOW MY WORK, BUT I'VE SEEN ALL YOUR MOVIES."

MIKHAIL GORBACHEV, introducing himself to Paul Newman in a Los Angeles hotel

"I was thinking of you last night, Helmut, because I watched the sumo wrestling on television."

BILL CLINTON to 280-pound German leader Helmut Kohl at a NATO conference

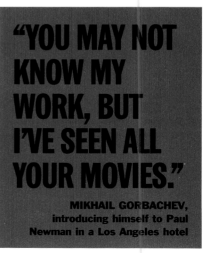

"IT'S A FAIRLY EMBARRASSING SITUATION TO ADMIT THAT WE CAN'T FIND 90 PERCENT OF THE UNIVERSE."

DR. BRUCE H. MARGON, astrophysicist, on missing matter in the universe

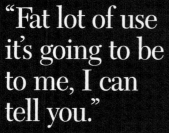

"Fat lot of use it's going to be to me, I can tell you."

PRINCE CHARLES, when informed by a Bedouin that camel's milk is an aphrodisiac

"IT'S NOT LIKE BILL TO PULL DOWN HIS PANTS."

GENNIFER FLOWERS, on Paula Jones' accusations against the President

"Al Gore is so boring his Secret Service code name is Al Gore."

AL GORE, at the Gridiron Club dinner

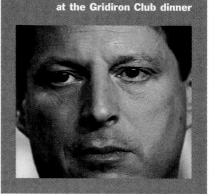

"Every time I'm about to go to bed with a guy I have to look at my dad's name all over his underwear."

MARCI KLEIN, Calvin Klein's daughter

handling something like that."

Richard Nixon, on Whitewater

"Mrs. Cédras was . . . attractive. She was slim and very attractive."

JIMMY CARTER, describing his peace efforts in Haiti

"I am not an Uncle Tom. . . I'm going to be here for 40 years . . . get used to it."

Justice CLARENCE THOMAS

"A long time ago being crazy meant something. Nowadays everybody's crazy."

CHARLES MANSON, to Diane Sawyer

"THIS IS SO CORNY, THIS IS SO DUMB. I HATE IT."

NANCY KERRIGAN, on being in a parade at Disney World.

RIGHT TURN

The Republicans stampeded to the biggest election sweep in years— but could they move beyond obstruction to create real change?

THE RUMBLING STARTED IN THE EAST, WHERE the polls opened first. Within hours the political seismologists at Voter News Service in Manhattan were getting off-the-chart readings from their exit polls. Tapping at rented computers in a windowless warren 30 floors up in the World Trade Center, analysts spent Election Day sifting the results of more than 10,000 field interviews by exit pollers who questioned voters as they emerged from 1,039 polling places across the country. By 11:45 a.m., Murray Edelman, the veteran director of the operation, expressed astonishment that for the first time in the 12-year history of exit polling, a clear majority of voters said they had cast ballots for a Republican candidate for Congress. Distrusting their data, Edelman and his colleagues double-checked individual precincts for glitches, but the rumbling only grew louder and spread westward. By 1 p.m., Edelman stated with confidence that "the Republicans will have a big win," taking control of the Senate and perhaps even the House.

The exit polls were right: the breadth and depth of the Republican victory—a 52-seat pickup in the House, nine in the Senate, 11 in the Governors' mansions— stunned Republicans as well as Democrats. Said David Wilhelm, departing chairman of the Democratic National Committee: "We got our butts kicked." A simmering American electorate, angry at a Washington establishment more concerned with serving the vested interests that pay for its campaigns than with the declining living standards and perceived moral decay of the rest of America, threw much of the country's governing class out of office. "We always vote for change, and we never get it," said Steve Douglas, 39, of Detroit, a house painter and Democrat who voted Republican this time.

Gone was 40 years of Democratic control of the lower house of Congress. Gone was the Speaker of the House of Representatives, the first holder of that office to be defeated at the polls since the 1860s. Gone were Democratic Governors in at least 11 states. Gone, perhaps permanently this time, was the once solid Democratic domination of the Southern states. Gone was the most eloquent defender of the liberal faith in America, New York Governor Mario Cuomo.

And if not gone, certainly drastically diminished was the prospect of William Jefferson Clinton's gaining a second term as President. "A national sea change," he called it, as he struggled to swim back into the ideological center. But he sounded more like a drowning man. Voters were saying they felt misled. "I voted for him, but he's just got it all wrong about where we stand on gays and guns and taxes. He sold us a bill of goods is what he did," said Jerry Smith, 42, a machinist in Oklahoma City, Oklahoma, and a new convert to the G.O.P.

Replacing the Democratic liberals was a herd of Re-

TWO HEADS BETTER? They scalded the Democrats on election night, but the future might see Newt Gingrich and Bob Dole battling each other to lead the resurgent G.O.P.

publicans ranging from the born again to the libertarian, led by the china-and-crystal-smashing Congressman from suburban Atlanta, Newt Gingrich, who would be the new Speaker of the House. After a short burst of conciliation on election night, he seemed disinclined to throw Bill Clinton a rope. The President, he said, would be "very, very dumb" to try to stand in the way of the new conservative agenda. And to sharpen the point of the election, he called the Clintons "counterculture McGovernicks." Weeks before the election, Gingrich had drafted detailed plans to help the Democrats clean out their desks and prepare the walking papers for more than 3,000 Democratic staffers. Like some kindly Scrooge, the Speaker-in-waiting explained that he wanted to let the staff members know where they stood as soon as possible, what with Christmas coming.

Already wheezing before the election, the New Deal coalition that had kept Democrats in power for most of the past six decades collapsed and would have to be replaced. Meanwhile, Republicans had achieved a pregnant moment when their 25-year realignment of party power seemed on the verge of success. At the White House, the finger pointing began. Blame fell heaviest on the President's most liberal advisers, including George Stephanopoulos, deputy White House chief of staff Harold Ickes and pollster Stan Greenberg. The trouble was, as an Administration centrist put it, "the liberal adviser who has got the President in the most trouble is the one he can't fire"—Hillary Clinton.

AND THE PRESIDENT *WAS* IN TROUBLE, AS THE full impact of the election on the Capitol Hill power structure became clear. Senator Alfonse D'Amato, the New York Republican, would become the next chairman of the Senate Banking Committee, from which position he could hector the White House with further investigations of Whitewater. The conservative Orrin Hatch would be vetting the President's judicial appointments as head of the Senate Judiciary Committee. And paleoconservative Senator Jesse Helms—who would later warn the President not to visit military bases in North Carolina without a bodyguard—would be tormenting the striped-pants set as chairman of the Foreign Relations Committee. Helms fired a shot across the bow in a letter to U.S. Secretary of State Warren Christopher after the election. He intended to work "in a spirit of mutual friendship and cooperation," he claimed, adding, "It would be less than candid of me to fail to acknowledge that there must necessarily be adjustments in the broad focus of the Administration's foreign policies."

Helms and the other Republicans had reason to be cocksure of their standing. Not a single Republican member of the Senate or the House was defeated; not a single Republican resident of a Governor's mansion was evicted. The anger of the electorate was anything but inchoate. It was neatly targeted. The Democrats were seen—not unreasonably, given their control of the White House and Capitol Hill—as the Establishment, and they were made to pay. The anger was not indis-

EDWARD KENNEDY
Senator • Massachusetts

Confounding widespread predictions that he would fail to win reelection at last, the embattled liberal Senator waged an energetic campaign against challenger Mitt Romney. Sounding sharp in two televised debates, Kennedy won his sixth term by the surprisingly large margin of 58% to 41%.

DIANNE FEINSTEIN
Senator • California

The first-term Democrat found herself in a tough campaign against a multimillionaire House member from Santa Barbara, Michael Huffington. The G.O.P. "Stealth" candidate poured $25 million into TV advertising and made few personal appearances. Feinstein's margin: a slim 123,000 votes.

GEORGE W. BUSH
Governor • Texas

Running against the highly popular and highly quotable Governor Ann Richards, the oldest son of the former President swept to victory in Clinton-unfriendly Texas. His brother Jeb, however, failed to win his race for Governor in Florida—though he lost to incumbent Lawton Chiles by only 75,000 votes.

criminate. The two most outrageous Republican offerings, the vacuous Michael Huffington and the felonious Oliver North, together spent more than $40 million on their egregious ambitions and lost anyway.

That voters were angry was not the surprise. They were plenty angry in 1992, when George Bush felt the pain after one term for failing to pay attention to the concerns of average Americans. But the Democrats had thought they were the solution, not the problem. They had become entranced with the big-picture economic statistics that showed a growing economy, rising employment, low inflation and a shrinking deficit. What they missed was the undiminished economic anxiety of the large working class. America might be No. 1 again in productivity, but the middle-class workers who made it so had seen many of their colleagues laid off, had been forced in some cases to settle for temporary jobs and in general had suffered an actual decline in disposable in-

& LOSERS

MARIO CUOMO
Governor • New York

Admired as the most eloquent liberal voice in America, Cuomo was also derided as the "Hamlet of Albany" for his indecision. He was soundly defeated by George Pataki, a state Senator who pledged to cut taxes 25% and re-institute the death penalty in New York, a step Cuomo had famously opposed.

TOM FOLEY
Representative • Washington

Foley earned an unenviable distinction: in losing to George Nethercutt, he became the first Speaker of the House to fail in re-election since William Pennington in the 1860s. Refusing to advance Congressional reform, Foley was seen as embodying the old-boy system voters blamed for gridlock.

OLIVER NORTH
Senator • Virginia

The conservative former National Security Office adviser—who was instrumental in operating the Iran-*contra* fiasco in the Reagan White House—was defeated by incumbent Charles Robb. North spent some $18 million, much of it raised from national direct-mail solicitation, in his losing bid.

modities trading and finagled a real-estate deal didn't exactly make them appear to be champions of the hard-pressed middle class.

The Republicans cast themselves again as enemies of Big Government, and thus as friends of the people. But the new G.O.P. majority on Capitol Hill was no less beholden to the special interests for campaign funds than were the Democrats. It had been no more willing to unravel the elaborate system of entitlements like farm subsidies and Social Security and a variety of tax preferences that favor the rich and the established and make real tax relief for the working class affordable. Some in the G.O.P. had as great a penchant for social engineering, in the form of making moral rules for the country to follow, as the Democrats did for contriving Great Society programs.

GINGRICH VOWED THAT IN THE FIRST 100 DAYS of the new Congress he would ram through votes on the central tenets of the "Contract with America" that he and his House candidates signed in September on the Capitol steps. The document was heavy with popular goodies like tax cuts and new defense spending. It was light on specific cuts in federal spending that would finance these apple pies without swelling the budget deficit, pushing up interest rates and leaving the bill for America's grandchildren. The Republican answer to this quandary was a device called the balanced-budget amendment: a proposed constitutional amendment that purported to force across-the-board spending cuts. Other key elements of the G.O.P. contract also looked likely to pass: a measure that would let the President veto individual items in the budget, a tax cut for capital gains on investments and some sort of tax cut for families with children.

Yet in victory the G.O.P. itself was still divided, between the excitable Gingrich and the more moderate Senate majority leader, Bob Dole; between the busybody moralists of the far right and libertarian problem solvers like Massachusetts Governor William Weld. While making war on Clinton, they would probably make war on themselves. Gingrich and Dole had never liked each other, especially since the time Gingrich called Dole "the tax collector for the welfare state." And soon the contest for the G.O.P. presidential nomination would begin to play out on the floors of the Senate and House.

It was certainly premature to declare a permanent Republican hegemony in the capitol. The G.O.P. had managed at last to discredit the Democrats, root and branch. What it had not done, however—and would have to accomplish over the next two years—was convince voters that Republicans in Congress could move beyond heckling and obstructing to meet the public demand for leaner, more effective, more accountable government. If not, the 1994 election would be remembered as just another blip, like the 1946 vote that won the G.O.P. only fleeting control of Congress. To paraphrase Victor Hugo: A great army can capture an enemy city, but to rule it requires a great idea. ■

come. At the same time, the upper class had actually increased its share of the nation's abundance.

Clinton did understand these facts as he campaigned for the presidency in 1992. His mantra was that people who "work hard and play by the rules" were getting worked over by pols who played around with the rules. But once in office, Clinton seemed not so much a friend of the working class as a captive of the economic and cultural élites. Most disastrously for the Democrats, he failed to understand that the most powerful expression of middle-class economic anxiety was an insistence that the government lighten the burden of taxation by shrinking itself and its role in the nation's life. Yet Clinton's top-down, bureaucratic health-care proposal, while rightly aimed at one of the prime causes of middle-class anxiety, was easily made to look like the epitome of tax-and-spend liberal programs. That he and his wife had benefited from a chummy round of com-

KING *of the* HILL
★ ★ ★ ★

How Newt Gingrich, rebel with a cause, rose to rule the House

OCTOBER 1994: AT THE AMERICAN LEGION HALL in Tullahoma, Tennessee, 200 people waited to hear Newt Gingrich rouse them with the message he would deliver in 137 congressional districts by Election Day: 1) Washington was the enemy; 2) the place should be dynamited; 3) he and his party held the torch. The message wasn't new: almost since he first came to Washington in 1979, from a House district in suburban Atlanta, Gingrich had preached and practiced a strategy of confrontation intended to break the Democratic hold on Congress by fracturing the place itself. Gingrich, a man willing to stick out his tongue at some venerable American institutions, had become a sort of Establishment guerrilla, attacking the House he so badly wanted to lead.

In the election that followed, Gingrich realized his dream. Surprising just about everyone but the fire-brand Representative, the Republican sweep capped Gingrich's long crusade with the honor he had sought for decades: he would be the new Speaker of the House. A good part of the credit for the romp went to Gingrich, who over the years had given ranks of younger G.O.P. candidates their model of armed Republicanism. Through GOPAC, the political-action committee he had led since 1986, Gingrich had conducted seminars and sent out thousands of tapes to candidates for everything from city council seats to statewide offices, instructing them on how to do in liberal opponents.

The son of an Army officer, Gingrich had his eye on elective office even before he finished work on his Ph.D. in history at Tulane University. After unsuccessful tries for a House seat in 1974 and '76, he entered Congress with the class of 1978 and soon founded the Conservative Opportunity Society, a group of right-wing Young Turks. In 1981 his 19-year marriage to his high school math teacher Jacqueline Battley broke up in painful circumstances. She was in the hospital recovering from cancer when he came to discuss the divorce terms. Remarried to Marianne Ginther, he remained close to his two daughters from his first marriage.

Once in Congress, Gingrich excelled at turning ordinary exchanges into blood feuds. He gained his reputation as a giant killer in 1987 when he brought the ethics charges against Speaker Jim Wright that led to Wright's resignation two years later—the same year Gingrich successfully ran for minority whip. More interested in plotting revolutions than in passing bills, Gingrich never made much of a mark as a legislator. His ideas, which often did not come to grips with the particulars of policymaking, were less important than his signature mood of righteous belligerence.

A onetime assistant professor of history who aspired to be "the leading teacher of 21st century American civilization," Gingrich offered a vision of the next century that bathed historical trend spotting in the glow of Alvin Toffler's futurism—and that often seemed just plain goofy. But in the '94 election, he came up with a grand strategy that tied up his favorite themes in a voter-friendly package, the "Contract with America." Among its promises: term limits, a balanced-budget amendment and some kind of welfare reform. Republican candidates embraced the contract, and when they swept to victory it became their action plan for the term's first 100 days, in which they claimed they would pass its provisions, dramatically reshaping the national agenda.

Gingrich was elated by the Republican sweep, so much so that he soon made a few of his typical overstatements. He denounced the Clintons as

Contract with America
★ ★ ★

1. FISCAL RESPONSIBILITY ACT
A balanced-budget/tax-limitation amendment.

2. TAKING BACK OUR STREETS ACT
Limit appeals in death sentences; provide more funding for prisons and police.

3. PERSONAL RESPONSIBILITY ACT
Limit funds to unwed mothers; impose "two years and out" provisions on welfare recipients.

4. FAMILY REINFORCEMENT ACT
Enforce child-support payments.

5. AMERICAN DREAM RESTORATION ACT
Provide a $500-per-child tax credit.

6. NATIONAL SECURITY RESTORATION ACT
Restore spending on national defense.

7. SENIOR CITIZENS FAIRNESS ACT
Repeal the 1993 Clinton tax hikes on Social Security benefits.

8. JOB CREATION & WAGE ENHANCEMENT ACT
Cut taxes on capital gains.

9. COMMON SENSE LEGAL REFORM ACT
Enact "loser pays" laws; limit damage awards in product liability and malpractice suits.

10. CITIZEN LEGISLATURE ACT
Impose term limits on Congress.

DID I SAY THAT? A strong communicator—but with more fervor than self-control—Gingrich often found his foot in his mouth.

"counter-culture McGovernicks" and claimed on a TV show, without offering proof, that one-fourth of the White House staff was guilty of drug use. He also created a firestorm when he declared that in the forthcoming session House Republicans would quickly introduce a constitutional amendment to permit school prayer, an item not included in the contract. Under pressure, Gingrich put the issue on a back burner.

MEANWHILE GINGRICH USED THE TIME BEtween the election and the convening of the new Congress to fashion House Republicans into a fighting unit. He skipped over some senior members when selecting committee chairmen. He said at least three committees would be abolished and staff reduced all around. He killed funding for 28 congressional caucuses, thus eliminating such potential foes as the Congressional Black Caucus. He also sparked a furor by advocat-

ing a return to an orphanage system for some welfare children, a proposal he defended in Ronald Reagan fashion— by referring critics to the sentimental movie *Boys Town.*

In December, Gingrich landed in more hot water, when he decided to accept a stunning $4.5 million advance from the publishing house of HarperCollins for writing two books. He was roundly criticized for this potential conflict of interest by Democrats and even by Senator Bob Dole, who noted that the book bonanza was hardly the most savvy political move as the party prepared to slash programs for the poor. Chastened, Gingrich decided to forgo the advance. But it was a rare retreat. More characteristic was his behavior on the morning after the election. When Bill Clinton called to discuss the future, the Speaker-in-waiting couldn't take the call—because, he claimed, he'd just been wired up to appear on CNN. Tell the President I'll call him back, he said. It was a sentence Newt Gingrich seemed to have been waiting all his life to utter. ∎

VICTORY BY THE NUMBERS

THE 10 BIGGEST SPENDERS

Senate

				Winners
	Michael Huffington	CA	$25,205,627	
	Oliver North	VA	$16,750,959	
	Dianne Feinstein	CA	$10,868,062	✓
	Edward Kennedy	MA	$7,782,333	✓
	Frank Lautenberg	NJ	$5,534,636	✓
	W. Mitt Romney	MA	$5,448,623	
	Kay B. Hutchison	TX	$5,256,624	✓
	Harris Wofford	PA	$5,228,428	
	Herb Kohl	WI	$5,152,501	✓
	Mike DeWine	OH	$5,004,269	✓

Financial activity Jan. 1, 1993 through Oct. 19, 1994 includes loan payments

House

				Winners
	Gene Fontenot	TX	$2,661,157	
	Dan Rostenkowski	IL	$2,247,746	
	Bob Schuster	WY	$1,966,131	
	Richard Gephardt	MO	$1,931,391	✓
	Robert Dornan	CA	$1,832,126	✓
	Enid Waldholtz	UT	$1,464,669	✓
	Newt Gingrich	GA	$1,426,232	✓
	Thomas Foley	WA	$1,400,626	
	Martin Frost	TX	$1,377,707	✓
	Margolies-Mezvinsky	PA	$1,376,357	

Source: Federal Election Commission

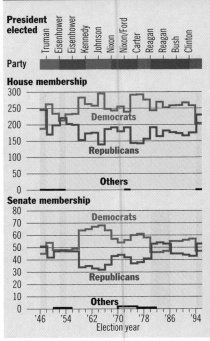

PARTY IN POWER

President elected: Truman, Eisenhower, Eisenhower, Kennedy, Johnson, Nixon, Nixon/Ford, Carter, Reagan, Reagan, Bush, Clinton

Party

House membership (Democrats, Republicans, Others) 300–0

Senate membership (Democrats, Republicans, Others) 80–0

Election year: '46 '54 '62 '70 '78 '86 '94

EXIT POLLS

How Americans voted in the race for the House

	Republican	Democratic
All	51%	49%
Males	57%	43%
Females	46%	54%
Whites	58%	42%
Blacks	8%	92%
Non–high school graduates	40%	60%
High school graduates	52%	48%
College graduates	55%	45%
Postgraduate study	42%	58%
Talk–radio listeners	64%	36%
Gun owners	69%	31%
Crime victims	53%	47%
Contributors to Perot's "United We Stand"	69%	31%

Do you want the President and the Congress to be of the same party?

Same	54%
Different	34%

Data are from an exit poll of 10,210 voters taken on Nov. 8 by Voter News Service. Margin of error is ± 1.5%

INITIATIVES

ILLEGAL IMMIGRANTS: California voters passed Proposition 187, 59% to 41%, which would bar illegal immigrants from receiving many state benefits. It would also require teachers, doctors and police to report illegal aliens to immigration officials.

ASSISTED SUICIDE: Oregon adopted the only measure in the U.S. to allow doctors to prescribe lethal doses of medication to terminally ill patients.

TERM LIMITS: Voters adopted them for congressional posts and other offices in Alaska, Colorado, District of Columbia, Idaho, Maine, Massachussetts, Nebraska and Nevada.

GAMBLING: Casino proposals were rejected in Colorado, Florida, Massachusetts, Rhode Island, Wyoming and the Navajo reservation. Missouri approved slot machines on riverboats, and New Mexico okayed video gambling and a lottery.

THE HOUSE

Current	New
	Republicans
178	230
	Democrats
256	204
	Independent
1	1

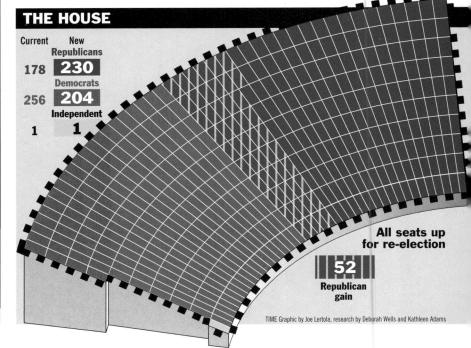

All seats up for re-election

52 Republican gain

TIME Graphic by Joe Lertola, research by Deborah Wells and Kathleen Adams

GOVERNORS

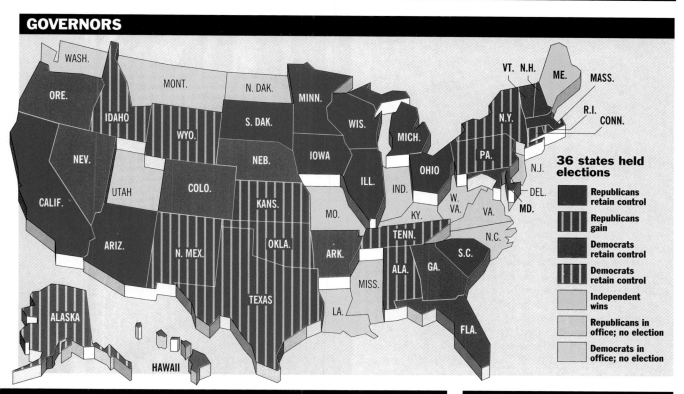

WASH.
ORE.
MONT.
IDAHO
NEV.
UTAH
CALIF.
ARIZ.
N. MEX.
WYO.
COLO.
N. DAK.
S. DAK.
NEB.
KANS.
OKLA.
TEXAS
MINN.
IOWA
MO.
ARK.
LA.
WIS.
ILL.
IND.
KY.
TENN.
MISS.
ALA.
MICH.
OHIO
W. VA.
VA.
N.C.
S.C.
GA.
FLA.
PA.
N.Y.
VT. N.H.
ME.
MASS.
R.I.
CONN.
N.J.
DEL.
MD.
ALASKA
HAWAII

36 states held elections

- **Republicans retain control**
- **Republicans gain**
- **Democrats retain control**
- **Democrats retain control**
- **Independent wins**
- **Republicans in office; no election**
- **Democrats in office; no election**

CRIME: Georgia approved a two-strike rule that mandates tougher penalties for violent felons. California adopted sentences of 25 years to life for three-time felons. Oregon stiffened mandatory sentences for violent crimes. Ohio eliminated the appeals-court phase in death sentences.

TAXES: Oregon, Missouri and Montana rejected a requirement to put all new tax proposals to public vote.

Nevada approved a two-thirds legislative approval for tax increases. Massachusetts rejected a graduated income tax in favor of the current flat rate. Arizona passed a cigarette-tax increase; Colorado rejected one. Oklahoma rejected a 1¢ entertainment tax that would have paid for breast-cancer research.

GAY RIGHTS: Oregon and Idaho defeated proposals that would have limited gay-rights protection.

VOTER TURNOUT

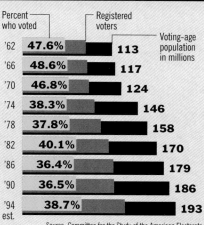

	Percent who voted	Registered voters	Voting-age population in millions
'62	47.6%		113
'66	48.6%		117
'70	46.8%		124
'74	38.3%		146
'78	37.8%		158
'82	40.1%		170
'86	36.4%		179
'90	36.5%		186
'94 est.	38.7%		193

Source: Committee for the Study of the American Electorate

THE SENATE

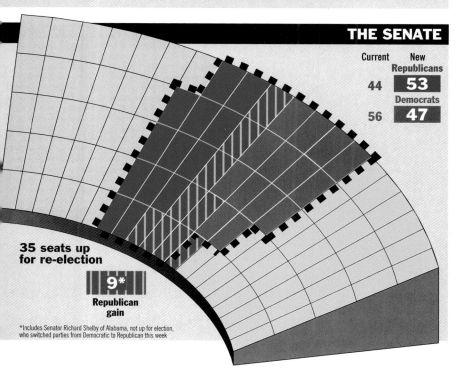

	Current	New
Republicans	44	53
Democrats	56	47

35 seats up for re-election

9* Republican gain

*Includes Senator Richard Shelby of Alabama, not up for election, who switched parties from Democratic to Republican this week

---

STATE LEGISLATURES

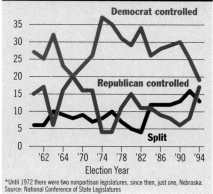

Democrat controlled

Republican controlled

Split

35
30
25
20
15
10
5
0

'62 '64 '70 '74 '78 '82 '86 '90 '94

Election Year

*Until 1972 there were two nonpartisan legislatures, since then, just one, Nebraska.
Source: National Conference of State Legislatures

By MICHAEL DUFFY, *TIME White House Correspondent*

THE DEFINING MOMENT OF BILL CLINTON'S SECond year in office came on November 9—the day after the midterm elections. The results were resounding enough: the voters had handed the Democratic Party its worst drubbing in 40 years. They turned both the House of Representatives and the Senate over to the Republicans and returned every Republican incumbent at the federal level to office. Exit polls around the country left little doubt that the voters were angry, alienated from Washington and anxious for smaller government and lower taxes. Clinton's presidency was half over, and the voters were running out of patience.

The next afternoon the President tried to explain the debacle. Typically, there was little consensus among his aides about what the landslide meant or foretold. So when he appeared in the East Room, running an hour behind schedule, Bill Clinton launched into an awkward defense of his first two years in office, suggesting repeatedly that the voters wanted him to do more of what he had been doing. A reporter pressed for clarification. "Are you essentially saying that the electorate yesterday was agreeing with you?" Replied the President: "I think they were agreeing with me, but they don't think we produced."

I think they were agreeing with me. It was hard to look at the 1994 election from any angle and come to that extraordinary conclusion.

And yet it often seemed that Bill Clinton, so well tuned to the nation's mood in 1992, was oddly out of touch with voters in 1994. What was intended as a watershed year of legislation and reform dissolved into an almost nonstop tide of scandal and disappointment and, in the fall elections, repudiation. The few accomplishments he had notched up by the end of his second year were largely overshadowed by mistakes, miscalculations and a startling misreading of the public mood. Clinton started the year near the top of his game and began a long, inexorable slide in the polls. By year's end he had fallen to a point (38 percent approval rating in one CBS News/New York *Times* survey) that sparked talk among party elders about whether he should, or could, be renominated in 1996. By mid-December, even Vice President Al Gore had to deny that he was contemplating a run for the top spot himself.

It was not supposed to go this way. Clinton had hoped to enact impressive new reforms of health care, welfare and campaign finance that would cement his party's tenuous hold on the middle class, burnish his credentials as a "New Democrat" and thus expand his thin electoral base. When piled atop his first-year accomplishments—the 1993 deficit-reduction package, the NAFTA trade accord and the Brady Bill—these achievements were supposed to constitute the results-oriented foundation of a re-election campaign. Instead, the President accomplished none of his top priorities,

Mistakes, miscues and misreadings seemed to put Clinton on the sidelines:

THE WHITE HOUSE

Who's in Charge?

Out of touch with voters and out of control in Washington, Bill Clinton seemed close to being out of time

Announcing his own plan for tax cuts after the election, Clinton seemed to ape Newt Gingrich, not outsmart him.

and reinforced impressions that he was not up to the job. And he now faced a hostile Republican Congress certain to torpedo any further initiatives.

Clinton often seemed more Prime Minister than President, a man who regarded legislation as the sole responsibility of office. He rarely used the White House pulpit to talk about matters beyond the ken of Congress and he diluted what majesty attended the office by talking in public about, among other things, his underwear. He played down—and, at times, completely ignored—the trappings of power as immaterial to his goals, when in fact they could confer a great deal of clout on the occupant of the Oval Office. And when he discovered that such tools existed, or that he wanted to employ them, he learned that the public had begun to tune him out.

It was a measure of his failure that Clinton faltered where he had hoped to soar: at home, on domestic affairs. Time and again he badly overestimated the voters' appetite for government. Much as he wanted to be seen as a moderate Democrat, his solutions were decidedly liberal. His plan to reform political finance was based on taxpayer-funded campaigns; his plan to "end welfare as we know it" would have cost more than the already expensive current system; the crime bill that took a year to enact wound up costing a stunning $32 billion over five years. But Clinton gave his weakest reading of the political mood on what was, ironically, the centerpiece of his agenda: health care.

HEALTH-CARE REFORM WAS A CLASSIC CLINTON undertaking: a bold, new, complicated solution to a problem that had festered for a generation. But, just as typically, the Clintons seemed to have designed it not for 1994 but for 1934, when the public badly needed—and trusted—government to make their lives better. At a time when hostility to federal solutions was already high, the Health Security Act would have created a vast new bureaucracy of unnamed regulators at the state and local level to decide who could provide care, at what price, and in what amounts. These features made the plan vulnerable to charges that it was intrusive government on a grand scale and a blueprint for rationing. The drawbacks in the end were probably no less damaging than the sheer size and mystery of the plan. With its "pools," "alliances," and "community ratings," the health program had the feel of a Rube Goldberg contraption, understood only by the mad scientists who designed it.

Add to this unpromising mix all of the trademark Clinton miscues—premature capitulation, internal bickering, party divisions—and the health plan began to unravel quickly. Clinton made big concessions whenever pressed. Inside the White House, cells of quiet opposition to the plan thrived, and seeded allies on Capitol Hill with doubts. Treasury Secretary Lloyd Bentsen and others felt the plan was too invasive, too punitive to business and doomed to fail in Congress.

"The wheels are coming off this Presidency," warned one White House aide

SECRETS? The First Lady shares her thoughts with the President at a health care forum in New Jersey; her closely held, overly complex plan failed.

quest into the Clintons' financial background would help diminish Clinton as an "agent of change" and establish him as just another politician.

PERHAPS THE MOST SURPRISING aspect of the Whitewater episode is how much it centered not on the President, but on his wife. Since Bill Clinton had spent much of the 1980s running for, and being, Governor of Arkansas, Mrs. Clinton played a larger role than her spouse in their investment in the Whitewater land deal. Unfortunately, the Clintons' partner in the deal, James Mc-Dougal, was also the owner of Madison Guaranty Trust, a savings and loan that would later go belly up and cost the federal taxpayers close to $50 million to salvage. Unfortunately too, Mrs. Clinton's firm—and at times Mrs. Clinton herself—would be found to represent the thrift in its dealings with the federal regulators who were forced to close it.

And then there was the matter of how, if the Clintons put so little money into the failed land deal, their tax deductions came to be so large. The lingering questions forced the Clintons to appoint a special prosecutor to look into the Whitewater affair. Attorney General Janet Reno turned to New York attorney Robert Fiske, a Republican, for the task; he was later replaced by Kenneth Starr, a more conservative, partisan Republican.

The scandal created a kind of open season on the Clintons. For Hillary, the most damaging revelation was that she had netted $100,000 in the early 1980s by trading commodity futures. Having conceived a health-care plan that was badly out of tune with the times, she was now seen as something of a hypocrite, for she, more than her husband, had railed against the go-go greed of the Reagan era.

Yet matters proceeded to go from bad to worse. In May, a former Arkansas state employee named Paula Corbin Jones charged the President with harassing her sexually at a Little Rock hotel in 1991. Clinton denied the allegation, but was forced to hire a second lawyer to defend himself in that case and set up a legal-defense fund to help cover his court fees.

Well before midyear incalculable damage had been done to the Clintons and their activist agenda. By the time Congress concluded its hearings into Whitewater in early August, the Clinton presidency was at a breaking point: the parade of failed memories, studied evasions and half-truths by White House aides in the

The White House promptly backed away from its health initiative, preferring to let Congress sort out the details. Soon many moderate Democrats in Congress joined in, arguing that there was no health-care crisis. Within just a few weeks—an astonishingly short interval—little was left of the Clinton proposal beyond the president's vow to stick by any plan that guaranteed universal coverage. By late spring health care was dead, and only the White House seemed not to know it.

The chief reason was that for much of the year the Clintons and their top aides were consumed by Whitewater, the name of the failed Arkansas real estate deal in which the Clintons had been a partner in the 1980s. What began as arcane questions about the propriety of the Clintons' tax deductions stemming from the investment—the First Couple insisted during the 1992 campaign that they'd lost their shirts in the deal—mushroomed into a full-blown scandal. Whitewater would paralyze the White House for months and leave a permanent scar on the Clinton presidency. The yearlong in-

With its "alliances," and "community ratings," the health program felt like a

Whitewater hearings went a long way toward explaining why Clinton's presidency had stalled and why voters—as well as the lawmakers on Capitol Hill—no longer took their marching orders from the President, his wife or their lieutenants. "The wheels are coming off this presidency," complained one senior official.

Once more, the President tried to start over. In June, he shuffled his senior staff, shunting aside Mack McLarty, his boyhood friend and ineffective chief of staff, for Budget Director Leon Panetta, who instituted a rough order at the chaotic Clinton White House. Panetta tightened access to Clinton, demoted and transferred personnel and took control of numerous White House operations that had enjoyed virtual autonomy under McLarty.

The most notable improvement came in foreign policymaking. National Security Adviser Tony Lake became more aggressive in formulating policy and teed up decisions more clearly for his boss. Clinton made a deal with North Korea to deprive it of nuclear-weapons capacity and oversaw steady progress in the Middle East peace talks. He rushed several thousand infantry to Kuwait in October to guard against another invasion by Iraqi leader Saddam Hussein. With an awkward assist from former President Jimmy Carter, Clinton dispatched nearly 20,000 troops to Haiti in September to oversee the peaceful transfer of power to Jean-Bertrand Aristide. The President ventured overseas six times himself in 1994 (breaking George Bush's record of five foreign swings in a single year). By autumn, the public preferred his handling of foreign policy to that of affairs at home.

SKELETONS? Busy as governor of Arkansas in the 80's, Clinton left the family financial affairs to Hillary, putting her at the center of the Whitewater mess.

BUT THE CHANGES WROUGHT BY PANETTA CAME at the margins of Clinton's presidency. The President was still slow to decide; he still preferred to talk problems to death; he didn't like to fire people. Autumn approached with almost no improvement in overall performance. Republicans in Congress demolished Clinton's legislative goals; health care atrophied and died; welfare restructuring went nowhere; campaign finance and lobbying reform ground to a halt; even formal ratification of GATT was postponed until after the election. Clinton won approval of his crime bill, but not before the Republicans had slapped a label across it reading PORK. Even White House officials despaired. As Al Gore noted at Clinton's private South Lawn birthday party in mid-August, "The two things people like about August are baseball and no Congress. Somehow, I think we got this wrong."

In the November elections, the voters tossed the Democrats overboard and delivered a stern message to the President: Shape up or ship out. As one senior official put it on New Year's Day, 1995, "The President has been totally marginalized."

Clinton tried once more to reinvent his presidency. He sought advice from top aides, pollsters, outside experts and even a pair of self-styled management gurus who had made millions selling books and videocassettes on late-night television. But his mid-December plan to cut taxes on middle-class Americans seemed like an attempt to mimic, rather than outsmart, House Speaker Newt Gingrich's Contract with America.

One official who quit the White House in frustration noted that Clinton doesn't really focus until "he's lying face down on the tracks as the train comes around the bend." Maybe so, but at times in 1994 it seemed that the train had already passed over and done its damage. And only the President didn't know it. ∎

Rube Goldberg contraption that only its mad-scientist designers understood

Trapping A Mole

The arrest of a longtime double agent within the CIA raised serious doubts about the spy agency

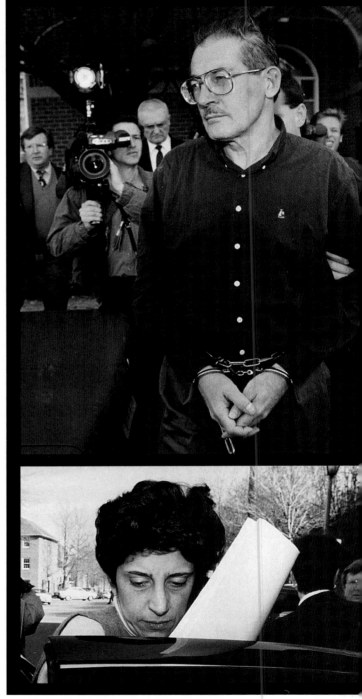

ALDRICH ("RICK") AMES WAS AN IMPROBABLE spy—which is probably why he made such a good one for so many years. Born in River Falls, Wisconsin, in 1941, Ames was part of a highly respected local clan. His interest in spy catching may have been stoked by his father Carleton, a pipe-smoking member of the CIA counterintelligence staff created and run by the monomaniacal mole hunter James Jesus Angleton. Carleton, now dead, had an undistinguished career tracking communist parties, but he left an important legacy to the CIA in the form of his son, who signed on as a trainee in 1962.

In the decades that followed, Aldrich Ames occupied a number of mid-level positions around the world—Ankara, Mexico City, New York City—for the spy agency, earning no special distinction. Then in 1985, divorced from his first wife, Nancy, who was also a CIA agent, he married Maria del Rosario Casas Dupuy, the daughter of a prominent Colombian family. They had met while Ames was posted to Mexico City, where Rosario worked as a cultural attaché at the Colombian embassy.

In the nine years following their marriage, according to U.S. federal prosecutors, Ames became the most serious foreign spy ever found within the CIA, allegedly selling to the KGB and its successor agency, the MBRF, the names of Soviet agents who had been recruited by the CIA, as well as valuable secrets about U.S. surveillance of the Soviet Union. During that time, while Mrs. Ames aided her husband in his illegal activities, the Ames couple made dozens of large cash deposits to banks in the U.S. and abroad. Eventually these transactions totaled $2.5 million—all of it allegedly paid to the Ameses, first by the Soviet Union, then by Russia, in exchange for national-security secrets.

Ames, 52, and his wife, 41, were arrested in Arlington, Virginia, on February 21 and charged with conspiracy to commit espionage. The arrest provoked an uproar. In Washington officials speculated that the case could prove to be the worst betrayal of intelligence agents in U.S. history. A veteran of the Soviet/East Eu-

rope division of the CIA, Ames knew the true names of virtually all the Soviet (and, later, Russian) agents working for the U.S., as well as those of new CIA recruits. As many as a dozen CIA operations may have been compromised as a direct result of the Ameses' activities.

Among the victims of Ames' betrayal was the CIA's most valuable foreign asset, General Dmitri Polyakov, a top officer of the Soviet military intelligence agency, the GRU. Polyakov began working for U.S. intelligence in 1961, and during the succeeding decades he passed increas-

Clockwise from top left: Aldrich Ames in custody; selections from bugged conversations between the spy couple; the $540,000 home of the $70,000-a-year man; Rosario Ames, once a highly regarded Colombian cultural attaché, under arrest.

military secrets, but the possibility that he had tipped off Moscow to virtually every CIA intelligence-gathering operation against the Soviets in recent years posed grave questions about America's security apparatus in the post–cold war era. Some in Washington even called for the abolition of the CIA. Hearings were held in both chambers of Congress, and spymaster Woolsey emerged from a two-hour grilling by the Senate Select Committee on Intelligence to announce that the Ames debacle was being treated not "as a single episode or incident but as a serious problem." He promised to launch independent investigations to determine how Ames eluded detection for so long and to study the CIA's security and counterintelligence practices. In October Woolsey demoted two senior officials who had actually commended one of Aldrich's superiors despite the mole's successful deceptions; they then resigned. Ultimately, Woolsey acknowledged the truth of a charge leveled extensively at the CIA in the wake of the scandal: that its "fraternity" culture of secrecy, protectiveness and loyalty helped shield Ames from earlier detection.

This was the most significant question: Why had Ames' activities gone undetected for so long? Given his GS-14 salary of $69,843, why didn't the couple's $540,000 house and $65,000 Jaguar set off alarms? Why did the agency neglect to inform the FBI of its suspicions about Ames after he gave deceptive answers in a 1991 polygraph exam? When did CIA and FBI investigators begin to catch on? If it was as early as 1986, as some reports suggested, and no later than 1991, why did investigators wait so long to make the arrests?

WHATEVER THE IMPETUS BEHIND THE CIA'S tardy concern over Ames' actions, the agency transferred him out of the Soviet/East Europe division to its counternarcotics center, something of an agency backwater, in 1991. From then on, both Ames' and his wife's activities were closely scrutinized. Agents retrieved papers and typewriter ribbons from their trash, bugged their phone and house, maintained visual surveillance and tapped into Ames' personal computer. In this way, according to prosecutors, they learned of unreported trips that Ames had made to Venezuela and Colombia and of a system for exchanging secret messages with his Russian handlers.

In late April Ames was sentenced to life in prison without parole after accepting a plea bargain that guaranteed Rosario a light term; in October she was given a sentence of 5½ years, allowing her to return more quickly to caring for the couple's five-year-old son Paul. In exchange, Ames agreed to cooperate with authorities in ascertaining the damage he had caused.

And the final question: What transformed this son of the CIA into a traitor? Defending himself, Ames later claimed that he had sold secrets not just for money, but also because he wanted to shorten the cold war by "leveling the playing field." The self-deceptive statement only highlighted the fact that Ames had left the field not level, but littered with the bodies of those he had betrayed. ∎

ingly precious secrets, at blood-chilling personal risk. Of all the secret agents the U.S. recruited during the cold war, Director of Central Intelligence R. James Woolsey later claimed, "Polyakov was the jewel in the crown." In 1990 the state-controlled Soviet newspaper *Pravda* reported that General Polyakov had been executed for espionage in 1988. He was only one of at least 10 people believed to have been put to death as a result of Ames' work for the Soviet and Russian intelligence agencies.

There was no indication that Ames had passed along

■ DISASTERS

STATE OF SHOCK

A major earthquake rocks a Los Angeles suburb—and shatters the waning confidence of Californians

PERHAPS THE SINGLE BEST EXAMPLE OF THE power of the earthquake that struck Los Angeles on January 17 involves the following brute subtraction: at 4:30 a.m. that Monday, Northridge Meadows was a three-story apartment building in a northwest suburb. Younger people lived on the second and third floors; the older folks generally lived downstairs so as not to have to climb steps. At 4:31 a.m., Northridge Meadows became a two-story apartment building, with all the carnage that suggests.

If this was just Atlas' shrug, as experts later suggested, one would hate to see the shimmy. In the aftermath of 30 seconds on that Monday, at least 58 people died. Local mountains may have risen more than a foot. Nine highways snapped like twigs. An oil main and 250 gas lines ruptured, igniting an untold number of fires. So many wires fell and circuits blew that 3.1 million people were plunged into total darkness. Water was denied to 40,000. There were more than 1,000 aftershocks, some considerable tremors in their own right. And the future of America's second largest city, as well as that of its citizens, may have been altered forever.

One could hardly watch the disaster unfold without wondering just how much more pain a place could bear. In a city long scorned for its lack of seasons, Los Angeles residents now say there are four: riots, earthquakes, fire and floods. The sturdy aerobic city of dreams was out of breath, its spirits fragile. "We don't call them disasters anymore," said Dan Schnur, an aide to Governor Pete Wilson. "We call them plagues. And we're just two behind ancient Egypt—frogs and boils."

Yet once the fires were out and the electricity back on, the residents of Los Angeles spoke both of terror and gratitude. Unlike other disasters of more nameless suffering, each death could be counted and mourned. A 20-year-old man died after the power failure cut off his

QUAKE! Until the earth moved, Northridge residents had no idea they lived above a fault line.

NOT THE BIG ONE? Not this time, geologists said, but the quake leveled buildings, freeways and dreams. *At left,* one of many collapsed apartment buildings. *At right,* the driver of this Honda survived.

hospital respirator. Another died in a fall from a sixth-floor window of a downtown hotel.

In the immediate aftermath of the quake, there were small graces everywhere. Though officials feared hooliganism and looting, crime dropped 80%. Drivers engaged in elaborate pantomimes as they arrived at intersections without stoplights. In Van Nuys Park, Tracy Calderone, a young rock-group cameraman, gave his tent to a Mexican family of total strangers who needed it more than he did. Neighbors in West Los Angeles found themselves sharing breakfast. "What a great way to meet people," one said. "We should do this more often." At a comedy club that offered free admission to anyone who brought something broken by the quake, Rick Alves presented his toe—broken during a barefoot dash from his rattling apartment.

For decades Californians have lived in fear of the Big One, the tectonic monster that inhabits the San Andreas Fault, a spectacular, 800-mile-long slash through the earth's surface that runs only 30 miles east of L.A. But this earthquake was a sobering reminder that the San Andreas is not the state's only seismic menace. A web of smaller cracks crisscrosses the fragile California crust. Many of these faults are well known. But others lie hidden deep underground, like the ones that gave Los Angeles this latest disaster. Until the earth moved, the residents of the suburb of Northridge, some 20 miles northwest of central L.A., had no idea that a deadly fault lay right below them, nine miles down. Registering 6.6 on the moment-magnitude scale, a measure of earthquake energy that among scientists has largely replaced the Richter scale, the Northridge temblor didn't qualify as a Big One. The San Andreas Fault could produce a magnitude-8 quake, which would be more than 85 times as powerful. But hypothetical situations were far from the minds of those in Northridge that morning.

AL MCNEILL WAS IN HIS YARD, IN FRONT OF what was once his house, a few miles from Northridge Meadows. Moments after the first upheaval, Al's son David smelled gas. Before he could turn off their line, a man in a pickup truck out front tried to start his engine. "There was a huge explosion," David remembers. A fireball leaped 50 feet in the air and then consumed the McNeill home and two others across from it. The same thing was happening all up and down the block, just as the local water mains were breaking. Later, people remarked on the peculiarity of seeing floods and flames in one and the same place. "We were pretty well prepared for an earthquake," said Al, tiredly. "But not the fire."

Robert DeFeo, battalion chief of the L.A. city fire de-

CHAIN OF DISASTER The earthquake unleashed other forces of destruction. As water gushed from underground pipes, gas from a broken main ignited, creating a deadly spectacle near Northridge.

partment, was grim-faced. He would like to be saving lives, but instead he was filling and refilling the coroner's station wagon in the driveway of Northridge Meadows, the collapsed apartment building. DeFeo's crew was using buzz saws, jackhammers and search dogs, and so far he had turned up nine corpses, each crushed while in bed. The heroics had occurred earlier, when residents pried neighbors from tight spaces or let them down from the roof with knotted fire hoses.

Jack Wiggens was probing the rubble of what was once a Bullock's department store. A structural engineer who was serving on L.A. Mayor Richard Riordan's blue-ribbon panel on retrofitting city buildings, Wiggens believed that the store probably should have been retrofitted. Many similar observations were made about the numerous major highways crippled by the quake. After the area's last big temblor, in 1971, L.A. swore it would strengthen its freeway bridges. But costs slowed the project, and the legislature voted down a 2¢ per gallon gas tax that might have goosed it along. Infuriatingly, I-10, one of the hardest hit of the freeways, had been scheduled to be retrofitted a month after the quake.

Following the disaster, Governor Wilson sent President Clinton an estimated bill to rebuild the city: between $15 billion and $30 billion. The President quickly pledged $41 million for immediate highway repair and

$639 million in low-interest small-business loans. A week later Clinton requested a $6.6 billion aid package for the earthquake victims and promised the money would not be held up by federal budget battles. Governor Wilson and Mayor Riordan joined the President in vowing fast action—and the trio kept their promise. The Santa Monica Freeway, the most critical commuter link, was reopened on April 11, 73 days ahead of its late June deadline.

Though the fast recovery buoyed the spirits of Angelenos, the earthquake may have done its greatest damage to the city's steadily eroding sense of itself as a privileged corner of America. If the Rodney King riots of 1992 ruined one of L.A.'s poorer sections, and the wildfires of 1993 singed some of its wealthier enclaves, the earthquake's effects were felt most strongly by the middle class. "We are in the process of rediscovering our reality, our ordinariness, aren't we?" observed Neil Morgan, a columnist for the San Diego *Union-Tribune*. "The uniqueness we assumed we had has come unraveled. We are so much more like the rest of the country. I mean, what the hell, they have snow and ice, and we have earthquakes. No, there's no redeeming uniqueness anymore." Scientists claimed the earthquake erupted around a hidden fault line—but it revealed fault lines of a different kind, running right through the shaken psyches of the citizens of Southern California. ∎

Murder Most

WHEN ASKED HOW THEY COULD HAVE let the most famous double-murder suspect in history slip away under their noses, the angry police commander and the tight-faced lawyer and the whole choir of commentators all said the same thing, without a trace of irony: "We never thought he would run."

In crisis, people condense into their essential selves. O.J. Simpson was, essentially, a very great runner. That was how a bowlegged kid with rickets had escaped the slums where he was born, how a football superstar had become a national icon: always outrunning his obstacles, finding daylight where there wasn't any.

But there was never a run like the one O.J. took on June 17 through the streets and highways of Los Angeles. The chase became a game, followed by millions as it unfolded on live TV: the police weren't really trying to overtake him, and he wasn't really trying to escape. He just wanted his mother. He wanted to go home. He found his blocker in his faithful friend and longtime teammate Al Cowlings, and together they slipped away from the lawyers and doctors and eluded the police, who had come to take O.J. into custody on charges of first-degree murder in the bloody stabbing deaths of his ex-wife Nicole and a young restaurant waiter, Ronald Goldman.

"I've had a great life. Please think of the real O.J. and not this lost person."

—O.J. SIMPSON

Word of the flight soon went out, and the crowds were on their feet, cheering. Police picked up Simpson's cellular-phone calls and began tracking his Ford Bronco along the San Diego Freeway. Reporters pursuing in helicopters overhead said he had a gun to his head. People pulled up their lawn chairs by the side of the road to wait for the cortege to pass. They lined the overpasses, waving, shouting, holding up signs—GO O.J. GO—as if he were trying to elude a pack of motorized tacklers.

Downtown at headquarters, the SWAT teams and crisis negotiators sat like everyone else, following the route of the Bronco on television and listening in on the calls: "He wants to head to his house." The 25-man SWAT team scrambled and moved out to O.J.'s Brentwood mansion in unmarked cars. When Cowlings drove up into the driveway, they could see O.J. in the backseat, holding a blue steel revolver pointed up against his own chin.

Simpson stayed in the truck, talking by phone to negotiator Pete Weireter about his successes and disappointments, about his demands. Finally he emerged, and when he reached the door of the house he collapsed into

CRIME

A brutal double slaying turned an American legend into a suicidal fugitive and accused murderer

Foul

the arms of the officers, looking sad and tired. They took him gently into the living room and waited while he telephoned his mother. "O.K., are you ready? We need to take you out," they said after a few minutes. They put the handcuffs on him and led him outside. "I'm sorry, you guys," O.J. kept saying. "I'm sorry."

It was terrible to watch and impossible not to. That was the nature of the entire week, as America stopped in its traffic to watch each clue scrape away another layer of the mystery. Where the facts were missing, suspicions kept the audience fed. Hearsay was not just admissible; it was broadcast live. Of course he did it—he had beaten his ex-wife before; he was high on coke; he had gone into a jealous rage. Of course he didn't do it—he loved her too much; he was incapable of such savagery; he had an airtight alibi.

"He's going to kill me. He's going to kill me. He's got guns. I want him arrested."

—NICOLE SIMPSON

Americans honor the principle of the presumption of innocence, especially when they want it to be true. And through the days of promiscuous speculation, in the sports bars and on the radio shows, O.J. Simpson's many admirers refused to suspend their disbelief. The most publicly shocking crime in years was received like a death in the family. Before it was all over, millions of fans were already passing through the stages of their grief—mourning not only two victims they had never known, but also the hero they thought they had.

He had smiled at them for years—first as one of the rare great sportsmen, unruined by his gifts or his fame, warm, grateful, ready to sign one more autograph when he was dog tired and overstretched. Later he ripened into the affable ABC commentator, the smooth corporate pitchman, even a plausible movie star.

Y ET FRIENDS WHO KNEW SIMPSON WELL UN-derstood that he was a creature of careful intention, his natural ease a measure of his discipline. He did not so much change, from the days of his painful childhood, as add layers, coats of polish that only occasionally peeled. Not that Simpson was a phony—he was just a man who had traveled a long way, accumulating public expectations. When his image was autopsied before the nation, the evidence supported both sides: that he was gentle and generous, violent and mean.

Simpson grew up in the San Francisco housing projects, stoning cars, fighting, getting hauled into juvenile hall. His talent saved him. "If it hadn't been for football," he said, "I wouldn't have come to school." By the

BLOODBATH Nicole Simpson was found with her neck severed to the spinal cord. Ronald Goldman received 22 knife wounds.

time Simpson was a junior at U.S.C., he was well along toward becoming the greatest running back college football had ever seen. He joined the Buffalo Bills and got a big house. He married his childhood sweetheart, Marguerite, and had three children before the first tragedy struck in 1979. Their two-year-old daughter Aaren fell into the backyard swimming pool and drowned. When O.J. heard about the accident, he rushed down the hallway screaming "She murdered my child! She murdered my child!" That year he and Marguerite were divorced, and he had knee surgery. His playing days were over.

But Simpson had long had his other lives: his friends, his movies, his television production company—and his new love. In 1977 he had found Nicole Brown, a beautiful, blond, 18-year-old waitress in Beverly Hills,

"It was the bloodiest crime scene I have ever seen," said a veteran cop

A maze of dog tracks painted a bloody mosaic around the victims' bodies

California. They married in 1985, shortly before the birth of their first child, Sydney. Another child, Justin, followed in 1988. The marriage was tempestuous (*see box*); they divorced in 1992, but Nicole moved to a townhouse not far from O.J.'s home, and he remained close to his children. As Nicole's ongoing calls to 911 would show, he continued a pattern of abusing his ex-wife.

In any domestic murder, the husband or lover is always the first to come under scrutiny. Police have learned, painfully, that women are commonly killed by the men closest to them. When the bodies of Nicole Simpson and Ronald Goldman were found outside Nicole's condo early in the morning of Monday, June 13, cautious officials announced they had no primary suspects. But they began building their case against O.J. even as he denied any involvement and went about his grieving for the mother of his children.

Some discerned a classic love triangle. O.J. and Nicole had been together that very day for Sydney's dance recital. But he was not included in the dinner celebration that followed at Mezzaluna, the local restaurant where Nicole's friend Goldman, an aspiring actor, was a waiter. She called the restaurant later that evening to ask if a pair of glasses had been left behind, and Goldman offered to drop them off at her nearby apartment.

Sometime after midnight, a neighbor out walking his dog found the bodies. Nicole, wearing only a nightgown, lay in a pool of blood, her neck severed to the spinal cord. A barefoot Goldman lay nearby, his body laced with signs of a ferocious struggle and 22 knife wounds. It was the neighborhood dogs that had sounded the first alarm, their paws spreading a bloody mosaic on the sidewalk around the house. One of the first cops on the scene, a longtime veteran, said, "It was the bloodiest crime scene I have ever seen."

"Ronald was a special human being. He didn't deserve for this to happen."

—GOLDMAN'S DAD

In the hours that followed, those who saw him say Simpson did not behave like a killer. He caught the 11:45 p.m. flight to Chicago for a meeting with executives of Hertz, his longtime employer, and ran into an old acquaintance, photographer Howard Bingham, on the plane. They chatted, mainly about golf, and O.J. seemed in a cheery mood. Employees at the O'Hare Plaza Hotel said Simpson arrived at dawn, tired but upbeat. He hung around the front desk for a few minutes, joking with the staff and signing autographs, before heading up to Suite 915. A few hours later, after getting news of the murder by phone, he returned to O'Hare Airport to catch a flight back to Los Angeles. He spent three hours with police and then went home; they described him as simply a witness, not a suspect.

Simpson remained in seclusion. He attended Nicole's wake on Wednesday and on Thursday her funeral mass, where he was treated as a mourner, not a murderer. But he engaged a well-known defense lawyer, the highflying Robert Shapiro, who called in a team to help him through his looming crisis. On Friday morning, L.A. District Attorney Gil Garcetti called Shapiro with word that the scientific tests were back, and that charges had been filed against Simpson of first-degree murder involving special circumstances—meaning that he could get the death penalty if convicted.

But Simpson still had some surprise moves to spring, even on his own team. The surrender deadline came and went, and when Los Angeles police department commander David Gascon finally appeared

MOURNING **While L.A. police investigated him, Simpson went to Nicole's funeral with their two children, Sydney and Justin.**

Behind the Smiles: Not What It Seemed

THE SIMPSONS
At a Hollywood gala, 1981

O.J. SIMPSON LIKED TO TELL INTERVIEWERS THAT "I'm a one-woman man." While that description fit the wholesome image of the former football star, friends described Simpson's relationship with Nicole Brown as far more complicated than Simpson admitted, or Hollywood mythmaking allows. They said his infatuation with Nicole did not prevent him from pursuing other women freely during their marriage. Occasionally Simpson would even order Nicole back to her parents for visits so that he could play the field for a while.

Friends called the relationship dangerous, dysfunctional, two passionate people goading and scrapping at each other. But the marriage—begun in 1985 shortly before the birth of their first child, Sydney—persisted through fights, separations, reconciliations. There were public explosions, including a New Year's Day 1989 incident when police answered a 911 call to the Simpson estate to find a badly beaten Nicole running out from the bushes, saying "He's going to kill me! He's going to kill me!" Though she later decided not to press charges, the city attorney brought up O.J. on a misdemeanor charge of spousal battery; he was placed on two years' probation after pleading no contest. The violence continued after their divorce in 1992. Police answered another 911 call in October 1993 when a jealous, ranting O.J. broke down the door of Nicole's townhouse. ∎

Friends saw a pair of passionate people

before reporters, he was in a quiet fury. O.J. had failed to surface, he announced, and was now a fugitive. The memorable Bronco chase was on.

After Simpson surrendered, the second, longer act of the O.J. saga began: the trial. To a large extent, it was initially waged in the court of public opinion, the place where everybody goes to plead in America's highest-profile trials. With the nation largely poised between affection for the former athlete and revulsion at the bloody slicing of his ex-wife and Ron Goldman, a public game began between O.J.'s accusers and his defenders. From the police came a flood of sometimes inaccurate leaks about bloody gloves and ski masks found after the crime. The defense described O.J.'s grief at not seeing his children on Father's Day. A Los Angeles TV station obtained the tape made of a 911 call in October 1993 when Simpson broke down the door of Nicole's house.

Meanwhile, Simpson's chief attorney Shapiro brought in the premium-brand lawyers Alan Dershowitz and F. Lee Bailey to aid the defense team. Later, perhaps anticipating race would figure in the trial, he added Johnny Cochran, a black attorney from L.A. with a reputation as a strong courtroom advocate. O.J. certainly needed help: in the first two days of the preliminary hearing to determine whether there was sufficient evidence to bring him to trial, it became apparent that lead prosecutor Marcia Clark and her team had gathered some devastating material, including enough scenes of blood to splice together a horror film. But with one challenge in particular—to the admissibility of bloody evidence gathered at O.J.'s home before police had obtained a warrant—Shapiro hoped to deprive the prosecution of some of its deadliest persuaders.

POLICE SAID THEY HAD GONE TO SIMPSON'S home after midnight on June 13 to tell him of his ex-wife's murder. On arrival they spotted bloodstains on the outside of the driver-side door of Simpson's Ford Bronco and a trail of blood leading from the driveway to the house. When it turned out that O.J. was not at home, homicide detective Mark Fuhrman vaulted a 5-foot fence onto the property—intent, he said, on foiling the Bronco's driver in the event that he might be stalking Simpson or his guests.

Midway through this entry he encountered Brian ("Kato") Kaelin, an aspiring actor who lived in a guest house in the Simpson compound. Kaelin reported being interrupted in the middle of a telephone conversation at 10:40 by a banging and shaking on the wall of his guest house. Fuhrman then rushed to the service path, where he discovered a bloody right-hand glove that closely resembled a left-hand glove, also covered in blood, that had been found at the murder scene. "My heart started pounding," Fuhrman told the court. "I realized what I had finally found"—presumably the possible key to the double murder. The officer stressed that it was not some-

goading and scrapping at each other

thing he had been looking for. Fuhrman also let in the other policemen, who proceeded to search the house and grounds. In all, they found 13 places where blood was splashed around the car, including a blood-stained footprint on the driver-side mat. Inside the house, there was blood in the foyer and on the master-bathroom wall.

Shapiro moved to suppress 34 important items collected at Simpson's home by the police, maintaining they were gathered illegally because the detectives searched the area for nearly six hours before obtaining a warrant. The prosecution stuck to Fuhrman's story that he entered the grounds only because he believed the murderer might be on the premises. Judge Kathleen Kennedy-Powell required only 30 minutes or so to issue her ruling in the preliminary hearing: Simpson would go to trial. There would be no bail.

BUT JURY SELECTION, PRETRIAL HEARINGS and other legal business put off the trial; it was scheduled to begin in mid-January 1995. The judge assigned to the case, Lance Ito, began pretrial hearings in late September. After heated arguments over the admissibility of the disputed evidence from Simpson's estate, Judge Ito ruled in the prosecution's favor on the vast majority of the items.

Procedural tussling and external events continued to dominate the center stage of the trial through the fall. Robert Shapiro began a campaign to portray detective Fuhrman, a critical prosecution witness, as a racist. In mid-October, Judge Ito suspended the screening of prospective jurors in order to ponder the impact of a sensational, allegedly tell-all book by a friend of Nicole Simpson's that accused O.J. of threatening his wife's life. By November, though, the jury was in place: it was composed of eight blacks, two Hispanics, one white and one person of white and American Indian background. Eight of the panelists were women, four men. The make-up of the jury was considered to be highly favorable to Simpson, since polls showed that blacks were more sympathetic to him than whites. It also led some to speculate the prosecution might settle for a plea bargain rather than put the case into the hands of the jurors.

After a very public period of deliberation, Judge Ito decided that he would allow the trial to be televised, despite his frequent complaints that the proceedings were becoming a media circus. In early January, 1995, the defense team surprised the court with a prominent about-face: they dropped their pre-trial challenge to the admissibility of key DNA blood tests that might link Simpson to the crime scene. Some believed the lawyers would challenge the reliability of the tests once they were admitted to the trial. As the new year began the jury was in place, the judge, lawyers and witnesses were familiar figures to most Americans, and the nation was bracing itself for more surprises in one of the most gripping murder cases in the annals of U.S. justice. ■

THE TRIAL

California v. Simpson: Faces in the Courtroom

LANCE ITO
Judge

A California superior court magistrate, Ito, 44 in 1994, was the son of Japanese-American parents who met in a U.S. internment camp during World War II. The former prosecutor's wife was Captain Margaret York, the highest-ranking woman in the L.A.P.D.

MARCIA CLARK
Prosecutor

Deputy Los Angeles District Attorney Clark, 41, grew up moving from city to city as her father, an FDA official, was repeatedly relocated. Twice divorced, Clark had prosecuted 20 murder cases and was considered an expert on DNA testing.

ROBERT SHAPIRO
Defense Attorney

A noted Los Angeles celebrity attorney, Shapiro, 52, was known as a skilled negotiator and a master of the plea bargain. His past clients included Johnny Carson, Christian Brando and Darryl Strawberry. Shapiro was married, with two children.

BRIAN "KATO" KAELIN
Witness

Permanently aspiring actor Kaelin, 35, lived in the guest house on O.J.'s estate and was a key witness to the events of the murder night. The case made a minor celebrity of this affable ladies' man, who was a fixture on the Hollywood party circuit.

D-DAY ANNIVERSARY

Return

THE LAST GREAT CANTONMENT OF THOSE who fought D-day and, as President Bill Clinton said, "saved the world" is a rich piece of history now—camp broken, tears, embraces and bugle calls fading into other memories. Those tens of thousands of veterans who went one more time to Normandy for the 50th anniversary of D-day in June 1994, to hear the thunderous echoes from the hours that shaped their souls and mortally wounded Hitler's monstrous evil, are home again to confront age and infirmity, and ultimately to yield to the death they evaded on June 6, 1944.

There was a beautiful sadness about the moment. The serenity of the thin crescent of beach as it lies today was seen at dawn by those on excursion boats in the English Channel and by the visiting President Clinton from the deck of the U.S. aircraft carrier *George Washington*. More than one waterborne spectator sensed how fragile the whole D-day operation must have been, successful finally because of its audacity and the spirits of young servicemen sustained by the singular strength that comes from freedom.

This memorial event defined democracy and liberty anew for a wondering world bogged down in complexities and cultural doubts. Scholars like Stephen Ambrose, author of a new book on D-day, put the meaning in simple but heroic terms: "The greatest event of this century." Some might argue, but not the men who

On the 50th anniversary of D-day, old soldiers—and
a young President—gathered to honor the past

of the Brave

struggled ashore through the slaughter and their individual terror.

More than he realized, Bill Clinton may have typified
a younger generation's response to this intense lesson
from another world, another war. It was as if he had
long been an indifferent son, blanking out for decades a
nation's old war stories, then awakening suddenly to the
heroics of a dim past and wanting to go back to nurture
the memories and understand them better.

By any measure, the President's speech commemo-
rating the veterans' sacrifice at Omaha Beach was one of
sensitivity and grace. Earlier he had paid tribute to the
Rangers who had climbed the forbidding cliffs at Pointe
du Hoc with ladders and grappling hooks. He stopped

MEMORY LANE A U.S. paratrooper walks from the
field near Ste.-Mère-Eglise
after repeating the jump he made a half-century before.

by Utah Beach before arriving at Colleville-sur-Mer,
where nearly 10,000 Americans from all of Europe's
battlefields are buried. The hand of Providence seemed
for once to touch Clinton, who has had his share of ceremonial glitches. Just as he began to speak, the sun
came out, etching in breathtaking brilliance the white
crosses against the tender green landscape.

The young President called to mind the sacrifices of
all the allies who "had come to free a continent—the
Americans, the British, the Canadians, the Poles, the
French Resistance, the Norwegians and others." Paying

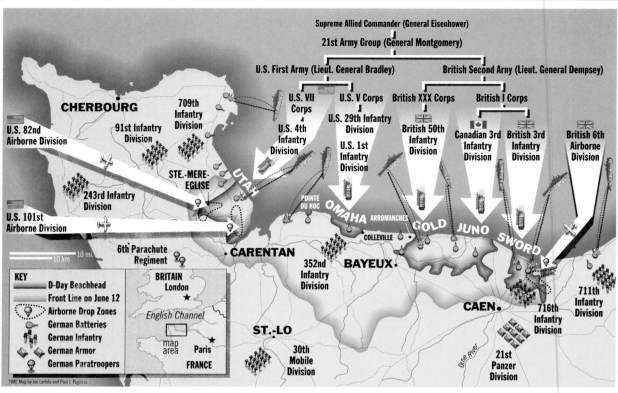

Supreme Allied Commander (General Eisenhower)

21st Army Group (General Montgomery)

U.S. First Army (Lieut. General Bradley)　　British Second Arny (Lieut. General Dempsey)

U.S. VII Corps　U.S. V Corps　British XXX Corps　British I Corps

CHERBOURG

709th Infantry Division

U.S. 82nd Airborne Division

91st Infantry Division

U.S. 29th Infantry Division

U.S. 4th Infantry Division

U.S. 1st Infantry Division

British 50th Infantry Division

Canadian 3rd Infantry Division

British 3rd Infantry Division

British 6th Airborne Division

STE.-MERE-EGLISE

UTAH

243rd Infantry Division

U.S. 101st Airborne Division

POINTE DU HOC

OMAHA

ARROMANCHES

GOLD

JUNO

SWORD

COLLEVILLE

10 mi.
10 km

6th Parachute Regiment

CARENTAN

BAYEUX

352nd Infantry Division

CAEN

711th Infantry Division

716th Infantry Division

KEY
- D-Day Beachhead
- Front Line on June 12
- Airborne Drop Zones
- German Batteries
- German Infantry
- German Armor
- German Paratroopers

BRITAIN
London
★

English Channel

map area

ST.-LO

30th Mobile Division

Paris ★

FRANCE

Orne River

21st Panzer Division

TIME Map by Joe Lertola and Paul J. Pugliese

THE GREAT ARMADA
The Allies assembled the greatest fleet in history to attack the German-held beaches of Normandy. 5,000 ships were accompanied by an additional 4,000 small craft, assembled into 59 convoys strung out over 100 miles, led by six battleships, 22 cruisers and 93 destroyers.

particular tribute to those survivors of the great invasion who had gathered for the commemoration, Clinton noted, "Today many of them are here among us. Oh, they may walk with a little less spring in their step, and their ranks are growing thinner, but let us never forget: when they were young, these men saved the world." Then the President asked the veterans to stand; they were greeted with ringing applause.

Nor was Clinton unmindful of those wartime adversaries—and an ally—who did not attend the commemoration. In some of the most exquisite language of the day, he turned their adversity into emancipation: "Germany and Italy, liberated by our victory, now stand among our closest allies and the staunchest defenders of freedom. Russia, decimated during the war and frozen afterward in communism and cold war, has been reborn in democracy."

Though in the company of host President François Mitterrand and other Allied leaders, including Queen Elizabeth II, Clinton made certain that the

men who fought the battle were at his shoulder all day. None was more gallant than hulking Joe Dawson, the captain of G Company, 16th Infantry Regiment, who in 1944 was the first officer to bring his shattered unit to the ridge above Omaha. Dawson used his native sense and energy to bring order and purpose out of chaos and confound the disciplined Nazi machine. D-day was a battle won by ones and twos and struggling gaggles of men who came out of the sea and moved inexorably up the small trails to defy Hitler's belief that they were too soft and self-indulgent to defeat his supermen.

Down on the beach with Dawson after the ceremony, Clinton stared out over the peaceful water, imagining the cauldron of 50 years ago. He bent to touch the sand, per-

IN THE LINE OF FIRE: More than 2,000 Allies gave their lives during the 24 hours of D-day.

haps a ritual of consecration for the simple virtues that propelled these young soldiers across such a distant fire zone: beaches are for families and picnics and laughter.

It was intriguing in this epic commemoration how most veterans could recall in minute detail those first 24 hours, then found their memories hazy as they tried to recapture the subsequent fighting that would continue for a year. Ambrose's interviewees could tell the exact size of the foxholes they dug, when they first relieved themselves after the long and tortuous journey to the beaches, or where they first hit ground, rolling beneath their billowing parachutes.

Richard Winters of Hershey, Pennsylvania, a first lieutenant in the 101st Airborne, came back to the outskirts of Ste.-Mère-Eglise and could identify every building, every wall, every swell of land where he had touched down. Jesse Franklin of Concord, New Hampshire, a military policeman sent to Omaha Beach to direct traffic, recalled that there was no traffic to direct. He hugged the sand on the orders of Colonel George Taylor, commanding the 16th regimental combat team of the First Division. Looking up, Franklin saw the colonel caked with sand and mud to his shoulders, bawling the now famous charge: "There are two kinds of men on this beach: the dead and those about to die. So let's get the hell out of here!" The colonel went up the ridge, but Franklin stayed to do his job, taking refuge in a captured German bunker.

Even as the vets fade away, the D-day anniversary may evolve into a continuous celebration of liberty. On the sunny afternoon in June when the modern paratroopers leaped from their huge C-130s near Ste.-Mère-Eglise, the hundred thousand spectators on the ground were in a picnic mood. Most of them were French families with grandfathers and kids, American flags tucked behind their ears and in their hair. They lolled on the grass, cheering the flawless parachute patterns. Such meaningful fun will doubtless endure.

This time his men had to push Major John Howard, 81, over Pegasus Bridge in a wheelchair as they marched to lay a wreath on the monument marking the landing of the British glider troops 16 minutes into D-day. They were the first Allied soldiers on the ground, and they captured the bridge in a few minutes, a distinction they do not want to lose in the crowded annals of history. Every year since, they have come back to give a champagne toast on the minute for their small but stunning victory. The champagne comes courtesy of the French villagers, just as it did on that fateful morning of what is now known as "the longest day." May the annual toast go on as long as freedom is cherished and champagne is at hand. ∎

The Man Who Beat Hitler

IF WORLD WAR II WAS THE CENTURY'S TURNING point, the turning point of the war was D-day. Once the Allied forces were successfully ashore, Hitler was doomed, caught between armies advancing against him from both the west and the Soviet east. The extraordinary undertaking of D-day reverberated into American politics, securing the reputation of an indifferent student from Kansas as a great military leader and propelling him into the White House eight years later. This was Dwight Eisenhower's invasion, the one he had planned and argued for and believed in completely.

IN COMMAND
General Eisenhower talks with paratroops of the U.S. 101st Airborne Division hours before they depart for France.

Americans who remember Ike at all tend to recall a do-little President or a mangler of sentences at press conferences. Military writers sometimes portray Ike the general as a genial and soothing Alliance board chairman at best, or at worst as a glad-handing bumbler. Eisenhower the Supreme Commander was none of those. He was a driving, demanding man of terrific energy: up before dawn, to bed after midnight, chain-smoking four packs of cigarettes, drinking 15 cups of coffee a day. He was a military perfectionist, impatient with his subordinates, and a peerless briefer. He had a volcanic temper that he struggled to control but sometimes used as a tool. He was naturally friendly, with a famous grin, and he inspired trust. But he was patient only when he had to be: to keep peace among the Allies. He made the coalition work, and some of his ablest and most loyal deputies were British.

In his old age and retirement, Eisenhower reflected on the fact that when he was planning the great invasion by sea, most of his colleagues thought the war would last two more years. His own bet—the end of 1944—was four months too optimistic. But he took pride in the fact that only "11 months from the day we landed in Normandy, the surrender took place." ∎

"I Have Never Been A Quitter"

Gifted yet never content, Richard Nixon spent his life falling and running and falling again

RICHARD NIXON'S FIRST CONSCIOUS MEMORY was of falling—falling and then running. He was three years old, and his mother had taken him and his brother out riding in a horse-drawn buggy, and the horse turned a corner too fast going home. The boy fell out. A buggy wheel ran over his head and inflicted a deep cut. "I must have been in shock," Nixon recalled later, "but I managed to get up and run after the buggy while my mother tried to make the horse stop." The only aftereffect, Nixon said, was a scar, and that was why he combed his hair straight back instead of parting it on the side.

In a sense, Nixon spent his whole life falling and running and falling again. A symbol of the politics of anger, he was one of the most hated figures of his time, and yet he was also the only man in U.S. history ever to be elected twice as Vice President and twice as President. In the White House he achieved many major goals: the U.S. withdrawal from Vietnam, restored relations with China, the first major arms agreement with the Soviet Union and much more. Yet he will always be remembered, as he was at his death on April 22 at 81, as the chief perpetrator—and chief victim—of the Watergate scandal, the only President ever to resign in disgrace.

The hallmark of Nixon's youth had been poverty—poverty and family illness and endless work. His father Frank was a combative and quarrelsome Ohioan who

DAYS IN THE LIFE: *Clockwise from bottom left,* Nixon joins Ike's ticket, 1952; gives the "Checkers" speech later that year; takes on Khrushchev in the "kitchen debate," 1959; bids farewell to the White House after resigning the Presidency, 1974; delivers his first inaugural address, 1969; meets Mao Zedong in Beijing, 1972; visits Boris Yeltsin on his last Russian journey, 1994.

HONOR GUARD: Though Nixon came close to impeachment and resigned the Presidency in disgrace following the Watergate affair, all four living ex-Presidents and their wives joined the Clintons to honor his memory at the funeral.

moved to Yorba Linda, California, in 1907. There Frank's pious Quaker wife Hannah gave birth on January 9, 1913, to a second son. She named him Richard, after the English King Richard the Lion-Hearted, plus Milhous, her own family name. When Dick Nixon was 12, his younger brother Arthur died of meningitis; later Harold, the eldest son, was stricken with tuberculosis, draining the family finances and sending Nixon into the work force at an early age. Upon graduating from high school, Nixon had to turn down a scholarship from Harvard (Yale was also interested in him) and attend a tiny local school, Whittier College. Duke University Law School was just starting when it offered the young college graduate one of the 25 scholarships available to a class of 44. There he lived in a $5-a-month room; later he shared a one-room shack that had no plumbing or electricity.

RETURNING TO WHITTIER, NIXON WAS TAKEN into the law firm of a family friend, where he bungled his first case, losing all his client's money in a real estate deal. But he persevered, began joining clubs and making speeches. He even joined a local theater group, where he met a schoolteacher named Thelma ("Pat") Ryan. It took two years of courtship before she agreed to marry him in 1940; she used her own savings to buy the wedding ring.

Nixon probably would have been content to stay in Whittier forever, but Pearl Harbor uprooted his whole generation. Despite the Quaker code of pacifism, he

> ## "We think ... when we suffer a defeat, that all is ended. Not true."

won a commission in the Navy in June 1942 and served creditably as a supply officer in the South Pacific. His most remarkable activity, though, was to become a master of bluffing in stud poker. By war's end, he had won and saved a stake estimated at as much as $10,000. He invested half of it the following year in launching his political career.

Jerry Voorhis, a popular liberal Democrat, had won five straight elections in California's 12th Congressional District, east of Los Angeles, but a group of local businessmen hoped to unseat him. Nixon implied—falsely—that Voorhis was virtually a communist. This kind of smear was to become a Nixon trademark. To one of Voorhis' supporters, Nixon later offered a very personal rationale: "Of course I knew Jerry Voorhis wasn't a communist, but I had to win. That's the thing you don't understand. The important thing is to win."

Win he did, with 56% of the vote. His climb to national office was spectacularly fast, spurred on by the exposure he won as a member of the House Committee on Un-American Activities as it investigated Alger Hiss as a communist informant. He ran for the Senate in 1950 against Helen Gahagan Douglas, a former actress who was an ardent New Dealer. Again smear tactics helped Nixon win: she was "pink right down to her underwear," he proclaimed. He had hardly begun serving in the Senate before the Republican leadership turned to him as a running mate for the immensely popular General Dwight Eisenhower. But during the campaign the press discovered that Nixon had a secret slush fund of $18,000 provided by California businessmen. At Eisenhower's urging, Nixon went before a TV audience with an impassioned defense of his honesty. The only personal present he had received was "a little cocker spaniel dog in a crate ... Black-and-white, spotted. And our little girl Tricia, the six-year-old, named it Checkers. And you know, the kids ... love the dog." Hundreds of thousands of listeners wrote their support of Nixon, and Eisenhower settled his future by saying publicly, "You're my boy!"

EISENHOWER WON 55% OF THE VOTE, AND the freshman Senator from California, only 39 years old, found himself the second youngest Vice President. Nixon soon turned himself into a latter-day Marco Polo, taking nine trips to 61 countries. Everywhere he went, he conferred, orated, debated, held press conferences. In Moscow to open a U.S. trade exhibit in 1959, Nixon got into a finger-pointing argument with Soviet leader Nikita Khrushchev in the kitchen of an American model home.

As Eisenhower's inevitable successor, Nixon was nominated to run against the Democrats' telegenic John F. Kennedy. The vote was incredibly close, with Kennedy winning 50.4% of the popular vote and Nixon 49.6%. He accepted the bitter defeat and returned to California. Then Nixon's legendary political shrewdness abandoned him. He let himself be talked into running for Governor against the popular Edmund G. ("Pat") Brown and tried to imply that Brown was a dangerous leftist. Nixon lost, and it was after this crushing defeat that he blew up at reporters and announced, "You won't have Nixon to kick around anymore."

Only 49 by then, he decided to move to New York City and make some money. He joined a prosperous Wall Street firm but never really retired from politics. He stumped loyally for Barry Goldwater in 1964, and when that campaign ended in disaster, he became the logical man to reunite the splintered party in 1968. In a year of assassinations and ghetto riots, Nixon spoke mainly in code words about "peace with honor" in Vietnam and "law and order" at home; he was reassuring enough to defeat Hubert Humphrey and the war-torn Democrats.

Nixon's first term included sweeping innovations, often surprisingly liberal. He was the first President in years to cut military spending, and the first to tie Social Security increases to the cost of living. He instituted "revenue sharing" to funnel $6 billion a year in federal tax money back to the states and cities. His imaginative measures were overshadowed, however, by Vietnam. Nixon had campaigned on a promise to end the war "with honor," meaning no surrender and no defeat, but the communists at first showed no interest in negotiations. Antiwar protests grew in size and violence, particularly after Nixon ordered bombing raids and made a temporary "incursion" into Cambodia. When a peace treaty was finally signed, it was too late to salvage America's interests in Vietnam.

Nixon brought to the White House an extraordinarily permanent anger and resentment. His fears led to the drawing up of an official "enemies list," the use of "dirty tricks" in his successful 1972 re-election campaign against George McGovern, and the creation of a group of "plumbers" to stop press leaks from the White House. It was this group that bungled the break-in at Democratic National Headquarters at the Watergate apartment complex. But it was Nixon and his aides who bungled the handling of the affair, engaging in the elaborate cover-ups and deceit of the "long national nightmare" that came to be known as Watergate. When public opinion, the Supreme Court and elder statesmen of his own party finally deserted him, Nixon resigned from the presidency on August 9, 1974, and returned to California.

For anyone else, departure in disgrace from the highest office in the land might have served as a public farewell. But Nixon, who proudly stated, "I have never been a quitter," climbed once more out of the abyss, re-creating himself as an elder statesman. He wrote his memoirs in 1978, then eight more books largely devoted to international strategy. After a year and a half in a New York town house, he moved to the wealthy suburbs of New Jersey and began giving discreet dinners for movers and shakers. Presidents Reagan and Bush called to ask his advice; so did Bill Clinton. In November 1989, Nixon became the first important American to visit Beijing after the massacre at Tiananmen Square.

Twenty years before his death, in his last meeting with his staff, the resigning President had burst into tears. "Always remember," he said, "others may hate you, but those who hate you don't win unless you hate them—and then you destroy yourself."

> **"What starts the process are the laughs and slights and snubs when you are a kid. But if your anger is deep, you learn."**

TAPS: At rest before the house his father built.

Rescue workers near Pittsburgh search for clues in the crash that killed 132.

Airline Safety: Under a Cloud

A SPATE OF 1994 AIRLINE DISASTERS led Secretary of Transportation Federico Peña to call for a conference on air safety in early 1995. Two crashes in February and March killed 61; they were followed by the July 2 crash of a USAir DC-9 near the Charlotte-Douglas International Airport in North Carolina, killing 37. More deadly was the crash of a USAir Boeing 737 on September 8 as it approached the Pittsburgh airport. When the jet smashed into heavily wooded hills northwest of the city, all 132 people aboard were killed. The human remains horrified and sickened rescue workers. The USAir crashes were followed by two crashes of American Eagle's small commuter planes, the first in Indiana in October, the second near Raleigh, North Carolina, in December; 83 people were killed in the two incidents. The Federal Aviation Administration banned a class of small commuter planes from flying in icy weather, and Peña vowed quick action to regulate the planes more strictly.

The White House Under Siege

Beginning with the bizarre crash of an airplane against the wall of the White House, a series of unlikely incidents raised concerns about the security of the Executive mansion. On September 11 Frank Corder stole a single-engine plane from an airport north of Baltimore, headed south to Washington, and skidded the plane across the White House lawn before crashing it into a wall two stories below the presidential bedroom. Corder was killed on impact.

On October 29 Francisco Martin Duran stood outside the fence surrounding the White House and shot 27 rounds of ammunition across the north side of the building. Duran was finally tackled by a bystander and arrested, *left*. Two other dangerous incidents followed, leading federal officials to call for a complete review of White House security.

Breyer: Voted In

HE FAILED TO GET THE PRESIDENTIAL nod the first time around, when Justice Byron White resigned from the Supreme Court. But the second time was the charm for Stephen Breyer of Massachusetts, who was chosen by President Clinton to assume the seat held for 14 years by Justice Harry Blackmun. The erudite Breyer, 55, was a former clerk for Justice Arthur Goldberg, and as a

BREYER: Quickly confirmed by the Senate.

congressional staffer was architect of the plan that deregulated the airline industry in 1978. Breyer breezed through confirmation hearings in the Senate Judiciary Committee—with a little help from longtime friend Senator Ted Kennedy.

Chavis: Voted Out

CHAVIS

WITH A VOICE VOTE and show of hands, the board of the National Association for the Advancement of Colored People, with 59 of 64 members present, overwhelmingly decided to oust its executive director, Benjamin Chavis Jr., 46, who was beset by charges of sexual harassment and financial mismanagement. Preparations for the meeting were tense, with the Nation of Islam providing security for Chavis even as 200 of his backers demonstrated their support. In spite of an hourlong speech to persuade the board, Chavis was unable to reverse his fate. Said a former high-level N.A.A.C.P. member: "Chavis and crew refused to deal with the reality that [this] is not a rich organization. The first thing they all did was ask for credit cards."

Protesters failed to stop the Prop.

Closing the Golden Gate

FOR YEARS CALIFORNIANS WELCOMED immigrants—illegal as well as legal—with few questions asked. Who else would perform menial labor for low wages? But in the November election, California voters passed the controversial Proposition 187, one of the most sweeping restrictions on aliens ever enacted in the U.S., by a vote of 59% to 41%. Among other items, the new law banned illegal immigrants from receiving prenatal services and from entering nursing homes. Opponents of the measure filed suits against it, counting on the U.S. Supreme Court to strike down the measure's restrictions on education for children of illegals.

Killing in the Name of Life

SALVI

MURDERS AT THREE clinics that offered abortion among their services shocked the nation and led to denunciation of the shootings by important supporters of the anti-abortion cause. In late July, gunman Paul Hill shot Dr. John Britton, who had replaced the murdered Dr. David Gunn as a circuit-riding doctor for several abortion clinics in northern Florida. In the second case, a man burst into a clinic in Brookline, Massachusetts, in late December and opened fire with a semiautomatic rifle, killing receptionist Shannon Lowney, 25. Ten minutes later he descended on a second clinic, where he fatally shot receptionist Leanne Nichols, 38. Days later, John C. Salvi III, 22, a hairdresser from New Hampshire, was arrested and charged with the crimes after he fired shots at another abortion clinic in Norfolk, Virginia.

Clinton 1, Saddam 0

RESTLESS, RECKLESS AND TIRED OF being rebuffed, Iraq's Saddam Hussein once again looked poised to carry out an epic feat of self-destruction. In October he sent 20,000 of his élite Republican Guards to join 50,000 regular troops in breathing heavily across Kuwait's border. But Bill Clinton surprised him, swiftly ordering 40,000 U.S. troops to the region and dispatching an aircraft carrier to the Persian Gulf. While Kuwait cheered, a chastened Saddam withdrew his soldiers.

Rush Rolls On

CANDIDATE BILL CLINTON'S SAVVY use of "new media," including talk radio and TV, was cited as one of the major reasons for his election in 1992. But in 1994 the worm turned: analysts cited liberal-bashing talk-

LIMBAUGH: The G.O.P.'s best weapon?

radio shows as an important factor in the downfall of congressional Democrats. Rush Limbaugh continued to lead the pack of right-wing cage-rattlers: his nationally-distributed radio show drew 20 million listeners daily. Limbaugh, twice divorced, celebrated by getting married, to a woman he met in Third Wave fashion: through online E-mail. ∎

Fighting the Flood

When major floods struck Texas along the San Jacinto River, Tannie Shannon, *above*, carried his granddaughter to safety, accompanied by his wife Frances and their dog Amadeus. The floods killed at least 20 people, forced some 13,000 residents to flee their homes and led to the explosion of two massive gasoline pipelines, sending thousands of gallons of flaming fuel racing down the river.

Free at Last

🇿🇦 "Voting is hard labor. But we

CIVIC DUTY: After waiting centuries to vote, blacks were patient with one last delay in Soweto.

have done our duty. " —GLADYS MSWELE, 60

When history delivers something that looks like a miracle—the fall of the Berlin Wall, for example, or the collapse of Soviet communism—the mind experiences a kind of electricity, the thrill of beginning, of seeing a new world. That was what it felt like to watch South Africa in April and May of 1994. Here was a spectacle of true transformation.

For the first time, South Africans of all races were citizens. Apartheid was gone, reduced to rubble, as if in one of those slow-motion demolitions that bring down massive, obsolete monstrosities to make way for new construction. Nelson Mandela, imprisoned for 27 years by

Mangosuthu Buthelezi, whose Inkatha Freedom Party had long boycotted the election. Only seven days before the polls were to open, the Zulu leader suddenly announced he had "decided to make compromises to avoid a great deal more bloodshed and carnage." He dropped his demand for an autonomous province that he could dominate and settled for constitutional recognition of the Zulu kingdom.

The Zulus' participation in the election, claimed a jubilant Nelson Mandela, "is a leap forward for peace." More than 20,000 citizens had died in the previous 10 years in South Africa, most of them not in the tensions between black and white but in the rivalry between Inkatha and Mandela's African National Congress.

Extremist whites did not follow the Zulus' lead. A group of bloody-minded white rightists tried—and failed—to disrupt the process of change. In the last few weeks before the election, they launched a campaign of small bombings against railways, power lines and A.N.C. offices in the conservative farm region west of Johannesburg. Then, as the election drew closer, they detonated powerful car bombs in downtown Johannesburg, in neighboring Germistown and at the international airport, killing a total of 21 people and injuring more than 150. By the end of that week the police had rounded up 34 suspects, all members of the neo-Nazi Afrikaner Resistance Movement.

HALLELUJAH! A church group proudly displays South Africa's new six-color flag, symbol of Nelson Mandela's rainbow nation, at an inauguration celebration in Cape Town.

the white regime for his violent advocacy of equal rights for all South Africans, was elected the first black President of his country.

During one memorable week in April, in a series of astonishing episodes beginning with all-race voting from the Limpopo to the Cape of Good Hope, the old South Africa of segregation and oppression peacefully dissolved itself and re-emerged as a tentatively hopeful, newly democratic nation. On Wednesday the 27th at 12:01 a.m., the old order formally ended, as cheering crowds in the nine new provincial capitals hailed the lowering of apartheid's blue-white-and-orange flag and the raising of a banner with six colors symbolizing the people, their blood, their land, the gold under the ground, the sky—and peace.

At the same moment, the country became whole again. The 10 black homelands, designed by apartheid architects as places of exile for surplus people with black skin, were abolished, including four that had pretended to independence. Most unexpected of all in this litany of surprises was the last-minute cooperation of Zulu Chief

Voters, especially blacks eager to embrace the day of their liberation, were not deterred. The election, astonishingly peaceful, succeeded beyond all expectations. Lines of determined voters stretched a mile and more at polling places. Many polls opened hours late or ran out of ballots or the invisible ink used to mark the hands of those who had already made their choice. The ballots, printed weeks before, did not include the late-entering Inkatha Freedom Party, and had to be updated with paste-on stickers; to ensure further fairness Chief Buthelezi demanded a fourth day of voting. Finally election officials requested and got an extension of the voting, originally scheduled to end Thursday, into Friday in several parts of the country.

The surprise was not that the election was carried out well but that it happened at all. Here was a white minority government, still with a monopoly grip on political power, handing over control of the country to the black majority it had held in servitude for 300 years. It was an event without historical precedent in the days of sweeping decolonization in Africa three decades before,

APARTHEID'S END: "Never, never, and never again shall this beautiful land experience the oppression of one by another," said Mandela at his inauguration.

or even in 1980, when the former British colony of Rhodesia became Zimbabwe, because this time the 5 million former rulers were not leaving.

South Africa's whites had methodically segregated blacks, paid them a pittance, ignored their housing and barely pretended to educate them. Blacks were not second-class citizens but third or fourth class. Yet after little more than two years of negotiations between President F.W. de Klerk and Nelson Mandela, the whites stepped back and passed the government to that eager if ill-prepared

who suddenly realized that the country's military machine now belonged to them. "Never, never, and never again," Mandela vowed, "shall it be that this beautiful land will again experience the oppression of one by another. The time for the healing of wounds has begun."

Once in office, Mandela delivered, building an inclusive government. In late June he announced that 10 former members of the Umkhonto we Sizwe, the military wing of the A.N.C., would become generals in the newly renamed South African National Defense Force. But in a move that telegraphed the new President's determination to assuage the fears of his white constituents, command of the SANDF remained with General Georg Meiring, who had headed the country's defense apparatus under the old regime.

There were other favorable signs: in the two months following Mandela's inauguration, crime was down dramatically, with political killings 60% under pre-election figures. The decline encouraged much-needed investment. Companies that had feared a bloodbath were beating a path to the new government's door. Among the big names were PepsiCo and Coca-Cola. Equally important to South Africa's long-term health, trading was

ARCHITECTS OF PEACE: The new President praised his predecessor F.W. de Klerk, who joined Mandela's unexpectedly broad Cabinet along with Finance Minister Derek Keys.

majority. "I feel a sense of achievement," said De Klerk, the Afrikaner who made himself into the country's last white President. "My plan has been put into operation."

WHEN THE VOTES WERE COUNTED, THE results were no surprise: Mandela and the A.N.C. swept to victory. Yet Mandela was moderate even in triumph, naming a 27-member coalition Cabinet that included his long-time A.N.C. supporters, De Klerk and several of his key lieutenants, and Zulu leader Buthelezi, who was named Home Affairs Minister.

Mandela's inauguration on May 10 transformed Pretoria from a dour police state to a city of brotherly love. Blacks and whites embraced, old political adversaries shook hands, and the crowds at a mixed-race concert swayed in unison to Zulu drummers, Afrikaner fiddlers and English-singing rock bands. A scintillating array of foreign guests—including Hillary Clinton, Yasser Arafat, Prince Philip, Fidel Castro and some 180 others—watched as a flight of South African air force jets streaked by overhead, streaming smoke trails of the redesigned flag's six colors, symbol of Mandela's new "rainbow nation." The sight brought tears to the eyes of many blacks

normal on the Johannesburg Stock Exchange; the flight of capital that reached a peak before the elections had slowed, and business confidence was soaring.

Mandela's most difficult task was to win economic parity for the people for whom he had won political equality. Apartheid left South Africa's blacks with almost nothing: the great majority live in such desperate poverty, in dusty, refuse-strewn townships or gritty rural backwaters, that their dreams are simply of clean water, paved streets, garbage collection, sewers. Most of them are without electricity or running water at home. Eight million live not in houses but in the squalor of squatter shacks. About 18 million black families earn less than $220 a month. Half the black population is illiterate, and half its work force has no job. Development experts say the national economy must grow at 3.5% a year to make even a dent in joblessness; the growth rate in the first year of Mandela's government was expected to hover between 2% and 3%.

Mandela's long walk to freedom ended in a jubilant, triumphant election week and the liberation he had worked 50 years to achieve. But his second struggle was just beginning. While he will be praised for the things he achieves, he will be held responsible for everything he does not do for the people, who expect the most. ∎

A Dirty Little War

A battle with rugged rebels in Chechnya shook Boris Yeltsin's Kremlin

THE OBSCURE LAND CALLED CHECHNYA IS ABOUT the size of Connecticut, a mere pinprick even on a large world map. The 1.3 million people of this oil-rich, predominantly Muslim enclave in Russia's North Caucasus region make up less than 1% of the population of the Russian Federation. Independent by nature, the Chechens under President Jokhar Dudayev declared independence from Russia in 1991. At first Boris Yeltsin was content to wage a proxy war against the rebels, giving covert support to Dudayev's pro-Moscow opponents. He was wary of picking a direct fight with the Chechens, a clan-structured people that still avidly pursued blood vendettas and were said to be the leaders of the Russian Mafia.

Even so, in late November Yeltsin took firmer action. A coalition of anti-Dudayev forces rolled into Chechnya's capital of Grozny, only to be repelled by Dudayev loyalists, who claimed to have destroyed 20 tanks and killed 350 people in the fighting. They also captured 120 Russian soldiers and paraded them on television, giving the lie to Moscow's insistence that it was providing only political backing for Dudayev's opponents. Yeltsin gave the rebels a 48-hour ultimatum to lay down their weapons, and as many as 40,000 Russian troops began massing on the borders of the mountainous, land-locked region. Meanwhile, sophisticated jet fighters—planes that could never have been procured or even operated without Russian help—bombed military bases and the Grozny airport. Yeltsin sent a Russian parliamentary delegation to meet with Dudayev in Grozny. But despite talk of cease-fires and amnesties, Russian forces continued to bombard the capital.

On Dec. 14, Dudayev broke off talks with the Russians and summoned his people to "a war for life or death." Yeltsin, stung by a worldwide outcry against the bombing of Grozny, promised to halt the air raids. But the bombs kept falling, and more protests followed. By year's end Grozny lay smoking and ruined, its main orphanage, hospital and dozens of apartment buildings destroyed. Neither Russian nor Chechen troops were in full control. More than 100,000 people were believed to have fled into the surrounding countryside.

In Moscow the invasion was condemned by communists, leaders of the once pro-Yeltsin Russia's Choice party and many other politicians. Rumors swirled that military factions might stage a long-predicted coup. Others said Yeltsin himself might stage a coup, supported by the group the Russians call the "power ministries": the more hawkish army generals, the Ministry of Defense under Pavel Grachev and the intelligence services. The rising influence of Alexander Korzhakov, Yeltsin's chief bodyguard—and drinking and tennis buddy—also alarmed Russian moderates. As winter settled over Moscow, there was a sense in the Russian capital that the seeds sown in the remote hills of the Caucasus might bear bitter fruit later in the year. ■

YELTSIN: Cracking down.

RUSSIA
CHECHNYA
Grozny
Caspian Sea
Black Sea
GEORGIA
Tbilisi ★
TURKEY
ARMENIA   AZERBAIJAN
Caucasus Mts.
0 —— 100 mi.
0 —— 100 km
TIME Map by P.J.P.

THE SHOT HEARD ROUND THE WORLD: Chechens take to the barricades near Grozny. "This whole thing is stupid and futile," said a Russian major. "They'll fight to the last."

THE FRAGILITY OF POWER: Though U.S. forces had occupied Haiti for a month before Aristide's return, he was guarded by a bulletproof shield at his reinstatement ceremony.

■ THE CARIBBEAN

Return of the Exile

The island rejoiced as U.S. troops finally reinstated Jean-Bertrand Aristide—and democracy—in Haiti

OR ONCE, THE DAY THAT HAITIANS WOULD RE-member was one of jubilation: their first freely elected President returning in triumph to vanquish the ghosts of the country's past. On that bright Saturday afternoon of October 15, as Jean-Bertrand Aristide paced through the ceremonies of reinstatement, his euphoric nation could reasonably embrace the vision he offered them—that it was their day of deliverance.

Aristide's joy-filled return marked more than a victory for the activist clergyman who had transformed Haitian politics. As he gratefully acknowledged, the moment would never have occurred without the persistence of Bill Clinton, who dispatched a peaceful army to pave the way. Now the U.S. and Aristide would depend on one another for success.

The Haitian leader's ceremonial return was visibly orchestrated by his muscular allies: when he arrived a few minutes before noon, it was aboard a U.S. Air Force jet. As it approached the island, crowds eager to catch a glimpse of their returning savior flocked to the National Palace, packing the streets so tightly that the faces of those standing closest to the fence were squeezed like lemons between the iron bars. When Aristide finally appeared before his cheering people, he was dwarfed by the bulletproof shield that surrounded the podium, another sign of his fragile safety in the divided society. A dozen U.S. soldiers with binoculars were perched atop the palace, scanning the crowds. And somewhere in the capital was a top-secret team of Delta Force commandos, ready to respond if an attempt were made on his life.

For a moment, the crowd seemed overwhelmed and strangely hushed. They waited with a stilled reverence that bordered on the mystical. When Aristide finally spoke, his message was unmistakable. In Creole, English, French and, finally, Spanish, he repeated words of peace

steeped in revenge and voodoo, its African-based spirit religion. U.S. troops had quelled civil disorder only by occupying the island from 1917 through 1934. In the years that followed, the nation endured the brutal reign of François "Papa Doc" Duvalier, who was freely elected in 1957 but became a dictator, using voodoo and the dreaded Tontons Macoutes to enforce his sway. Papa Doc died in 1971 and was succeeded by his 19-year-old pleasure-loving son Jean Claude "Baby Doc," who fled the country in 1986 when the people rose up against him. After a confused period of coups and short-term leaders—Namphy, Manigat, Avril—the country held a truly democratic election in December 1990. To the joy of most Haitians, the leftist Aristide was chosen to lead the country. But his rule was divisive, for he appeared to encourage revenge among his followers—the *Lavalas*, meaning flash flood—for the past misdeeds of the country's ruling business and military élites. In September 1991 he was forced from power and fled the island in a coup led by Lieutenant Colonel Michel François, police chief of Port-au-Prince, and Lieutenant General Raoul Cédras.

Following the coup, the U.S. under President George Bush led U.N. sanctions against the impoverished nation, pushing the junta into an agreement to let Aristide return to power on October 30, 1993. That agreement, concluded in July 1993 under Bill Clinton's Administration, was known as the Governor's Island Accord for the small island on which it was signed, a U.S. military outpost in New York Harbor. But the junta failed to live up to its promises, and Aristide did not return to power.

THE FIRST ATTEMPT TO REINSTATE ARISTIDE HAD foundered, in an incident that embarrassed the Clinton Administration. Under U.N. authority, the U.S. dispatched a troopship, the U.S.S. *Harlan County*, to Port-au-Prince on October 11, 1993. It carried 193 U.S. and 25 Canadian engineers and specialists who were to repair roads, hospitals and schools and train a new police force to prepare the way for Aristide's return. But instead of the grateful Haitians the Administration expected to greet the ship, the *Harlan County* was met by a howling, rioting mob. In a demonstration organized by the junta, thugs ranged along the Port-au-Prince docks, banging on cars carrying U.S. diplomats and chanting anti-U.S. slogans. Beleaguered by the recent deaths of U.S. troops in Somalia, Clinton ordered the ship into an ignominious retreat.

But the crisis in Haiti continued to fester, as waves of Haitian refugees, demanding political asylum, set out on homemade rafts to cross the Caribbean to the U.S. During his campaign against Bush in 1992, Clinton had denounced Bush's policy of sending Haitian refugees back to their land. But once in office, he followed his predecessor's policy: the new Administration feared that accepting the refugees would lead to a flood tide of immigrants that the U.S. could not accommodate. The Haitian rafters were sent off to Guantánamo Bay, the U.S. Navy's outpost in Cuba, where they were quarantined, later to be joined by Cuban boat people. Clinton's

and nonviolence over and over. "Honor. Respect," he intoned. "Honor. Respect." The crowd cheered wildly as he promised, "Never again will blood be shed in this country."

As he stepped down from the podium, there was a feeling that the little priest had somehow been propelled by a miracle. In returning to reclaim his place as Haiti's first freely elected leader, he had the support of a U.S. government that distrusted his competence and character. The very men who pushed him from the country three years before had been forced into exile, and the ruling minority that loathed him was contained by military force. Aristide had been given an opportunity that few could have foreseen only months before: to put on the path to democracy a country whose history reflects decades of dictatorship.

A violent society since its slaves revolted against French colonial rule in the 19th century, Haiti seemed

Carter to the Rescue

FOR A MAN WHOSE ADMINISTRATION IS WIDELY considered to have failed, Jimmy Carter has been a very popular former President. He captured the public eye, post–White House, with his work as a carpenter helping to build low-cost housing; his Carter Center, which runs a number of other housing programs, launched the Atlanta Project to revitalize the Georgia city. Overseas, Carter has quietly worked for human rights and monitored elections for fairness in many countries. Though some critics charged he was a softy who coddled dictators, admirers claimed he was a tireless crusader for peace. All in all, few would deny he had been a deeply involved ex-President.

In 1994 Carter acted as a special envoy from Washington, helping to resolve some crises that

PEACE MISSION: Jimmy Carter and defense expert Senator Sam Nunn, *above*, were joined by General Colin Powell as the ad-hoc diplomatic team in Haiti.

bedeviled Bill Clinton. When the former President insisted on accepting an invitation to visit North Korea in June "as a private citizen," his fellow Democrat Clinton had him briefed on what to tell Kim Il Sung—because, said a resigned U.S. official, he would have gone and talked to Kim anyway. Greeted like a visiting head of state, Carter publicly embraced Kim and denounced Clinton's threat of sanctions against North Korea. But his diplomacy appeared to pay off when Pyongyang later agreed to dismantle its nuclear-bombmaking capability.

The former President's last-minute mission to Haiti convinced Raoul Cédras to leave the country peacefully, but Carter was accused of being overly cordial and too lenient with the dictator. As 1994 neared its end, he travelled to the Balkans, where he persuaded the Serbs and Muslims to agree to a four-month cease-fire. This journey, too, was controversial, but it capped an extraordinary year for the ever-smiling ex-President. ∎

policy switches on Haiti were one of the factors contributing to the widespread belief, reflected in opinion polls, that the President was wavering and uncertain in his conduct of foreign affairs.

Through the summer Clinton rattled his saber at the illegal Haitian regime, promising a U.S.-led invasion to restore Aristide to power. But many—including, for some time, Cédras and his henchmen—believed the U.S. would not act. Clinton had made the same noises about intervening in Bosnia without acting. But as September came, the U.S. threats grew louder, and an invasion ultimatum loomed. Alarmed at last, Cédras began a search for an American intermediary to step in and negotiate a settlement with Washington. At the same time, former President Jimmy Carter, who had turned his energies to conflict resolution since leaving the White House, had been trying to establish contact with Cédras. To bolster his peacemaking team, Carter recruited General Colin Powell, the former Chairman of the Joint Chiefs of Staff, and Senator Sam Nunn, at that time the powerful head of the Senate Armed Services Committee. He then lobbied President Clinton for the diplomatic assignment; Clinton accepted.

CARTER AND HIS TEAM ARRIVED IN PORT-AU-Prince on Saturday, September 17, and immediately entered into negotiations with Cédras and other officials. After two days they were close to an agreement: the junta would step down, and Aristide would return. But by late Sunday afternoon, with no accord signed, President Clinton upped the pressure, ordering the invasion to begin. Cédras, feeling double-crossed, refused to sign the document; the de facto president—81-year-old Emile Jonaissant, caricatured as a spineless puppet of the junta—signed it instead. Though Clinton had demanded Cédras' signature, the President seized the opportunity, instructed Carter to accept the agreement, then halted the invasion.

Many Americans initially criticized the pact as too lenient on Cédras and his colleagues, whose murderous regime had left 3,000 dead since the 1991 coup. The agreement called for a general amnesty and did not require the dictators to leave Haiti after they resigned, though Clinton strongly believed they would.

The following day U.S. forces arrived, carrying out a peaceful invasion of the island that was met with enthusiasm and celebration among most Haitians. As troops poured in—12,000, then 15,000, finally more than 20,000—they were hailed as liberators. American MPs moved into five of the capital's most notorious police precincts. That same day, the Coast Guard returned the first shipload of what it hoped would be a reverse wave of returning refugees. Aristide's supporters showed restraint. The little violence that did arise was aimed not at the minions of the junta, but at its symbols. At the main army barracks in Cap Haitien, crowds stripped buildings as if they were exorcising evil spirits.

As the U.S. forces fully occupied the island, they helped rebuild its infrastructure—in some cases literal-

The Population Bomb: Castro's Boat People

THE CUBANS CAME TO the U.S. in rafts made of ropes and inner tubes, catamarans built in living rooms, boats made from beds and old car engines. One young boy survived the journey to Florida after his parents gave him their only life jacket and handed him over to another boat—before they disappeared beneath the waves.

They were called *balseros*, or rafters, and their exodus followed nearly five years of turmoil in Cuba after the fall of its Soviet patrons. Fidel Castro, faced with a failing economy in the grip of a U.S.-led embargo and angered over the death of a policeman in a refugee hijacking in early August, opened the ports and unleashed the population. As groups of *balseros* began to take to the sea, Castro's police did nothing to stop them. By mid-August, Castro had succeeded in making his problem Bill Clinton's problem.

Finally, on August 19, Clinton revoked the special status Cuban refugees had long enjoyed, which guar-

NOT WELCOME: Reversing 30 years of U.S. policy, Clinton refused admission to some 25,000 refugees.

anteed them asylum if they reached American shores. Navy ships began collecting refugees intercepted by the Coast Guard and ferrying them to Guantánamo Bay Naval Station, the base on Cuba's southeastern shore that has remained officially under American control since 1903, despite Castro's revolution.

The crisis was resolved in September by American and Cuban diplomats meeting in New York City. The Cubans settled for what the U.S. wanted: a narrow agreement on immigration, and no lifting of the devastating embargo. The deal amounted to a simple swap: the U.S. would take in at least 20,000 legal Cuban immigrants each year—many more than were typically admitted annually—and Havana would halt the exodus. The biggest losers: the 25,000 Cubans who risked their lives at sea only to wind up under quarantine at Guantánamo Bay or—even farther from home—in Panama City, Panama. ∎

ly paving the road to a restoration of democracy. Lieutenant General Hugh Shelton became the de facto proconsul in Port-au-Prince; his 10th Mountain Division was for the moment Haiti's replacement army, civil service, utility company and public relations firm. In the countryside, 31 U.S. Army Green Beret A Teams, each made up of about 12 soldiers, quietly fanned out to key villages, where some held town meetings and others completed "Operation Light Switch," getting a generator up and running to restore some power.

Close to a month after U.S. troops entered Haiti—and five days before Aristide's return—Cédras finally flew into exile in Panama, but only after he had been assured that the U.S. would recompense him for taking over his various residences on the island. Again, critics charged Clinton with buying off a dictator who should have been punished.

Overall, though, the occupation of the island brought the sweet taste of victory to the White House. For once, a risky venture had rebounded favorably to a grateful Clinton Administration. Critics of the President's previously wavering policy were forced to concede that his firm actions had carried the day for the short run. But many worried about the long-term prospects for getting U.S. soldiers back to American shores. Remembering Somalia, Clinton's critics feared "mission creep," in which Americans would be forced to remain in Haiti for

months, even years. In early October, both the Senate and the House voted to urge a prompt, orderly pullout of U.S. forces, but did not set a date for the withdrawal.

BEHIND THE CHEERING CROWDS AND SMILING faces that accompanied Aristide's triumphant return lay a complex, highly polarized society. If the President was to heal those divisions, which had defied similar efforts for centuries, the keystone to his success would be reconciliation. Aristide, who resigned from the Catholic priesthood shortly after his return, had to show from the start that he could work with a prickly parliament. He needed to persuade an entrenched business élite that distrusted him that it should contribute to a new kind of Haiti. He would have to quell those of his followers who lusted for revenge, and back up American soldiers if they had to use force against looters or other mobs. Crucial importance would be placed on his ability to reform the judicial system and give Haitians a sense that the rule of law existed.

Since Aristide had promised not to run again, he had barely a year to give his nation a new political architecture. If the reborn President could transform the system sufficiently so that power passed peacefully to his successor, the one-time priest from the impoverished village of Port Salut would have truly liberated his country from the terrible legacy of its past. ∎

The Perils of Peace

Vowing eternal warfare, terrorists attacked the fragile movement to build lasting harmony between Arabs and Jews

FEBRUARY 25: AT 5:20 A.M. ON FRIDAY, THE HOLIEST day of the Islamic week, about 700 men, women and children rose in the dark to down a hurried breakfast. They jammed into the Ibrahim Mosque at Hebron—the Tomb of the Patriarchs Abraham, Isaac and Jacob—for the dawn prayers that mark the start of the sunrise-to-sunset fast on each of the 30 days of Ramadan, the holy month. That same morning Dr. Baruch Goldstein, an Israeli settler on the West Bank, also entered the mosque, armed with a military-issue assault rifle. Taking up a position close to the backs of the worshippers in the rear row, he opened fire—and continued shooting for 10 minutes. "I saw seven people die immediately," said an eyewitness. "They were hit in the head, and their brains spilled out. It was total chaos."

July 1: In blazing Mediterranean sunshine, Yasser Arafat crossed the border from Egypt into the Gaza Strip, dropped to his knees and kissed the sandy soil. As the welcoming crowd cheered and waved black-red-green-and-white flags, he and his aides piled into a convoy of cars and trucks carrying armed guards and sped along the main north-south road into Gaza City. Thousands of supporters roared a welcome outside the building where the Israeli army of occupation had maintained its local headquarters until May.

October 19: Sallah Abdel Rahim Nazal Souwi, a 27-year-old Palestinian from the West Bank, boarded the heavily traveled No. 5 bus in downtown Tel Aviv, carrying a 22-pound package of TNT. At 8:55 a.m., just after the bus passed Dizengoff Square in the heart of the shopping district, he stood up and blew himself, the bus and 21 of its passengers to pieces. The force of Souwi's bomb was so intense that the bus was reduced to fragments. Parts of victims were blown through windows. Police officers fainted; reporters sobbed at the sight.

As these scenes remind us, the balance between war and peace, civilization and terrorism, is very fine in the Middle East. In recent years there have been tremen-

dous breakthroughs toward peace. Yet peace has its perils: the response of terrorists is to heighten their attack on stability. Treaties are answered with bombs, handshakes with hand grenades. The year 1994 saw momentous events: the arrival of Arafat to assume P.L.O. control of Gaza, the signing of a peace treaty by long-time enemies Israel and Jordan, the unprecedented visit of an American President to Syria in hopes of extending the peace process. Yet Israeli extremists such as Baruch Goldstein and Arab terrorists like the militant Palestinian group Hamas continued to sow fear and terror, subverting the welcome movement toward peace.

AS THE YEAR BEGAN, THE REGION COULD LOOK forward to the promise of Palestinian self-rule, sealed before the eyes of the world in a moving ceremony in September 1993 on the White House lawn. The Clinton Administration and the government of Yitzhak Rabin in Israel were hoping to expand the ripples of peace to Israel's other neighbors in the region. But the process was almost derailed in late February with the massacre at Hebron. Its perpetrator was so blinded by enmity toward Arabs that he seemed "batty" even to some of his ultranationalist, fervently religious neighbors in the Jewish settlement of Kiryat Arba, near Hebron in the West Bank.

Goldstein was a fanatic who took precise, carefully calculated steps to reach a clear, if evil, goal. His intention was not just to kill Arabs, but to destroy the peace process. He chose time, place and method well to produce the most inflammatory effect, firing repeatedly inside the mosque. The final toll of the dead: 29 Arabs and Goldstein, who was beaten lifeless. Many more—as many as 70 Muslims—were wounded. Later inquiries by the Israeli government revealed that security procedures were surprisingly lax at a shrine that had been a notorious flash point of tension.

Goldstein's death mission was successful at first: the P.L.O. withdrew from its talks with Israel over the promised transfer of power in the West Bank, and riots swept through occupied West Bank towns. It was not until the U.N. Security Council unanimously condemned the Hebron massacre that Syria, Jordan and Lebanon agreed to resume their own talks with Israel, and the P.L.O. returned to the conference table. Goldstein had succeeded in exacerbating the tensions between Muslim and Jew.

Yet so strong was the movement toward peace in the region—and so deep were the risks mutually shared by Yasser Arafat and Yitzhak Rabin—that though the Hebron massacre delayed the timetable toward peace, it did not halt the process. About four months after the incident, a long-awaited day dawned in Palestine, when Arafat returned to the Gaza Strip and stepped onto Palestinian land for the first time in 27 years. On this day Arafat acknowledged the challenge that faced him: to switch roles from guerrilla leader to head of government.

The P.L.O. boss's belated decision to make the visit was vintage Arafat: solitary, sudden and unpredictable. But that operating style was becoming a liability.

Arafat's ingrained, lifetime habits of secrecy and high-handedness had already caused serious splits among the P.L.O. leadership and deep concern among the rank and file. Civilian administration of Gaza and Jericho—on such matters as education, health, taxation—had remained in limbo. After spending a lifetime in the cause of Palestine, Arafat risked rejection if he could not learn to share power with the people he had led for a quarter-century.

In late July the center of the Middle East peace process turned from Palestine to Washington where, in a historic meeting, Prime Minister Rabin and Jordan's King Hussein signed an agreement ending their 46-year state of belligerency. The Washington Declaration called for direct telephone lines, an electrical power-grid link and the opening of two new border crossings as the first steps toward friendlier relations. The agreement also gave Jordan "high priority" as custodian over the Muslim holy sites in Jerusalem, which set up a potential conflict between Jordan and the P.L.O. Arafat insisted that the agreement did not undermine Palestinian claims to East Jerusalem as its capital.

On October 14, Rabin and Arafat, along with Israeli Foreign Minister Shimon Peres, were named the recipients of the 1994 Nobel Peace Prize. But the day was spoiled when Nahshon Waxman, 19, a corporal in the Israeli army, was kidnapped by the militant Hamas group and held hostage. When Israeli special forces attacked the West Bank house where Waxman was being held, one Israeli and three Hamas soldiers died—as did Waxman, who was executed by his captors. All parties agreed that a real peace could not be reached until Arafat succeeded in controlling Hamas and other terrorists in Gaza and the West Bank.

Only a few days later those violent forces struck again, when the Hamas "martyr" Souwi blew up the bus in Tel Aviv, killing himself and 21 passengers. The force of his bomb was so intense the bus was reduced to fragments.

GOT A LIGHT? Longtime enemies, Jordan's Hussein and Israel's Rabin surprised diplomats with their easy friendship.

asphalt strip in the middle of a minefield. An area had been paved and fenced in specifically for the ceremony. "Walk 15 yards beyond that barbed wire," a U.S. Secret Service agent warned onlookers, "and you won't be coming back."

THAT HEADY AFTERNOON BUILT EXPECTATIONS OF more good news; Israel especially hoped the President's most daring stop—a peace pilgrimage to Damascus to meet with Syria's President Hafez Assad—would speed up its glacially slow negotiations with Syria over the Golan Heights. Clinton was taking a chance on Assad, rewarding him up front with a telegenic official visit by a U.S. President even though Syria was still listed by the State Department as a sponsor of terrorism. Clinton minimized expectations before the meeting, predicting there would be no "dramatic breakthrough." He was right: the Syrian leader refused to condemn terrorist attacks publicly, even though U.S. officials claimed Assad had agreed to do so in his private talks with the President. Clinton ended the journey to Damascus by speaking of the possibility of progress, rather than of any real progress. Yet, given the region's blood-soaked recent history, 1994 was a year of continuing growth in the Middle East, a year when the worst perils that terrorists could hurl in its path failed to halt the slow but determined march toward a lasting peace. ∎

But Rabin strongly insisted that he would continue the peace process, thus denying Hamas the victory it sought: an end to the talks.

Only one week after the bus blast, President Clinton visited the Middle East in hopes of accelerating the peace process. His first stop was a desert border crossing, where he met Hussein and Rabin to co-sign the treaty of friendship agreed to in Washington. The symbolism surrounding the President's witness-for-peace visit was almost too perfect. At the border crossing, the table for the signing was set up on an

HAMAS HAVOC: After the Tel Aviv bus blast, Israeli police were faced with gathering body parts to identify the victims.

Devalued Dreams

Revolt, assassination and a falling peso mock the nation's progress

REBELS: Zapatistas, led by Comandante Marcos, center, launched Mexico's first violence from the left in 20 years.

AS MEXICO'S PRESIDENT CARLOS SALINAS DE GORTARI surveyed his nation on New Year's Day, 1994, he could take pride in his achievements. During his five years in office, Mexico's economy had flourished, and Salinas had crowned his success with the signing of the NAFTA trade pact. In the year ahead, he would hand the presidency to his hand-picked successor in the long-ruling P.R.I. party, Luis Donaldo Colosio. But 1994 would be a year of turmoil in Mexico, marked by a peasant uprising, the assassination of Colosio and a devastating year-end financial collapse.

The troubles began on that New Year's Day, in Chiapas, the southernmost state of Mexico and one of the nation's poorest. The last fireworks had fizzled when the people of San Cristóbal de las Casas were treated to an even more dramatic spectacle. Into the square of the town of 80,000 marched 300 armed peasants, most of them wearing army fatigues and the face-covering bandannas that have become the trademark of Latin American revolutionaries. Led by a man known only as Comandante Marcos, and calling themselves the Zapatista National Liberation Army—after Emiliano Zapata, the legendary hero of Mexico's 1910 revolution—the rebels said that their goal was to stop the "genocide" of the nation's Indians.

Before the uprising was over, as many as 2,000 guerrillas had occupied San Cristóbal and six other towns in the highlands of Chiapas. Though a series of skirmishes between government forces and the Zapatistas left an estimated 150 dead, Salinas met the rebellion with restraint. Only days after it had begun, Salinas declared a unilateral cease-fire, proposed talks and offered amnesty to any guerrillas who would lay down their arms. He succeeded in achieving a March peace accord in which the government agreed to such reforms as providing more housing and schools for the southern Indians.

The agreement thrilled Mexicans—but euphoria soon gave way to despair when Salinas' chosen successor, Colosio, was assassinated on March 23 while campaigning in Tijuana. Although police caught Mario Aburto Martinez, 23, a poor factory mechanic, and tried and convicted him of the crime, suspicions ran high that a political conspiracy was behind the murder.

The country's honor was partially restored when the presidential election, monitored by outside observers, was hailed as the fairest in Mexico's history. When Colosio's successor, Ernesto Zedillo Ponce de Leon, assumed the presidency on December 1, his goal was to ensure stability. But his plans immediately went awry; determined to devalue Mexico's inflated currency slightly, he let the peso float against the dollar. The peso went into a tailspin, at the worst point losing 40% of its value. Within nine days as much as $8 billion—12% of Mexico's vital foreign investment—may have fled the country. The assassination, the rebellion and the economic tailspin revealed an underlying poverty and instability that mocked Salinas' year-old vision of Mexico as a modernizing nation. ■

WAR WITHOUT END

While Bosnia's Muslims die under
Serb guns, NATO and the U.N.
talk tough but carry a small stick

THE TABLES WERE SPREAD IN BRUSSELS AT THE
end of November for a grand conclave charting
the future of NATO. Foreign ministers repre-
senting the 16 partners in one of history's
strongest, most successful alliances arrived with
words intended to reaffirm its solidarity, even as
the war in Bosnia was testing its inner strength. In
suffering Bosnia, the first test case of cohesion following
the Soviet Union's collapse, the great powers had cer-
tifiably failed. Western impotence in the face of the latest Serbian assault—this time on the U.N.-designated
"safe haven" of Bihac in northwest Bosnia—was the cul-
mination of more than two years of ineffectual wrangling
among Washington, its European partners and the U.N.
over how the horrible ethnic conflict could be stopped.

Indeed, much of the discussion in Brussels focused on
ways to withdraw the 24,000 U.N. peacekeepers should
the need arise quickly, an undertaking that could pose
appalling dangers. Lost amid the recriminations was a
firm grip on how the order of battle in Bosnia really
stood. After 31 months of fighting that followed the
breakup of Yugoslavia into independent republics, more
than 200,000 were dead or missing and some 2 million
were homeless. Yet the main conflict at stake had not

been resolved: the Serbs, an Orthodox ethnic group out-
numbered by Muslims and others in the republic of
Bosnia and Herzegovina, were still fighting to escape becoming a permanent minority inside an independent,
Muslim-led Bosnia. Bosnian Serbs, led by Radovan
Karadzic and supported by their comrades in the neighboring republic of Serbia, effectively controlled 70% of
the territory of Bosnia. Partition plans had been drawn
up time and again; the parties had met in countless
peace talks; cease-fires had come and gone. Bill Clinton
and NATO talked tough against the militant Serbs at
times, but seldom backed up their words with action.

For the first time in the war, the Bosnian Muslims
made gains against the Serbs in late October. After a
period of training and refitting with weapons smuggled
in from their allies in Croatia, the heavily Roman
Catholic neighboring republic, a reinvigorated Bosnian
army conducted sharp, sustained attacks, driving the
rebel Serbs back from the Bihac area and also gaining
ground around the long-besieged capital of Sarajevo.

But by the time of the Brussels summit, the Serbs had
engaged in a strong counterattack, recovering territory
they had lost and almost overrunning Bihac. Serb jets
operating from an air base in Croatia had joined in the

CROATIA
Velika
Kladusa
Danube
KRAJINA
Bihac
Banja Luka Doboj
BOSNIA
AND
Tuzla
HERZEGOVINA
CROATIA
Kupres
Brgule
Zepa
Sarajevo
Gorazde
Trnovo
Mostar

SERBIA
Drina

Muslim and
Croat control
Serb-controlled
Bosnia
MONTENEGRO
Serb-controlled
Croatia
Dubrovnik
25 mi.
50 km
Recent fighting
Adriatic Sea
TIME Map by Paul J. Pugliese

DEADLY AIMS: *Left,* in Sarajevo a Ukrainian member of a U.N. antisniper team aims at Serb sharpshooters, who renewed their attacks on the Bosnian capital in the summer.

attack. For once, NATO retaliated—but once again the allies pulled their punches. When NATO jets roared across the Adriatic from Italy to bomb the base, they punched a few craters into concrete runways but avoided hitting Serbian planes or soldiers.

The half-hearted offensive was a particularly galling demonstration of the allies' reluctance to use sufficient force to challenge Serb aggression. The U.S., which ordinarily exercises crucial leadership in such affairs, had stumbled. A cautious George Bush had avoided becoming entangled in the region's problems, spurring demands by presidential candidate Clinton for an iron-fisted approach toward the Serbs. But once in office Clinton proceed to soft-sell the get-tough strategy among NATO allies. When the Serbs continued to shell and "cleanse" Muslims out of their homes, the alliance belatedly declared "safe areas" like Bihac to be protected by air strikes—but then rarely ordered them.

Yet military threats had worked once during the conflict: in besieged Sarajevo in February, after a horrifying Serb bombardment of the capital's marketplace. A cease-fire had gone into effect at 9 one morning in order to let a convoy of refugees leave the city. As relieved citizens thronged the market, a mortar shell slammed into a table surrounded by shoppers and exploded with dreadful force, killing 68 and wounding more than 200. An outraged world was galvanized into action. The allies announced a "total exclusion zone" for heavy weapons, backed up by a strong threat of bombing. The Serbs complied with the 10-day ultimatum set by NATO, and the Bosnian capital spent the spring and early summer enjoying a welcome semblance of peace.

The success of the deadline ultimatum in Sarajevo was not to be repeated. The Europeans, along with Bill Clinton, flinched at the thought of risking even one of their soldiers in confronting an enemy so inscrutable and remote. The next move on the chessboard came just before Christmas, when the Clinton Administration allowed former president Jimmy Carter to engage in one of his rounds of freelance diplomacy. The master of nice-guy negotiating met with Karadzic; describing the Serbs' cause as misunderstood by Americans, Carter emerged with Karadzic's promise to accept a cease-fire, which went into effect at the end of the year and was scheduled to last until May 1. For the most part, the guns were silent in Bosnia. But the central question—the final disposition of the Bosnian land so brutally fought over by Serbs and Muslims—seemed no closer to settlement. ■

SHOWDOWN IN

"The U.S. has not sought, does not seek and will not seek to establish any international right to abortion."

—VICE PRESIDENT AL GORE

IT RAN THE COURSE OF A TYPICAL FAMILY argument, opening with fierce disputes, even threats of violence, and ending in a surprising display of peace and harmony. But this time the family doing the shouting was the Family of Man, and the occasion was the International Conference on Population and Development in Cairo, sponsored by the United Nations. For once, those nations were truly united: no attending country voted against the final draft of a 113-page plan calling on governments to commit $17 billion annually by the year 2000 to curb population growth.

The triumphant show of harmony at the close of the conference came as a surprise, for the months leading up to it had promised a melee. An unusual convergence of interests between Roman Catholic and Muslim leaders put the organizers of the conference on the defensive around the flash points of abortion and sex education for teens. In the weeks before the conference opened, Vatican sources directed an unusual personal attack at U.S. Vice President Al Gore, several Muslim leaders declined to attend, and Islamic fundamentalist extremists in Egypt threatened to disrupt the proceedings with violence.

The goal of the meeting was to reach general agreement on how to control the world's population, which reached 5.7 billion in 1994 and is swelling toward a disastrous 10 billion by the year 2050. The host city itself provided a sobering reality check for the significance of the conference: crowded, chaotic Cairo is the capital of a country that jams 62 million people into a narrow strip of arable land the size of the Netherlands.

Heading into the conference, many issues were not in dispute: more than 90% of a draft document had been agreed upon by 180 U.N. member countries. Its centerpiece was a plan to curb population growth by enhancing the status of women around the world. The plan, strongly supported by the U.S., called for channeling funds into local programs that would give women better access to family-planning services and improved health care, while urging men to shoulder more responsibility for contraception and child rearing. Said Nafis Sadik, executive director of the U.N. Population Fund and the guiding force behind the conference: "There is a strong focus on gender equality and empowering women to control their lives—especially their reproductive lives."

That language drew early and fervent protests from the Vatican, which saw "control their reproductive lives" as a code phrase calling not only for access to artificial birth-control methods but also to abortion on demand. Sadik maintained that the conference plan did not endorse or encourage abortion,

CAIRO

A conference on population growth pits the U.S. against a surprising religious alliance

but only declared that the millions of abortions now taking place every year must be performed more safely.

The draft document also sparked an uproar in the Islamic world, where abortion is generally forbidden. Saudi Arabia's highest body of religious authorities condemned the conference as a "ferocious assault on Islamic society." Sudan, Lebanon and Iraq announced that they would send no delegates to Cairo, and the leaders of Turkey, Bangladesh and Indonesia bowed out. Only Pakistan's Prime Minister Benazir Bhutto supported the conference: she not only attended, but gave a major address.

While Muslim leaders withdrew, the Vatican strongly pressed its objections. The week before the conference, the chief spokesman for Pope John Paul II, Joaquín Navarro-Valls, accused Vice President Gore of misrepresenting the U.S. position on abortion. Referring to a speech in which Gore

"The draft document, which has the United States as its principal sponsor, contradicts, in reality, Mr. Gore's statement."

—A VATICAN SPOKESMAN

stated that "the U.S. has not sought, does not seek and will not seek to establish any international right to abortion," Navarro-Valls said, "The draft document, which has the United States as its principal sponsor, contradicts, in reality, Mr. Gore's statement." As proof, Navarro-Valls cited a U.N. proposal that women "have access to safe, effective, affordable and acceptable methods of fertility regulation." That language, he contended, was meant to include the right to abortion.

But once the Vatican had made its key point, it performed a stunning reversal by endorsing much of the program. The final draft of the document recognized that unsafe abortions are a public-health problem that should be addressed. But the draft steered clear of encouraging abortion as a means of family planning. The Vatican's conciliatory step may have been a response to the anger aroused by its earlier attempts to rally nations against the meeting. The Holy See had courted fundamentalists in Iran, for example, but instead of bashing the West, the Islamic republic delighted delegates by working harmoniously to resolve differences over the language in the final document.

The unexpected consensus in Cairo left delegates bubbling about a "watershed in world history." But it was far from certain that the conference would have lasting impact. Many U.N. action programs, however fiercely debated and intricately crafted, are allowed to fade into oblivion over the years. Yet whatever the practical benefits of the conference, few denied its symbolic importance. The harmony achieved in Cairo may signal a new, more mature approach to confronting a potential global disaster, allowing the world family to move beyond divisive debates about abortion and contraception in dealing with the population juggernaut. ∎

Bombs and Bombast

A new boss signs an agreement to end the nuclear smokescreen

GLOBAL VISION: His father tried to burnish his reputation, but defectors told tales of Kim Jong Il's penchant for Portuguese oranges, French brandy and Swedish women.

GRANT AT LEAST THIS MUCH TO KIM IL SUNG: HE certainly knew how to go out with a bang. The last Stalinist dictator managed to die just when the parts of the world least sympathetic to him would miss the ultimate totalitarian the most. A god-king to his own people, a monster to those he waged war on and a riddle to almost everyone else, the only leader that communist North Korea had ever known perished at such a delicate point of diplomacy that even his sternest ill-wishers were praying that it was not true. On July 8, as Radio Pyongyang sobbed the obituary, key questions were left hanging: What would become of the stalemate between North Korea, the U.S. and the U.N. over Kim's dreams of building an atomic bomb? Would Kim succeed in becoming the first communist dictator to pass leadership to his son, Kim Jong Il?

By the end of the year, the world knew the answer to the first of those questions, but not the second. Thanks to strong U.S. diplomacy, Pyongyang reached an agreement on the future of its nuclear program. But inside hermetically sealed North Korea, the future of Kim Jong Il, 52, was still very much in doubt.

Kim Il Sung died just as U.S. and North Korean negotiators were beginning talks in Geneva on the dangerously mounting dispute over the north's nuclear program. For 16 months, North Korea had played a complicated game of nuclear now-you-see-it, now-

you-don't, and in June Kim had blocked the International Atomic Energy Agency from verifying whether North Korea had already secretly diverted enough plutonium for a bomb or two. In response, President Clinton for the first time asked the U.N. Security Council to take up the issue of economic sanctions against North Korea. At this point of stalemate, former U.S. President Jimmy Carter entered the scene, paying a "private visit" to Kim in his capital, Pyongyang, and emerging to claim a diplomatic breakthrough. Sure enough, the North Koreans confirmed in late June that they would freeze their nuclear program and engage in talks in Geneva with the U.S. over its nuclear future.

At this moment, when the 82-year-old dictator suddenly seemed to be reaching out to the world at last, Kim Il Sung died. The future of his recent agreements was put in doubt—as was the future of the nation itself—for Kim Jong Il was as spectacularly mysterious as his father. The bouffant-topped heir was rumored to be a lightweight with a yen for cognac and women. Yet Kim Jong Il did assume top posts in party and government and announced that talks would continue. Finally, on October 21, North Korea signed an accord with the U.S. under which it agreed to stop violating the Nuclear Nonproliferation Treaty and replace old nuclear power plants that produce weapons-grade plutonium. The payoff: Pyongyang would receive free fuel oil and $4 billion (mostly from South Korea and Japan) to build safer light-water reactors that yield a type of plutonium harder to use in building atom bombs. Critics called the pact a bribe, claimed it might encourage others to nuclear blackmail, and noted that it allowed Pyongyang five years before it had to open its suspect sites to inspection.

Meanwhile, Kim Jong Il remained aloof, not speaking to his citizens and not meeting with representatives of foreign countries, fueling rumors that his grasp on power was slight. Ahead lay a policy dilemma that might carry the seeds of his destruction: keeping the country isolated and politically rigid might result in widespread starvation, while serious efforts at reform could either topple the regime or lead to a coup by hard-liners. ■

■ RWANDA
Kingdom of Revenge
A centuries-old feud erupts into massacres and mass migrations

ON THE MARCH: Leaving everything behind, whole villages fled together; tribal elders took charge of rationing scarce supplies, priests reassembled their congregations and mini-marketplaces sprang up everywhere.

N ORMALLY IN SPRING, WHEN THE RAINS COME TO the lush valleys of Rwanda, the rivers swell with a rich red soil. In 1994 they were more swollen than ever. First came the corpses of men and older boys, slain trying to protect their sisters and mothers. Then came those of the women and girls, flushed out from their hiding places and cut down. Last were the babies, whose bodies bore no wounds; they had been tossed alive into the water to drown. The bodies, or pieces of them, glided by for half an hour or so at a time, about as long as it takes to wipe out a community, carry the victims to the banks and dump them in. Then the water would run clear for a while, until men and older boys drifted into view again, then women, then their babies, all reuniting in the shallows.

Aid workers estimate that anywhere from 500,000 to 1 million died in Rwanda in 1994. The bodies not rotting by the roads were buried in mass graves or floated down the rivers, far from the arithmetic of history.

How did so much hatred accumu-

MASS EXODUS: As if infected with sorrow, refugees spread woe to Rwanda's neighbors

UGANDA
10,500

Goma
over 1 million
Gisenyi ● Byumba
RWANDA
ZAIRE Lake ★ Kigali
Kivu
Safe
Zone
Cyangugu Butare Benaco
& Ngara
Bukavu 460,500
250,000
TANZANIA

Uvira Bujumbura Ngozi, Kirundo
350,000 ★ & Muyinga
200,000
AFRICA

BURUNDI
0 50 mi.
0 50 km Lake RWANDA
Tanganyika

Source: U.N. High Commissioner for Refugees TIME Map by Paul J. Pugliese

late in so small a nation? Europeans who stumbled into Rwanda a century ago found a country ruled by tall, willowy Tutsi cattle lords under a magical Tutsi king, while darker-skinned, stockier Hutu farmers tended the land, grew the food and kept the Tutsi clothed and fed. The tribes lived in symbiotic harmony—until the Europeans came. First the Germans and then, after World War I, the Belgians ruled this small African colony. Based on their notions of racial hierarchy, the Belgians upheld the dominance of the Tutsi, with their lighter skin and aquiline, almost European features, over the majority Hutu population. A minimum height was set for the sons of chiefs who wanted to go to school, which effectively disqualified many of the shorter Hutu. The Tutsi received the best government jobs, even as the colonists drained Rwanda's wealth.

The years of colonialism essentially destroyed the social and political structures that had kept tribal peace for centuries. By 1959 the aggrieved Hutu majority had risen up in rebellion; in some villages machete-wielding gangs set upon the Tutsi and hacked off their feet, cutting them down to size. The fearful Belgians abruptly abandoned their Tutsi agents and sided with the Hutu majority. Having inflamed the Hutu's resentment of the Tutsi élite, the colonizers left the once ruling minority to the mercies of the mob. Thousands of Tutsi fled into exile in Uganda, where they waited for 30 years for the chance to reclaim their power.

By the time the Belgians ceded independence to Rwanda in 1962, the foundations for slaughter had been laid. From 1973 onward, Rwanda was led by President Juvenal Habyarimana, a Hutu who grabbed power in a coup and worked hard to hang onto it, in part by further demonizing the Tutsi. But by the late 1980s his economy was gasping, famine was spreading and his hold on power looked increasingly fragile. A number of exiled Tutsi formed the Rwandan Patriotic Front and devoted themselves to overthrowing Habyarimana. In 1990 the R.P.F. invaded from Uganda and launched a holy war that came to a halt only in August 1993 with the Arusha accords, signed by the R.P.F. and the Rwandan government. The accords mandated that Tutsi would finally be allowed into a national-unity government, and that a new army of both Hutu and Tutsi soldiers would enforce the peace.

> "First it was politics. Then it was genocide." How can so much hatred have accumulated in so small an area?

THE PROSPECT OF RECONCILIATION WAS TOO much for Hutu hard-liners, who began plotting against Habyarimana. On the night of April 6, the plane carrying the President and his neighboring head of state, Cyprien Ntaryamira of Burundi, was shot out of the sky over Kigali, the capital. The two were on their way back from a peace conference in Tanzania that was meant to further advance the coming truce between the Tutsi and Hutu. Instead, with Habyarimana's death, the conflict turned into massacre after massacre after massacre. Though U.N. officials believed the Hutu presidential guard was behind the assassination, the Hutu instantly blamed it on the Tutsi rebels of the R.P.F. Within minutes of the crash, soldiers of the presidential guard, who most resisted any sharing of power with Tutsi, took to the streets. Joined by mobs of drunken young men, they began hunting down Tutsi civilians, killing them where they stood. There were no sanctuaries: blood flowed down the aisles of churches, where many sought refuge, and five priests and 12 women hiding out in a Jesuit center were slaughtered. Toddlers lay sliced in half, and mothers with babies strapped to their backs sprawled dead on the streets of Kigali. The fighting was hand to hand, intimate and unspeakable, a kind of bloodlust that left those who managed to escape it hollow-eyed and mute.

Beneath the killing frenzy, something more systematic and sinister was happening. Moderate members of the Hutu government, those who had favored making some accommodation with the Tutsi, were among the first to be hunted down. Thousands of Tutsi took refuge in the Kigali sports stadium; U.N. refugee officials said that each night, armed Hutu with lists of professionals and intellectuals would arrive at the stadium, haul out dozens of Tutsi and execute them, in a kind of intellectual ethnic cleansing. Much of the most vicious killing was done not by the army but by Hutu death squads, young men in street clothes, armed with anything from a screwdriver to an Uzi to a machete, with whistles around their necks. If one spotted a fleeing Tutsi family, he blew his whistle, and his comrades sealed off any escape. "First it was politics," said an eyewitness. "Then it was genocide."

The population grew so desperate that in a single 24-hour period in May a quarter of a million people streamed across the border into Tanzania, creating an instant city, the second largest in that country. Some of the refugees were Tutsi, but many were Hutu who

NO ESCAPE: More than 2 million exiles fled the country, only to find that disease ruled the refugee camps. Typhoid, dysentery, malaria and cholera conspired to kill those who had escaped the young men in the death squads, at left.

feared that the Tutsi rebels of the R.P.F., now controlling much of eastern Rwanda and threatening to capture Kigali, would exact revenge for the massacres. By August at least 2.2 million people had fled the country, including 1 million Hutu refugees who pushed northwest into the Zaire town of Goma in one five-day period. In early July Goma was a town of 80,000 on the shores of a lovely lake; by the end of the month it held more than 1 million sick and starving newcomers, who camped on doorsteps, in schoolyards, in cemeteries, in fields so crowded that people slept standing up. In the refugee camps, sanitation was impossible; typhoid, dysentery and cholera menaced the refugees, especially the children. Malarial mosquitoes swarmed above the swamps, and the dry coughs of pneumonia and tuberculosis echoed through the camps.

From the beginning of the crisis, the Clinton Administration stoutly resisted leading a full-scale relief effort. But in late July, as the magnitude of the refugee problem became apparent, the President took stronger measures, ordering a round-the-clock airlift of food, water and medicine and dispatching U.S. soldiers to distribute them. Ultimately the U.S. contributed $570 million in relief aid.

In late July the R.P.F. declared victory in the civil war and formed a new, inclusive government. Relief officials maintained that the Tutsi victors showed great restraint in their conduct of the four-year war and their prescriptions for peace. In a gesture of reconciliation, the R.P.F. named a moderate Hutu as President and Prime Minister, though the real power rested in the hands of R.P.F. General Paul Kagame, now Vice President, who masterminded the military victory. The proud and reserved Kagame, 37 in 1994, was a brilliant guerrilla tactician who had broadened his movement to include members of all factions who shared his views. More than half the posts in Kagame's new government went to non-R.P.F. members. But the habits of hatred die hard: many Hutu leaders grew only more belligerent in defeat and vowed revenge. In this land of tribal rivalries, the rivers could once again run with blood. ∎

An End to "The Troubles"?

After 25 years of terrorism and tears, a fragile peace comes to Ulster

BURNING ISSUES: A lasting peace will have to take root in children nurtured by hatred. After debasing this Loyalist flag, these boys in a Catholic section of Belfast will burn it.

ACCORDING TO AN OLD STORY, THE PILOT OF AN AIRliner flying into Belfast once advised his passengers to turn their watches back to local time—1690. The Irish on board surely savored this morsel of black humor. But in 1994, as the sorrow of centuries marched in review before Irish eyes, the gallows wit gave way to the fugitive elixir of hope. In Northern Ireland, 25 years of civil strife punctuated by acts of mayhem seemed near expiring when leaders of the two militant groups, the pro-Catholic Irish Republican Army and the pro-British Loyalists, agreed to lay down their arms.

The cease-fire in "the Troubles" was spurred by the Downing Street Declaration of December 1993, under which Prime Ministers John Major of Britain and Albert Reynolds of Ireland offered Sinn Fein, the political wing of the I.R.A., a seat at the bargaining table if the guerrillas permanently renounced violence.

After months of groundwork and tantalizing hints by Gerry Adams, the charismatic leader of Sinn Fein, the I.R.A. announced a "complete cessation of military operations" on August 31. "We've won! Up the I.R.A.!" cried cheering paraders in impromptu motorcades in the Roman Catholic section of Belfast, capital of British-ruled Northern Ireland. Said Maura Collins, 28: "I have known little else but the Troubles. I am optimistic this

will bring peace for my children to grow up in a better environment." Conversely, the unseen hand of some Protestant militant scrawled an ominous piece of grafitti: WAR HAS ONLY BEGUN.

Begun? With 3,168 killed and more than 36,000 wounded in political violence since 1969, this brutalized society could hardly expect the momentum of vengeance to shift gears sharply as the result of a single proposal. The day after the I.R.A. announcement, assailants from the Protestant paramilitary Ulster Defense Association shot dead a Catholic in northern Belfast and claimed responsibility for an attempt to kill a taxi driver. Unsurprisingly, the Rev. Ian Paisley, the firebrand Protestant orator, rejected the I.R.A. offer as bunk.

Yet six weeks after the I.R.A.'s cease-fire declaration, the two most important paramilitary groups of Protestant Loyalists announced that they too would "cease all operational hostilities" at midnight October 13. "It's a great day for the people of Northern Ireland," said John Hume, leader of Ulster's Social Democratic and Labour Party.

Spokesmen for the Protestant groups—the Ulster Volunteer Force, the Ulster Freedom Fighters and the Red Hand Commandos—linked their truce to the I.R.A.'s continued adherence to its cease-fire. Yet like the I.R.A., the Loyalists avoided using the word permanent to describe their cease-fire, as called for in the Downing Street Declaration as a precondition for any talks. After the I.R.A. cease-fire, Reynolds backed away from the condition, but Britain's Major had Protestant Unionists' fears to assuage. Nonetheless, Major made the next move. Calling the quiet of the I.R.A.'s guns "more compelling than words," he announced in mid-October that the talks including Sinn Fein could start before Christmas.

True peace remained an elusive goal. Politically, the two camps were as bitterly opposed as ever, with the I.R.A. demanding a united Ireland—whatever the 1 million-member Protestant majority in Northern Ireland might say. In November the Reynolds government fell in a domestic crisis, casting further doubts on the future. Even so, after enduring 25 years of hatred, Northern Ireland seemed eager to give peace a chance. ■

WORLD BRIEFS

From Russia, with Venom

WITH RUSSIA ENSNARED IN A FINANcial, political and spiritual crisis as great as any in its thousand-year history, ultranationalist demagogue Vladimir Zhirinovsky saw his support edge toward the mainstream. His followers now included military officers, well-groomed young men from the new commercial classes and middle-aged, postcommunist apparatchiks. Part showman, part shyster, Zhirinovsky continued his outrageous high jinks in 1994: he heaved a potted plant at Jewish protesters in Strasbourg, took his entourage to an exotic-dancing club in Helsinki and posed—au naturel—for photographers while cavorting in a steam bath in Serbia. Yet his astonishing displays of excess only seemed to endear him to his followers—even as Boris Yeltsin's power appeared to be shaken by the military quagmire in rebellious Chechnya.

STRONGMAN? As Yeltsin's grip on power loosened, Zhirinovsky pressed ahead.

22 bodies were found in this ritual room.

Cult of Death

IN CANADA AND SWITZERLAND, INvestigators probed the deaths of 53 members of the Order of the Solar Temple, an apocalyptic religious cult. The cult headquarters in Switzerland was consumed by fire; officials called the deaths mass murder followed by mass suicide. Among the dead: Luc Jouret, 46, leader of the cult, and co-leader Joseph di Mambro, 70.

Rescue in Marseilles

A BLOODY CATASTROPHE WAS AVERTED in Marseilles as a team of French antiterrorist commandos stormed a hijacked Air France jetliner, saving all 173 hostages aboard and killing four gunmen who, disguised as security officials, had seized the plane at Algiers airport on Christmas Eve. Three hostages were murdered before Algerian authorities permitted the plane to take off for Marseilles. French police found 20 sticks of dynamite on the plane, confirming an earlier tip that the hijackers intended to blow it up over Paris. Several hours after the rescue, the Armed Islamic Group (G.I.A.), the militant fundamentalist movement that claimed responsibility for the hijacking, retaliated by murdering four Roman Catholic priests—three French and one Belgian—in the Algerian city of Tizi-Ouzou.

The Jackal: Caged at Last

CARLOS

AFTER A 20-YEAR MANhunt that extended throughout Europe and the Middle East, one of the world's most wanted terrorists was arrested in Sudan and flown to France. Ilich Ramírez Sánchez, a.k.a. Carlos the Jackal, had masterminded the kidnapping of 11 OPEC ministers from a Vienna conference hall in 1975. He has also been linked to a 1982 Paris bombing that had killed one person and wounded 63, and to the fatal shootings of two French counterintelligence agents in 1975.

Sayonara and Ciao

THEY CAME TO POWER PROMISING TO carry out government reforms, yet both resigned in failure in 1994. The government of Japan's President Morihiro Hosokawa fell in April, under mounting allegations of corruption. Across the globe former media magnate Silvio Berlusconi, besieged by scandal, left the Italian presidency in December after seven months in office. ∎

The Cruel Sea

In one of the century's worst maritime disasters, the passenger ferry *Estonia*—bound for Sweden from Estonia across the chilly Baltic Sea—capsized and sank just before midnight on September 28. Of the roughly 1,000 people aboard, more than 900 were confirmed drowned. The suspected cause: a leaky front door for loading passenger cars.

Boom for Whom?

FAST TRACK: North Carolina's Nucor can forge a ton of steel four times faster than most mills; it's the most productive in the world.

Companies cheered as the U.S. finally beat its business rivals around the world, but for ordinary Americans, the victory carried a bitterly high price

TO PROFESSIONAL ATHLETES AND THEIR ADORING fans, there is nothing so exultant as the chant of "We're No. 1!" In 1994, American business executives were getting somewhat the same feeling. Finally, finally, they were beating their Japanese, German, South Korean, Taiwanese, name-the-country rivals—and in products like autos, machine tools and computer chips, where a few years ago they were being trounced. The U.S. firms were not only turning back an import invasion of American markets but also triumphing in so-called third-country export markets and even swiping some sales in Japan and other tormentor countries. The closest thing to an official world championship of business is top rank among the nations studied by the Swiss-based World Economic Forum, and in September 1994 the forum made the announcement: after eight years of Japanese domination, the U.S. in 1993 had the world's most competitive economy.

But many ordinary Americans, and even some corporate middle managers, greeted that news with a shrug and a "So what?"—or a skeptical obscenity. The price of beating overseas competition had been bitterly high: wave after wave of downsizing layoffs, wage increases limited or forgone, replacement of full-time workers by part-time or temporary hired hands. Even those who had hung on to regular jobs were often too exhausted by long hours of overtime and weekend work to enjoy the extra money they were earning.

The upshot, according to TIME's Board of Economists, was this: the increases in productivity, or output per worker hour, that had helped make the U.S. No. 1 again also laid the groundwork for an unprecedented period of steady growth in output and employment, with little inflation. Said Stephen Roach, senior international economist at the investment firm of Morgan Stanley: "Ultimately, that could be translated into the long-awaited improvement in the standard of living of the American worker." But, as he and other board members noted, that didn't hap-

pen in 1994. Making it do so, said Roach, "is the real challenge" facing the economy.

Meanwhile, the public mood seemed confused and contradictory. Among 800 people questioned in October in a TIME/CNN poll, 81% thought their own family's finances were doing either fairly well (69%) or very well (12%). Yet when asked "Do you personally feel better off as a result of the recent improvement of the economy?" 58% answered no, 37% yes.

Even to experts, the economy displayed two faces, both of which were on view in Flint, Michigan. Flint is the site of General Motors' Buick City works, which is central to all GM auto production because it makes parts for assembly plants throughout the country. But Buick City was also the scene in late September of a strike that, said Roach, "was symbolic of an issue that is really at the core of the debate right now: Do workers get to reap the benefits of the improved efficiencies they are delivering to employers?"

Eight years ago, after the closing of GM's Fisher Body plant, Michael Moore's sarcastic film *Roger & Me* portrayed Flint as a dying community. But since then U.S. automakers had turned themselves from the world's highest-cost producers to those with the lowest costs: only $42 in wages for each $100 in product turned out, about a third below Toyota or Mercedes-Benz. They had won back so many motorists who formerly bought only foreign cars that the share of the U.S. market going to imported autos had fallen from 22% in 1991 to less than 14% in late 1994. Profits were booming; GM had turned a record $4.9 billion loss in 1991 to a profit of $2.5 billion in 1993 and $3.3 billion for the first three quarters of 1994. Buick City was running flat out to meet demand.

But workers complained that for them expansion spelled exhaustion. Companies throughout American industry were using overtime to wring the most out of the labor force: the factory workweek was averaging a near record 42 hours, including 4.6 hours of overtime. Americans, ob-

The key question: When would the surging gains in the economy be translated into benefits workers could feel in their lives?

WORN OUT: Strikers shut down GM's Buick City plant when overtime hours left nearly 10% of the work force ailing.

served Audrey Freedman, a labor economist and member of TIME's board, "are the workingest people in the world." The Big Three automakers pushed this trend to an extreme. The workers at their plants were putting in an average of 10 overtime hours a week and laboring an average of six 8-hour Saturdays a year.

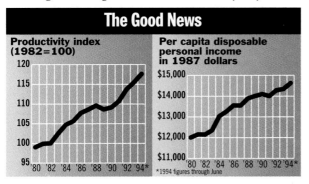

The Good News

Productivity index (1982=100)

Per capita disposable personal income in 1987 dollars

*1994 figures through June

Worse still, the Buick City employees griped, each was being asked to do what used to be several jobs. That complaint was echoed by workers, blue collar and white collar, all over the country. In Chicago, Gamma, the city's largest commercial photo lab, turned a loss into a profit partly by dismissing 25 employees and leaving the remaining 160 to carry the same workload. Said sales manager George Burns: "Everyone has to do everyone else's job in addition to his own. I sell, supervise and jump into the lab whenever that gets busy." His workdays had lengthened from eight or nine hours to 12 to 14. "You feel it," he said. "It's like a football player at the end of the season. You get out of bed a little slower. It gets a little tougher every day."

For Gamma, GM and other companies, the economics worked out. Overtime was expensive, of course; many autoworkers were earning $65,000 to $70,000 a year, and electricians on plant-maintenance crews working seven-day weeks could push their take above $100,000. But the combined wage, fringe benefit and training costs of hiring new workers would have been more expensive still. Consequently, GM had done no major hiring since 1986, pushing to an extreme a common trend. Since the recovery from the last recession began in March 1991, the U.S. had created almost 6 million new jobs, but in a sense that left it 2 million short; had companies hired at the rate of past expansions, the increase would have been 8 million jobs or more.

Finally, when it absolutely could not avoid adding workers, GM at Buick City and elsewhere turned to temporary-help agencies, which now were supplying blue-collar workers as well as stenographers, computer operators and other office hands. Once more the reason was economics: "temps" drew only wages, not health insurance and other expensive fringe benefits, and they could be used and let go as needed, without drawing the supplementary unemployment benefits GM and other companies must pay to laid-off regular workers.

Again, GM's strategy was typical of American companies generally. About the only way in which the Buick City situation was atypical, in fact, was that the workers

finally rebelled—and won. First, to hear them tell it, they had literally worked themselves sick; by late September, more than 1,000 of the 11,500 workers were on sick leave. At that point, Local 599 of the United Auto Workers called the workers out, aiming to force GM to hire some permanent employees to relieve the overtime crush. Workers responded enthusiastically, and after three days GM settled with a pledge to hire an additional 779 regular laborers. Whether that victory would set any kind of precedent remained to be seen. Not many other workers had been pressed as hard as those in Buick City, nor were many as strategically placed to cripple their company's production by walking out.

Though many employees were overworked, experts like Allen Sinai, chief global economist at the investment firm of Lehman Bros., believed "the world is better than it was." The unemployment rate in 1994 had dropped to a four-year low of 5.9%, and new claims for unemployment insurance—a measure of how many jobs are being lost—had fallen to an average of just over 300,000 for a four-week period in the fall, a five-year low.

THERE WAS MUCH EVIDENCE, HOWEVER, THAT the U.S. was developing into something of a two-tier society. While corporate profits and executive salaries were rising rapidly, real wages (that is, discounted for inflation) were not growing at all. Indeed, the government reported that in 1993 real median household income in the U.S. fell by $312, while a million more people slipped into poverty; those officially defined as poor were 15.1% of the U.S. population vs. 14.8% in 1992. These were astonishing developments for the fourth year of a business recovery that was steadily gaining strength.

The intense drive for productivity was raising the reward for training and education higher than ever. Between 1979 and 1989, calculated labor economist Freedman, median real income for year-round, full-time workers age 25 or older did not change significantly, but within that enormous group there were some dramatic shifts. College-educated women increased their earnings 16%, college-educated men only slightly. Earnings of women with a high school education or less held about even. The big losers were men who never got past high school. Their inflation-adjusted earnings fell 14%.

Freedman's analysis of the reasons for these disparities indicated that they may have widened further since

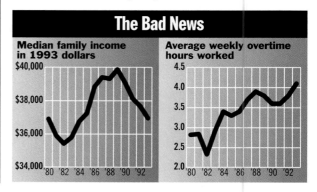

The Bad News

Median family income in 1993 dollars

Average weekly overtime hours worked

WORLD BEATERS: In South Carolina, BMWs can be built for substantially less than it costs to build them in Germany.

1989. She noted, "It's the blue-collar, production-worker jobs that were high-paying and secure and unionized that are much less available" to men with a high school education or less—a trend that corporate downsizing had accentuated even more. At the same time, "the jobs that are being created are computer-using jobs. They're service, white-collar types of work, and they are more likely to go to women." Freedman identified some other profound changes in job markets that held back wage growth. Full-time, full-year workers were no longer as dominant as they had been. There was more self-employment and part-time employment.

RIGID WAGE STRUCTURES HAD BEEN BROKEN UP. Gone, for example, were the days when a raise for truck drivers would quickly be translated into raises for supervisors, warehousemen and trucking-company office employees to maintain standard differentials. Career-long service with a particular company, involving year-after-year raises for doing essentially the same work, was becoming a thing of the past too.

Fine for the companies. But could gains in productivity and competitiveness be translated into enough wage hikes and additional employment to raise the average citizen's standard of living? There were some

signs in '94 that such a turn might be coming. True, downsizing seemed to have become a way of life. Among 713 companies polled by the American Management Association, 25% planned staff reductions in 1995—the largest proportion in the eight-year history of this survey. And at some companies, downsizing showed signs of turning into a fixation, an almost pathological urge to cut whatever the circumstances.

But Big Business knew that in the long run, continually cutting back was obviously no way to grow. Even in the short run, downsizing carried to an extreme could reduce the very productivity it had at first enhanced. Downsizing could also anger customers who found the remaining workers too busy to pay attention to them. Even middle managers, coping with the pervasive insecurity generated by wave after wave of cutbacks, might respond not by working harder but by adopting a to-hell-with-this-company attitude. Said one: "I keep my head down so it doesn't get chopped off."

Such tension and turmoil should not have to continue. Year-by-year fluctuations aside, economists and executives generally agreed that the U.S. had built the best-balanced, leanest, most efficient base for steady growth the country had seen in decades. Workers could only offer the fervent wish: after all the pain it cost to get us here, don't blow it now. ∎

GREENSPAN'S Rates of Wrath

Would the Fed's rate hikes stave off inflation—or kill the recovery?

HIGHER! Greenspan stood tall, defending his jacking up of interest rates against charges he was fighting a phantom.

E VEN AS A SAXOPHONE PLAYER IN A 1940S SWING band, Alan Greenspan had a passion for staying in control. While some of his fellow musicians smoked marijuana or snorted stronger drugs, the future Chairman of the Federal Reserve Board kept track of the band's money. "Some people used to complain that the band was smoking these funny hand-rolled cigarettes," recalled Washington lawyer Leonard Garment, another sober-sided member of the touring ensemble. "But Alan was as clean as Clark Kent: he handled the books and never ran a deficit."

Fifty years later, Greenspan was still firmly in charge of the books. As Chairman of the Fed, he raised short-term interest rates on six separate occasions in 1994, placing himself smack in the middle of a storm of controversy. Greenspan defended his succession of rate hikes—cumulatively the largest in 14 years—as preventive medicine against an overheating of the surging U.S. economy that, if left unchecked, would lead to inflation. But critics charged that he was blocking the recovery rather than slowing it down, and paying too much attention to Wall Street bond traders rather than the daily struggles of the middle class.

On November 15, when Greenspan raised short-term interest rates for the sixth time, it was the largest percentage hike since 1981. Once again his intention, as it had been the previous five times, was to curb anticipated inflation. The Fed chief and his supporters claimed to see real signs of incipient inflation: recent rises in sensitive commodity prices and delays in deliveries of goods, which suggested tightening supplies that might enable some sellers to make price increases stick. Such pressures would abate, they thought, if the Fed made clear that it would raise interest rates enough to deprive inflation of the tinder of cheap loans. Central to their strategy was the bond market. Unlike stocks, which fluctuate in price and dividend depending on company performance, bonds are in essence long-term contracts issued by companies and government bodies, guaranteed to pay a fixed rate of interest. As a kind of long-term loan, they had been financing the recent recovery. Greenspan's strategy was aimed at keeping the bond market stable, thus preventing long-term rates from rising to a level that could abruptly kill the economic expansion.

But no sooner had the Fed acted than bond investors began to worry that the 0.75% hike might not be enough to keep inflation at bay. "There's more to do, so what's the point in being a hero and buying bonds at this rate when it still has a way to go," said David Glen, 37, the manager of $6.5 billion in bond funds for Scudder, Stevens & Clark. So after a brief period of euphoria, the bond market tumbled.

This vote of no confidence gave the bond market the aspect of a fierce pagan idol that could never be appeased. No sooner did it receive one more form of tribute than it found fresh problems to worry about. Among other things, investors saw a new threat of inflation in promises by House Speaker-in-waiting Newt Gingrich—and later, Bill Clinton—to cut taxes in 1995 without any credible program for restoring lost revenues. The stock market, meanwhile, suffered a steep 96.24-point fall in the Dow Jones industrial average the day after Greenspan's first rate hike. But once investors understood the Fed's strategy and saw that the economy was continuing its strong recovery, the stock market grew modestly through the end of the year.

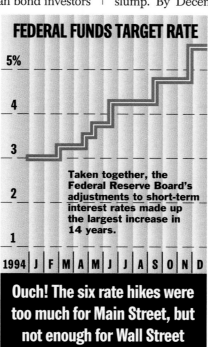

FEDERAL FUNDS TARGET RATE

Taken together, the Federal Reserve Board's adjustments to short-term interest rates made up the largest increase in 14 years.

1994 J F M A M J J A S O N D

Ouch! The six rate hikes were too much for Main Street, but not enough for Wall Street

GREENSPAN SEEMED TO BE BESIEGED ON TWO fronts by the fall: he was receiving little credit from the bond market for his five previous elevations of the interest rate, and he was unintentionally deepening an old fault line in the American economy. "Never before has there been such a huge gap in perception between what is going on in the real economy and what the financial markets think is going on," said Robert Hormats, the vice chairman at Goldman Sachs International. In November the two sides of the argument, accustomed to fighting with statistics, came as close as they could to meeting face to face: while Fed members deliberated over the sixth increase, some 200 protesters led by the AFL-CIO gathered outside in the first such demonstration against rate hikes since farmers blocked the street with tractors in the early 1980s.

Less partisan Fed watchers argued that Greenspan should declare victory in the war against inflation and stop driving up rates. But defenders of the rate hikes made the following case: with unemployment at just 6% in the third quarter and factories humming along at nearly 85% of their capacity, the U.S. economy was in a dangerous zone. In this view, the Federal Reserve was likely to keep tightening credit until the economy slowed from a feisty 4% growth rate to a more sustainable 2.5%. If the Fed could achieve that goal, it would accomplish a rare "soft landing," the jargon for slowing just enough to restrain inflation without sending the economy into a slump. By December, only one month after the sixth hike, Greenspan was already strongly suggesting another increase would come in early 1995.

But Fed critics argued that there was no need for such maneuvering, which risked bringing on a recession, because inflation was already under control. They gained support when the government reported that the Consumer Price Index, a key gauge of inflation, had risen only 2.7% cumulatively over the year before. In addition, the Fed's critics insisted that traditional warning signs of inflation, such as high rates of factory utilization, were no longer reliable because the U.S. economy had become so productive that companies could build more of everything, from cars to computers, without pushing up prices.

Despite the bond market's cool reception, the Fed's sixth hike promised to slow consumer spending at a time when stagnating incomes had forced millions of Americans to use credit cards for everything from dental bills to trips to the supermarket. Consumers owed more than $4 trillion at the end of the second quarter; that equaled more than 80% of their disposable income, the highest such ratio on record.

Rising interest costs would also slow the expansion of small companies, which generate lots of jobs but because of their size must borrow from banks at more than the prime rate. No sooner had the Fed moved in November than many banks boosted their primes from 7.75% to 8.5%. Home buyers and car buyers were already talking of postponing rather than purchasing. Yet even as the rising rates hurt borrowers, they proved a boon to many savers. Economists say that for every percentage-point increase in short-term rates, holders of securities ranging from Treasury bills to money-market funds gain nearly $20 billion in annual income.

Would Greenspan's gamble pay off? According to David Blitzer, chief economist of Standard & Poor's Corp., there have been nine U.S. recessions since World War II—and only two soft landings. But that didn't seem to bother the Fed's No. 1 horn, who had learned how to keep cool in the '40s and never lost the knack. ∎

Golden Harvest

One year after the great floods, U.S. farmers raise a bumper crop

ATE OCTOBER 1994: STRETCHING ACROSS AMERICA from the foothills of the Alleghenies to the high plains of the West, the greatest harvest spectacle the world had ever seen rushed toward its finish. Half a million thundering combines with dust devils spiraling like proud sentinels above their clattering jaws were cutting through 140 million acres of U.S. corn and soybean fields, night and day, lifting a golden bounty that broke every record in the book.

Official estimates from the U.S. Department of Agriculture put the corn crop at 9.6 billion bushels, up a staggering 52% over 1993's flood-ravaged crop of 6.3 billion. As the the sun rose day after day in mild, cloudless skies, only to be followed by soft, moon-washed nights, the private estimates climbed even higher, to 10 billion bushels, about 500 million beyond the old record set in 1992. Add to this overflow 2.5 billion bushels of soybeans—almost 240 million more than the historic crop of 1979. And when cotton, rice and a hefty 2.3 billion bushes of wheat were counted, it was no won-

der that usually taciturn agronomists and economists turned lyrical over the continuing capacity of America to astound itself with the production of staples. "It is just truly remarkable that farmers could bounce back from the floods and replenish the coffers like this," said Keith Collins, the USDA's chief economist.

The sheer bulk of the harvest rolling into the towering prairie elevators and barges along the great rivers was not the entire story. The yield per acre of land was phenomenal. Early government estimates were for 33.5 bushels per acre of soybeans. That went up to 40.5 bushels per acre before the harvest began. "That is the distinguishing feature," claims economist Collins. "I've never seen an estimate move so far above the trend line. Statistically, it is one chance in a hundred." The average for corn leaped from 127 bushels to 134 bushels per acre.

The choreographers of this production miracle combined a bit of capitalism with salubrious weather. Like their corporate brethren, farmers have learned and leaned. It took only 600,000 farmers to plant, nurture and

MOUNTAINS IN IOWA? As the record harvest swept in, grain elevators like this one in Ralston, Iowa, were filled to overflowing.

crops had all been stuffed with surplus were largely empty because of last year's poor crop and exceptionally high worldwide demand for grain. There appeared to be adequate storage capacity for this year's harvest. Here and there, while trucks, barges and trains maneuvered into position, it was necessary to build mini-mountains of corn on rail sidings and streets, but the 1986 scenes of corn piled on tennis courts and around village squares were not repeated.

There was a temporary downside to such production. In late October corn slid below $2 per bushel for the first time in two years. Soybeans at $5.40 per bushel were a dollar down from 1993. The effect rippled throughout the American food chain. Hogs were $35 per hundredweight—a 14-year low—and live cattle, which had brought $85 per hundredweight just two years before, were selling at $65. The government would cushion the blow of falling prices by paying farmers, for example 65¢ per bushel of corn when it slipped below the target price of $2.75. And in October the USDA announced it would require farmers to take 7.5% of their corn acreage out of production in 1995 to prop up the price of the crop. But in the short term, exports were the remedy. Already in 1994 South Korea had increased its U.S. corn imports fivefold, while Japanese imports had risen 20%.

> **Usually taciturn agronomists turned lyrical over the nation's continuing capacity to astound itself with the production of staples**

Ultimately, when subsidies, exports and ingenuity were taken into account, the income of farmers was expected to grow from $17.5 billion in 1993 to $23 billion in 1994. And it looked as if those cash-happy farmers were on a spending spree: U.S. sales of big (100-horsepower and over) tractors jumped 73% in September compared with 1993.

The final irony of this great harvest drama lies beyond the shores of the U.S. Lester Brown, head of the Worldwatch Institute, predicts that unless there are dramatic changes in population growth and food supply, the world soon will not be able to feed itself. "Food security will replace military security as the principal concern of many nations over the next 40 years," he claims. But others, like Dennis Avery, director of the Center for Global Food Issues at the Hudson Institute in Indianapolis, Indiana, believe that the American harvest miracle may help feed the world, particularly if more money is spent on research in food production. Grain and meat output have been keeping pace with population growth for decades, and Avery claims that eliminating price supports and trade barriers and, above all, increasing the American farm yield even further can feed the livestock of prospering nations as they move to improve their diets. If Avery's vision is realized, America might replace its uneasy role as the world's policeman with a more welcome one: the world's farmer. ■

collect most of this crop, compared with 1 million only 20 years ago. These survivors, almost all of them educated landowners plugged in by computers to the latest technologies of soil, fertilizers and cultivation, were ready but wary. The terrible floods of 1993 had left them convinced that the sand-covered bottomlands—some abandoned in discouragement—would cut into the yield.

Many farmers held their breath as the spring thaws came to a land still saturated with water. But the weather profile in the 1994 growing season was near perfect. After the thaw there were dry, mild days, so the farmers could plant almost without interruption. Most of them used the no-till method, in which seeds were drilled or chiseled into matted stubble left from the year before; this residue forms a weed-retardant layer and a sponge for moisture. The right rains came at the right time. Only in isolated corners of the country were there scorching winds or floods.

There was yet another dividend from smiling Providence. The grain bins that in earlier years of bumper

Asia Reaches for

SHOULDERING INTO THE CLOUDS, SKYSCRAPERS are the modern world's cathedrals of aspiration: the greater the dreams of commercial glory, the higher the towers reach toward heaven. Since the beginning of the 20th century, North America has been the cradle for the tall-taller-tallest buildings, from Manhattan's Woolworth and Empire State buildings to the Sears Tower in Chicago. As the 20th century fades, however, North America is ceding its skyscraper supremacy to Asia. In Malaysia construction is under way on twin towers that will be the tallest edifices on earth when completed in 1996. China is planning a colossus that will reach an even greater height, if not by much. Japan and Taiwan are racing to start their own giants.

If architecture is frozen music, as Goethe wrote, then the tune being sounded across Asia is a triumphant anthem for the coming millennium. Rising skylines in Guangzhou, Shanghai and Wuhan reflect both the world's plunge into investing in China and the commitment of internationally renowned architects, whose new designs reflect a distinctly Asian æsthetic.

"Skyscrapers are symbolic buildings," says Witold Rybczynski, a noted architecture critic who teaches at the University of Pennsylvania. "They aren't big for functional reasons." Transcendent wonders rising above the cityscape, the great buildings exert irresistible allure. When Yokohama's Landmark Tower opened in July 1993, it became not only the tallest building in Japan but also the newest tourist attraction: more than 1.7 million people have taken the ride on the 30-m.p.h. elevators—the world's fastest—to the 69th-floor observatory. Takanori Adachi, 35, a businessman, wishes he had an office there: "I'm sure such a view would bring tranquillity to your mind and raise your productivity."

For 20 years the Sears Tower has stood in Miesian superiority alongside Lake Michigan, unchallenged as the tallest building in the world. Malaysian Prime Minister Mahathir Mohamad aims to change that: he is the mastermind behind the Kuala Lumpur City Center, whose two gleaming, symmetrical skyscrapers, the Petronas Towers, will surpass the U.S. landmark by 23 feet. Mahathir was a member of the jury that chose the architect for the towers, which will be occupied principally by the state-owned Petronas oil company. The winner was

HIGH, HIGHER, HIGHEST

A sampler of the world's tallest, old and new, suggests that, for the master builders of the future, only the sky is the limit.

Messeturm
FRANKFURT, GERMANY
The European record holder is the work of Chicago architect Helmut Jahn. Once likened to a lipstick, the red granite obelisk is a beacon for the city's trade fair.

Tallest existing building (Sears Tower)

Landmark Tower
YOKOHAMA, JAPAN
The project known as Minato Mirai 21 is part of Yokohama's bid to rival Tokyo as an urban center. Its first structure is the Landmark Tower, which is topped by a 603-room hotel.

Central Plaza
HONG KONG
The colony's 78-story Central Plaza nosed past the Bank of China to become Asia's giant—but only by a few meters and not for very much longer.

Empire State Building
NEW YORK CITY
Sleek and streamlined, it was the first office tower to be the symbol of a metropolis and reigned supreme for four decades. Admirers say it still defines skyscraper aesthetics.

Jin Mao Building
SHANGHAI
For the energetic city, the U.S.'s Skidmore, Owings & Merrill gave the exterior a pagoda-like effect.

259 METERS

296 METERS

310 METERS

381 METERS

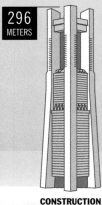

421 METERS

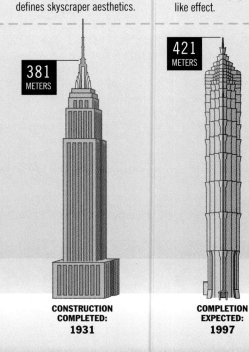

CONSTRUCTION COMPLETED: 1991

CONSTRUCTION COMPLETED: 1993

CONSTRUCTION COMPLETED: 1992

CONSTRUCTION COMPLETED: 1931

COMPLETION EXPECTED: 1997

the Sky

In Asia buildings are piling up as fast as wealth; soon the East will be home to the tallest skyscrapers in the world

Argentine-born Cesar Pelli, whose glass-sheathed World Financial Center has been a glistening gem on the tip of lower Manhattan since 1984.

Pelli's Kuala Lumpur towers, with their lofty spires and horizontal ribbons of glass and stainless steel, will be a striking and romantic update of 1930s Art Deco skyscrapers. "I tried to capture some of the feeling I had when I was in Malaysia," says Pelli, who believes his design embodies the image of a dynamic, rapidly growing country. Halfway up the towers' 88 stories, a sky bridge will connect the buildings, symbolizing a gateway. Islamic geometric forms of squares and circles symbolizing unity, harmony and rationality are incorporated into the floor plan, and the interior will be decorated with local stone, wood and fabric, so that "the buildings will be perceived at all levels as being rooted in Malaysia."

By the year 2000, the Petronas Towers may well be eclipsed. The city of Chongqing, in southwestern China, is planning to construct a 114-story building designed by the New York City firm of Haines Lundberg Waehler. Its team of architects honors the ancient principles of geomancy the Chinese call feng shui in its plans. For example, the architects based their overall concept on the number eight, for good luck: above an eight-story public lobby, offices are located on the eighth through the 80th floors and are punctuated by eight-story atriums.

Britain's Sir Norman Foster, who designed the high-tech Hong Kong and Shanghai Bank in Hong Kong, is planning an audacious project that could move Asia into an authoritative lead in the worldwide race for vertical ascendancy. He and his associates have completed a second-stage development study for Millennium Tower, a conical behemoth in Tokyo that would loom twice as high as the Sears Tower. As yet, Foster's scheme is only a tantalizing theoretical proposal, but along with the skyscrapers already completed or abuilding, it evokes Asia's soaring dreams for the next century. ■

Millennium Tower
TOKYO
Imagine a spike-in-the-sky with such a multitude of diverse spaces and an array of facilities that it would be a vertical version of Tokyo's Ginza or Paris' Champs Elysées.

800 METERS

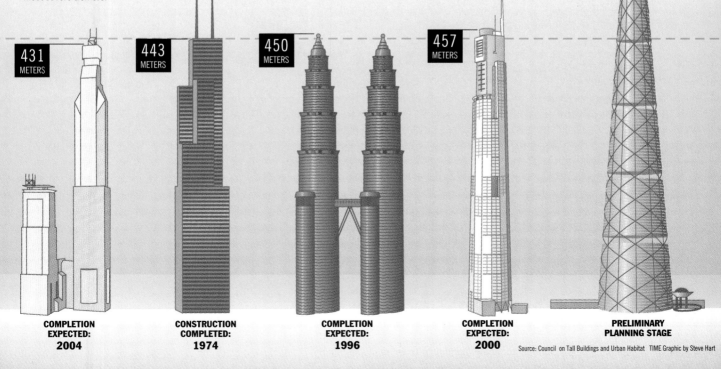

Asia Plaza
KAOHSIUNG, TAIWAN
In an earthquake-prone country, the major concern about the planned 103-story tower is that it must be able to withstand the most severe tremors.

431 METERS

COMPLETION EXPECTED: 2004

Sears Tower
CHICAGO
The austere corporate style, as exemplified by Skidmore, Owings & Merrill's 110-story Sears Tower, was stamped on hundreds of structures around the world.

443 METERS

CONSTRUCTION COMPLETED: 1974

Petronas Towers
KUALA LUMPUR, MALAYSIA
When completed, they will be the pride of the country's 18 million people and a monument to Pharaonic expansion.

450 METERS

COMPLETION EXPECTED: 1996

Chongqing Tower
CHONGQING, CHINA
In a crowded city, a hotel will begin above the clouds on the 80th floor. The glass top will be an illuminated signal in the evening sky.

457 METERS

COMPLETION EXPECTED: 2000

PRELIMINARY PLANNING STAGE

Source: Council on Tall Buildings and Urban Habitat TIME Graphic by Steve Hart

The Walls Come Down

Business applauds as the U.S. fights to open markets around the world

ALL TOO SELDOM DOES WASHINGTON INSPIRE U.S. business leaders to dream out loud about the economic frontiers that suits and pols can conquer together. But as Dick Gady, the chief economist of agriculture giant ConAgra, awaited final approval of the General Agreement on Tariffs and Trade (GATT), he was moved to talk in terms of manifest destiny. "We're going to grow more grain," he boasted. "We're going to grow more beef. We're going to be slaughtering more hogs. We're gonna get that European market!"

Call it NAFTAmath. After Bill Clinton, a committed free-trader, won congressional approval of the North American Free Trade Agreement in 1993, reducing trade barriers among Canada, the U.S. and Mexico, the movement toward free trade caught fire around the globe. Still, 1994 began with a failed attempt at freeing markets. In February, Japanese Prime Minister Morihiro Hosokawa came to Washington for trade talks with Clinton, who was determined to win ironclad agreements to open Japan's markets, which are tightly closed against many U.S. goods. Japan's trade surplus with the U.S. stood at a near record level of $60 billion. But Hosokawa would not give ground; no agreement was reached. In return the U.S. threatened to impose sanctions against Japan. They were averted when Japan agreed to open up markets in four areas in October.

In June, Clinton faced another tough call: whether to continue to give Beijing some form of the most-favored-nation status under which Chinese goods enter American markets at low tariff rates. Citing China's woeful record on human rights, lawmakers and others pressured Clinton to remove the MFN status. But the President, endorsing industry's view that prosperity is the best route to freedom, renewed it.

In November the free-trade winds blew Clinton to Indonesia for a summit meeting of the 18-nation Asia-Pacific Economic Cooperation group. Once again Clinton's commerce-oriented policy set his drive for ever increasing trade with the nations of Asia against his concerns for human rights. Working conditions in Southeast Asia often include a sweatshop pace, low wages and long working hours. To his credit, Clinton tried but failed to enlist U.S. companies in a voluntary set of principles to govern activities in the region. "Trade does take a priority," conceded a White House official.

Returning to Washington, Clinton struggled to pass the GATT treaty. In the last days of 1993, the U.S., along with 123 other nations, had agreed to this breakthrough accord, which would lower worldwide tariffs by a third, remove trade quotas, and protect intellectual property. But the treaty required congressional approval—and the Republicans balked. First Newt Gingrich in the House delayed discussion of the bill until after the November elections. Then Bob Dole in the Senate demanded that a review panel be created to monitor the fairness of trade-dispute decisions. The White House agreed, but rejected Dole's attempt to link approval of GATT to a cut in the capital-gains tax. Congress finally gave approval to GATT, passing it with large bipartisan majorities.

Fresh from this victory, Clinton journeyed to Miami for yet another free-trade love-in, the 34-nation Summit of the Americas. There the leaders of the hemisphere—except Fidel Castro—rounded out the Year of Free Trade by setting a date of 2005 as a deadline for signing a final agreement on a New World common market, with "real progress" to be made on lowering hemispheric trade barriers before the turn of the century. ■

DON'T LOSE YOUR SHIRT: Free-trader Bill Clinton goes native with his fellow conferees at the trade summit in Indonesia.

TOP TRIO: Katzenberg, Spielberg, Geffen.

A Meeting of the Moguls

HOLLYWOOD CALLED IT THE DREAM Team: award-winning director Steven Spielberg, dealmaker extraordinaire David Geffen and Jeffrey Katzenberg, the hardworking executive who had driven Disney studios to prosperity and critical acclaim in a renaissance of its animated features, combined to form a new production company. Katzenberg bolted Disney when he was passed over by boss Michael Eisner for the late Frank Wells' position as president. The team's first deal: developing television shows for Cap Cities/ABC.

Renaissance Nerd

GATES

"BILL GATES: WHAT *Doesn't* He Want?" asked a '94 FORTUNE magazine headline. A billionaire nine times over, Gates *did* want the Codex Hammer, an illustrated collection of musings by *ur*-hacker Leonardo da Vinci. So the master of Microsoft bought it anonymously at a Christie's auction—for $30.8 million.

Red Ink for Japan Inc.

A SURGING STREAK OF ACQUISITIONS in the 1980s left some of America's most famous icons in Japanese hands. But in 1994 Japanese firms reeled from setbacks in the U.S. The chief loser: Sony, which took a $2.7 billion write-off on its money-losing Columbia film studio and reported an overall second-quarter loss of $3.2 billion. Meanwhile, Mitsubishi—80% owner of New York City's Rockefeller Center—was threatening to default

on its five-year-old $1.3 billion mortgage, and Matsushita was locked in management struggles with executives Lew Wasserman and Sidney Sheinberg over the firm's troubled Hollywood studio, MCA.

Danger: Derivatives

AMERICAN INVESTORS DISCOVERED A new financial instrument in 1994—but some were burned in the process. Wall Street's newest offering was the derivative, a computer-generated, hyper-sophisticated and volatile investment. It used the public's massive bet on securities to create a parallel universe of side bets and speculative mutations derived from the value of more traditional investments like stocks and bonds. Derivatives could be as straightforward as options to buy or sell securities or as fancy as unregulated and customized agreements to purchase oil futures in Nigeria while selling dollars in Indonesia and graphite in Madagascar. Derivatives could also be dangerous. In December, archconservative Orange County in Southern California filed for bankruptcy after treasurer Robert Citron lost $1.5 billion on leveraged investments in derivatives and other instruments. The unexpected bankruptcy threatened county pensions, payrolls and schools, and sparked a federal inquiry.

Oranges fell in this market.

MURDOCH: Another steal from CBS.

Rupert Scores Again

MEDIA MOGUL RUPERT MURDOCH WAS never one to agonize over a decision. It took him less than two weeks of negotiations to announce what some called the most sweeping shake-up of affiliates in network-TV history. In return for an investment of $500 million from Murdoch's upstart 7-year-old Fox network, Ronald Perelman's New World Communications agreed to align 12 of its stations— in such major markets as Detroit, Dallas, Atlanta and Phoenix, Arizona—with Fox. The biggest casualty: CBS, which owned eight of the affiliates—many in major markets—and which had been stung in 1993 when Murdoch's Fox network outbid it for rights to N.F.L. football. Immediately after the deal, CBS stock dropped 11%. ∎

Lights! Camera! Dial Tone!

A battle raged in America's $250 billion telecommunications industry as the seven "Baby Bells," cable-TV suppliers and long-distance phone companies fought to wire the nation's home computers, phones and television sets. In 1994 the Walt Disney Co. teamed up with three Bells to develop movies and games for home viewers, while other Bells bought up cable companies. Meanwhile, cable outfits like Time Warner and TCI Inc. planned to offer phone service. Stay tuned.

■ BEHAVIOR

SEX
IN THE
U.S.A.

My, my! It's mainly for the married

I S THERE A LIVING, BREATHING ADULT WHO HASN'T AT TIMES FELT THE nagging suspicion that in bedrooms across the country, on kitchen tables, in limos and other venues too scintillating to mention, other folks are having more sex, livelier sex, better sex? Maybe even that quiet couple right next door is having more fun in bed, and more often. Such thoughts spring, no doubt, from a primal anxiety deep within the human psyche. It has probably haunted men and women since the serpent pointed Eve toward the forbidden fruit and urged her to get with the program.

Still, it's hard to imagine a culture more conducive to feelings of sexual inadequacy than America in the 1990s. Tune in to the soaps. Flip through the magazines. Listen to Oprah. Lurk in the seamier corners of cyberspace. What do you see and hear? An endless succession of young, hard bodies preparing for, recovering from or engaging in constant, relentless copulation. Sex is everywhere in America—and in the ads, films, TV shows and music videos it exports abroad. Although we know that not every ZIP code is a Beverly Hills, 90210, and not every small town a Peyton Place, the impression that is branded on our collective subconscious is a sexual banquet to which everyone else has been invited.

Just how good is America's sex life? Nobody knows for sure. Don't believe the magazine polls that have Americans mating energetically two or three times a week. Those surveys are inflated from the start by the people who fill them out: *Playboy* subscribers, for example, who brag about their sex lives in reader-survey cards. Even the famous Kinsey studies—which caused such a scandal in the late 1940s and early '50s by reporting that half of American men had extramarital affairs—were deeply flawed. Although Alfred Kinsey was a biologist by training (his expertise was the gall wasp), he compromised science by taking his human subjects where he could find them: in boardinghouses, college fraternities, prisons and mental wards. For 14 years he collared hitchhikers who passed through town and quizzed them mercilessly. It was hardly a random cross section.

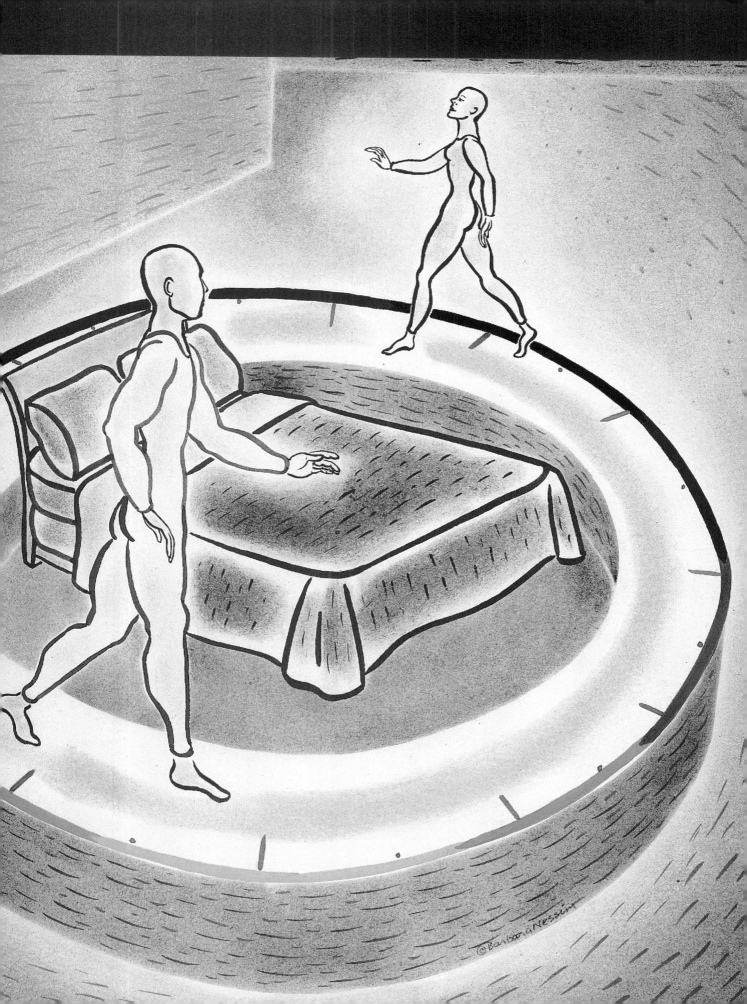

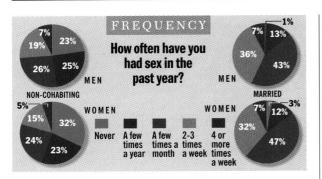

Now, more than 40 years after Kinsey, we finally have some answers. In October 1994 a team of researchers based at the University of Chicago released the long-awaited results of what is probably the first truly scientific survey of who does what with whom in America and just how often they do it.

THE FINDINGS—BASED ON FACE-TO-FACE INterviews with a random sample of nearly 3,500 Americans, ages 18 to 59, and employing techniques honed through decades of political and consumer polling—smashed a lot of myths. While the scientists found that the spirit of the sexual revolution was alive and well in some quarters—they reported that about 17% of American men and 3% of women had had sex with at least 21 partners—the overall impression was that the sex lives of Americans were about as exciting as a peanut-butter-and-jelly sandwich. Among the key findings:
● Americans fall into three groups. One-third have sex twice a week or more, one-third a few times a month, and one-third a few times a year or not at all.
● Americans are largely monogamous. The vast majority (83%) have one or zero sexual partners a year. Over a lifetime, a typical man has six partners; a typical woman, two.
● Married couples have the most sex and are the most likely to have orgasms when they do. Nearly 40% of

found vaginal sex "very or somewhat appealing." Oral sex ranked a distant third, after an activity that many may not have realized was a sex act: "Watching partner undress."
● Adultery is the exception in America, not the rule. Nearly 75% of married men and 85% of married women said they have never been unfaithful.
● There are a lot fewer active homosexuals in America than the oft-repeated 1 in 10. Only 2.7% of men and 1.3% of women reported that they had had homosexual sex in the past year.

The full results of the survey were published as *The Social Organization of Sexuality* (University of Chicago; $49.95), a thick, scientific tome co-authored by Laumann, two Chicago colleagues—Robert Michael and Stuart Michaels—and John Gagnon, a sociologist from the State University of New York at Stony Brook. A thinner companion volume, *Sex in America: A Definitive Survey* (Little, Brown; $22.95), written with New York *Times* science reporter Gina Kolata and aimed at the general reader, was published at the same time.

When details of the survey were revealed, critics and pundits were happy to put their spin on the study. Promoters of the sexual revolution were vociferous:

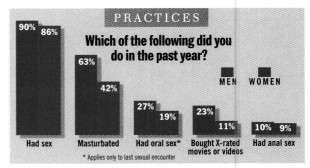

"Positively, outrageously stupid and unbelievable," growled *Penthouse* publisher Bob Guccione. "I would say five partners *a year* is the average for men."

"It doesn't ring true," insisted Jackie Collins, author of *The Bitch, The Stud* and other potboilers. "Where are

54% of men think about sex daily. 19% of women do

married people said they have sex twice a week, compared with 25% for singles.
● Most Americans don't go in for the kinky stuff. Asked to rank their favorite sex acts, almost everybody (96%)

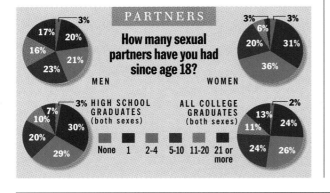

the deviants? Where are the flashers? Where are the sex maniacs I see on TV every day?"

"I'm delighted to hear that all this talk about rampant infidelity was wildly inflated," declared postfeminist writer Camille Paglia. "But if they're saying the sexual revolution never happened, that's ridiculous."

"Totally predictable," deadpanned Erica Jong, author of the 1973 sex fantasy *Fear of Flying*. "Americans are more interested in money than sex."

"Our Puritan roots are deep," said *Playboy* founder Hugh Hefner, striking a philosophical note. "We're fascinated by sex and afraid of it."

"Two partners?! I mean, come on!" sneered *Cosmopolitan* editor Helen Gurley Brown. "We advise our Cosmo girls that when people ask how many partners you've had, the correct answer is always three, though there may have been more."

Europeans seemed less surprised—one way or the other—by the results of the survey. The low numbers confirmed the Continental caricature of Americans as flashy and bold onscreen but prone to paralysis in bed. Besides, the findings were pretty much in line with recent studies conducted in England and France that had also found low rates of homosexuality and high rates of marital fidelity.

Scientists, on the whole, praised the study; but like every statistical survey, this one had its weaknesses. Researchers cautioned that the sample was too limited to reveal much about small subgroups of the population—gay Hispanics, for example. The omission of people over 59 was regrettable, said Shirley Zussman, past president of the American Association of Sex Educators, Counselors and Therapists. "The older population is more sexually active than a 19-year-old thinks, and it's good for both 19-year-olds and those over 59 to know that."

SEX ABROAD

In your lifetime how many sex partners have you had?

	One		Five or more	
MEN				
WOMEN			56%	
U.S.	20%	31%		30%
Britain	21%	39%	44%	20%
France	21%	46%	45%	14%
Finland	12%	28%	60%	34%

From foreign studies cited in this survey.

where Woody Allen tells his psychiatrist that he and Annie have sex "hardly ever, maybe three times a week," and she tells hers that they do it "constantly; I'd say three times a week." In the Chicago study, 54% of the men said they think about sex every day or several times a day. By contrast, 67% of the women said they think about it only a few times a week or a few times a month.

But the basic message of *Sex in America* was that men and women had found a way to come to terms with each other's sexuality—and it is called marriage. "Our study," wrote the authors, "clearly shows that no matter how sexually active people are before and between marriages . . . marriage is such a powerful social institution that, essentially, married people are all alike—they are faithful to their partners as long as the marriage is intact."

Americans, it seems, have come full circle. It's easy to forget that as recently as 1948, Norman Mailer was

Of married people, 94% were faithful in the past year

The Chicago scientists admitted to another possible defect: "There is no way to get around the fact that some people might conceal information," said Stuart Michaels of the Chicago team. The biggest hot button, he said, was homosexuality. "This is a stigmatized group. There is probably a lot more homosexual activity going on than we could get people to talk about."

MUCH OF WHAT IS GENERALLY ACCEPTED as conventional wisdom was confirmed. Kids *do* have sex earlier now; by 15, half of all black males have done it; by 17, the white kids have caught up to them. There *was* a lot of free sex in the '60s: the percentage of adults who had racked up 21 or more sex partners was significantly higher among the fortysomething boomers than among other Americans. And AIDS *has* put a crimp in some people's sex lives; 76% of those who have had five or more partners in the past year said they have changed their sexual behavior, by either slowing down, getting tested or using condoms faithfully.

But more intriguing twists emerged when sexual behavior was charted by religious affiliation. Roman Catholics were the most likely to be virgins (4%) and Jews to have had the most sex partners (34% have had 10 or more). The women most likely to reach orgasm each and every time (32%) were, believe it or not, conservative Protestants. But Catholics edged out mainline Protestants in frequency of intercourse.

Elsewhere in the study, the perceptual gulf between the sexes was reminiscent of the scene in *Annie Hall*

still using the word fug in his novels. There may have been a sexual revolution—at least for those college-educated whites who came of age with John Updike's swinging *Couples*, Philip Roth's priapic *Portnoy's Complaint* and Jong's *Fear of Flying*—but the revolution turned out to have a beginning, a middle and an end. "From the time of the Pill to Rock Hudson's death, people had a sense of freedom," said Judith Krantz, author of *Scruples*. "That's gone."

It was the first survey—Kinsey's—that got prudish Americans to talk about sex, read about sex and eventu-

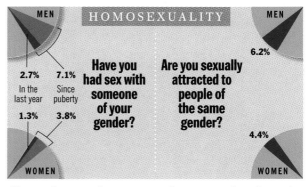

HOMOSEXUALITY

MEN — 2.7% In the last year — 7.1% Since puberty

Have you had sex with someone of your gender?

WOMEN — 1.3% — 3.8%

MEN — 6.2%

Are you sexually attracted to people of the same gender?

WOMEN — 4.4%

ally watch sex at the movies and even try a few things (at least once). Kinsey's methods may have been less than perfect, but he had an eye for the quirky, the fringe, the bizarre. The new report, by contrast, revealed itself to be a remarkably conservative document. It put the fringes on the fringe and concentrated on America's heartland, where life, apparently, is ruled by marriage, monogamy and the missionary position. ∎

The Butt Stops Here

Antismoking forces assailed the weed, but some sniffed a witch hunt

FOR YEARS, SMOKERS AND nonsmokers managed an uneasy truce: Live and let live (or let die). You stay in your section; I'll stay in mine (but don't blow in this direction). Yet in 1994 that truce was stubbed out. A rash of new restrictions, legislation and governmental tough talk elevated the antismoking campaign to new heights. Before, it was a matter of health warnings, moral persuasion and segregation of the warring parties. Now smoking was in danger of being legislated virtually out of existence—or at least shoved into the realm of behavior so socially reviled that it must be practiced only in private. The process was pushed forward on many fronts:

● Tobacco companies came under increasing fire for alleged misconduct and cover-ups. In March, Representative Henry Waxman, a California Democrat, charged that tobacco giant Philip Morris had discovered the first strong evidence that nicotine is addictive in 1983 but suppressed the study. Waxman called the top brass from Philip Morris and six other firms to testify before his House Subcommittee on Health and the Environment, where they faced six hours of sharp questioning and agreed to give Congress previously unpublished research on nicotine and addiction. The executives denied that cigarettes were addictive but admitted that they would rather their children did not smoke.

● Smoking drew new attention from federal regulators. The activist Food and Drug Administration was examining whether to classify nicotine as a drug—a move that

What restrictions should be applied to smoking?

	NONSMOKERS	TOTAL
BANNED	44%	35%
SPECIAL AREAS	52%	59%
NO RESTRICTIONS	3%	5%

Which do you agree with more?

SMOKING IS A BAD HABIT AND SOCIETY SHOULD DO EVERYTHING POSSIBLE TO STAMP IT OUT.	31%	25%
IT'S BAD, BUT EVERYONE SHOULD HAVE THE RIGHT TO MAKE HIS OR HER OWN CHOICE WHETHER TO SMOKE.	67%	73%

would effectively remove cigarettes from the over-the-counter market. FDA Commissioner David Kessler told Congress he believed that nicotine is a "highly addictive agent" and that cigarette producers control the level of nicotine "that creates and sustains this addiction."

● An increasing number of private companies were moving to satisfy the antismoking mood. McDonald's banned smoking in 1,400 of its company-owned fast-food restaurants in the U.S.

Instead of arguing on health grounds, the tobacco industry often recast the debate as a freedom-of-choice issue. And it came down hard on its foes. Philip Morris filed a $10 billion libel lawsuit against ABC for the network's report on the *Day One* newsmagazine show charging that the tobacco industry "artificially adds nicotine to cigarettes to keep people smoking and boost profits."

But more than just tobacco industry executives and die-hard smokers raised questions about the antismoking frenzy. Some feared the crusade had turned into a witch hunt. For all the new efforts to enact tough restrictions on smoking, a TIME/CNN poll found evidence that the American public did not widely support them. The poll found that only 31% of nonsmokers agreed with a statement that our society should do everything possible to stamp out smoking. And just 44% thought smoking should be forbidden in offices. Amid all the new sound and fury over cigarettes, it seemed, the majority of the public came down in favor of an old-fashioned virtue: tolerance. ■

Battle for the Soul of the

INTERNET

BASEMAN

THERE WAS NOTHING VERY SPECIAL ABOUT THE message that made Laurence Canter and Martha Siegel the most hated couple in cyberspace. It was a relatively straightforward advertisement offering the services of their husband-and-wife law firm to aliens interested in getting a green card—proof of permanent-resident status in the U.S. The computer that sent the message was a perfectly ordinary one as well. But on the Internet, even a single computer can wield enormous power, and in April 1994 this one stirred up a controversy that may continue for years.

The Internet, for those who are still a bit fuzzy about these things, is the world's largest computer network and the nearest thing to a working prototype of the information superhighway. It's actually a global network of networks that links the large computer-communications

services (like CompuServe, Prodigy and America Online) as well as tens of thousands of smaller university, government and corporate networks. The Net reaches an estimated 25 million computer users—and is growing like Jack's beanstalk.

Now, just when it seems almost ready for prime time, the Net is being buffeted by forces that threaten to destroy the very qualities that fueled its growth. It's being pulled from all sides: by commercial interests eager to make money on it, by veteran users who want to protect it, by pornographers who want to exploit its freedoms, by parents and teachers who want to make it a safe and useful place for kids. The Canter and Siegel affair, say Net observers, was just the opening skirmish in the larger battle for the soul of the Internet.

What the Arizona lawyers did that fateful April day

SPAMMERS vs. CANCELBOTS
What happens if advertisers spew unwanted solicitations through the Net like so much Spam hitting a fan—and don't respond to entreaties and mail bombs? Militant Net vets send in ad-seeking "cancelbots" to zap the commercial pitches.

was to "Spam" the Net, a colorful bit of Internet jargon that evokes the effect of dropping a hunk of Spam into a fan. They wrote a program called Masspost that put the little ad into almost every active bulletin board on the Net—some 5,500 in all—thus ensuring that it would be seen by millions of Internet users, not just once but over and over again. One writer compared the experience to opening the mailbox and finding "a letter, two bills and 60,000 pieces of junk mail."

In the eyes of many Internet regulars, it was a provocation so bald-faced and deliberate that it could not be ignored. All over the world, Internet users responded spontaneously by answering the Spammers with angry electronic-mail messages called "flames." The volume grew so heavy that the computer delivering the E-mail crashed. A Norwegian programmer even wrote a piece of software that came to be known as the "cancelbot"—a sort of information-seeking robot that roamed the Net looking for Canter and Siegel mass mailings and deleting them before they spread.

The Green Card Incident, as it came to be known, brought to the surface issues that had been lurking largely unexamined beneath the Net's explosive growth. The Net was not designed for doing commerce, and it does not gracefully accommodate new arrivals—especially those who don't bother to learn its strange customs or, worse still, who openly defy them.

The Internet evolved from a computer system—a network of networks—built 25 years ago by the Defense Department to link academic and military researchers and enable them to continue to work even if part of the network were taken out in a nuclear attack. It eventually linked universities,

the government and corporations via phone lines, and all the institutions using it shared the costs of running it. The scientists who were given free Internet access soon discovered it was good for more than official business. They used it to send each other private messages (E-mail) and to post news on electronic bulletin boards. Over the years the Internet became a favorite haunt of graduate students and computer hackers, who loved to stay up all night exploring its weblike connections and devising novel applications for it.

Until quite recently it was painfully difficult for ordinary computer users to reach the Net. Not only did they need a PC, a modem to connect it to the phone line and a passing familiarity with a computer operating system called Unix, but they could get on the Net only with the cooperation of a university or government research lab. In 1993 and 1994, most of these impediments disappeared. There are now dozens of small businesses that sell access to the Net at a base rate of $10 to $30 a month. And in the summer of 1994, mainstream computer services like America Online began to reach parts of the Internet through easy-to-use menus.

But with floods of new arrivals have come new issues and conflicts. A large part of the problem is cultural. The rules that govern behavior on the Net were evolved by computer hackers who largely ignore formal rules. Instead they subscribe to a sort of anarchistic ethic, stated most succinctly in Steven Levy's *Hackers*. Among its tenets: access to computers should be unlimited and total; all information should be free; authority should be mistrusted and decentralization promoted.

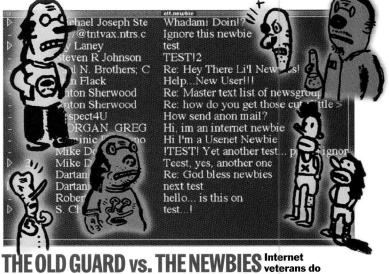

THE OLD GUARD vs. THE NEWBIES
Internet veterans do not take kindly to refugees from the real world ("clueless newbies") who don't bother to learn the Net's strange language and droll customs. Newcomers may be greeted with jeers and rude "flames," especially if they hail from a middle-of-the-road service like America Online.

SPOOKS vs. CYPHERPUNKS

There is a group of hackers who believe that powerful encryption will set them free. Government spooks don't mind if these so-called cypherpunks use codes to lock up secrets, so long as the spooks hold a back-door key like the Clipper Chip.

As long as the community was relatively small, it could be self-policing. Anybody who got out of line was shouted down or shunned. But with massive growth, those informal rules of behavior started to break down. The Internet is becoming Balkanized, and where the mainstream culture and hacker culture clash, open battles are breaking out. Among them:

● Tensions between old-timers and new arrivals—or "newbies"—flare up every September as a new crop of college freshmen is loosed upon the network. But the annual hazing given clueless freshmen pales beside the welcome America Online users received in March 1994, when the company opened the doors of the Internet to its nearly 1 million customers. The result was a verbal conflagration—message boards consumed in "flame" mailings from veterans to newbies—that smoldered for months.

● For those interested in pornography, there's plenty of it on the Internet. It comes in all forms—hot chat, erotic stories, explicit pictures, even XXX-rated film clips—and the newsgroups that carry it are among the top four or five most popular. The salacious stuff is clearly an embarrassment to the Clinton Administration, which has been trying to make a virtue of getting the Internet into schools. For purely technical reasons, it is impossible to censor the Internet at present. But some clever antipornography activists post messages in newsgroups devoted to X-rated picture files, drawing flurries of angry responses that fill the message boards and thus pushing out the sexy items.

● No battle on the Internet has been as public as the one waged over the Clipper Chip, the U.S. government–designed encryption system for encoding and decoding phone calls and E-mail so that they are protected from snooping by everyone but the government itself. The information-should-be-free types on the Internet were strongly opposed to Clipper from the start, not because they were against encryption but because they wanted a stronger form of encryption—for which Uncle Sam will not have a back-door key.

● Hackers hate ads, but the Internet represents a surging new market, filled with bright, upwardly mobile people. Though the Net is still not entirely ready for business, commerce is on its way. The hottest product of 1994 was Mosaic, an Internet navigation system that can be understood at a glance by anybody who can point and click. Hundreds of companies are using Mosaic to establish an easy-to-find presence on the Net. In 1993 there were a handful of these Mosaic "sites"; by mid-1994 there were more than 10,000.

The Internet has grown too large to think of as a single place, says Esther Dyson, a board member of the Electronic Frontier Foundation, an Internet watchdog group. "It needs to be subdivided into smaller neighborhoods. There should be high-class neighborhoods. There should be places that parents feel are safe for their kids." San Francisco's Whole Earth 'Lectronic Link (the WELL) is perhaps the most famous of these new virtual communities. It is protected by a "gate" that won't open without a password or a credit card. The danger of this trend is that people will withdraw within their walled communities and never venture again into the Internet's public spaces. The magic of the Net is that it thrusts people together in a strange new world, where they get to rub virtual shoulders with characters they might otherwise never meet. The challenge for the citizens of cyberspace will be to carve out safe, pleasant places in which to work, play and raise their kids without losing touch with the freewheeling, untamable soul that attracted them to the Net in the first place. ■

PORNOGRAPHERS vs. FUNDAMENTALISTS

It's hard to block anything on the Internet, which is designed to interpret censorship as damage and route around it. So the folks who want the network to be safe for children invent clever schemes to thwart the flesh merchants, like crowding out sexy pictures and graphics with E-mail.

How Mac Changed the World

Macintosh made cyberspace as homey as Apple pie

THE MACINTOSH COMPUTER HAS NEVER LACKED enthusiasts ready to paint the machine with cosmic significance. More than any other personal computer, the Mac comes wrapped in hype, most of it directly traceable to Steven Jobs, the former chairman of Apple. He loved to tell his designers that the computer they were building—with its icons, its pulldown "menus" and its "mouse"—would not only change the world, but also "put a dent in the universe." To hammer his point home, Jobs launched the new machine in January 1984 with the famously melodramatic commercial—aired just once, during the Super Bowl—in which a woman clad in a Mac T shirt smashed a screen image intended to represent the brain-dead

PCs of archrival IBM, the Big Brother of computing.

Such grandiose marketing worked for a while, and then backfired. After an initial spurt of sales, word got out that the new machine was underpowered and overpriced—a yuppie toy. Although Apple eventually solved most of the computer's problems, today IBM compatibles dominate the personal-computer business. The Macintosh remains stuck in a niche, with a market share that hovers around 10%.

But a look at the information landscape 10 years after the launch suggests that the Macintosh may turn out to be almost as important as Jobs promised. Not only have the icons and pointing devices pioneered by Apple become ubiquitous—both on rival computers and on

Pocket Computers

Some of the folks who built the original Macintosh are now designing metaphors to sort through the E-mail, faxes and other information services coming to hand-held gizmos like the Newton.

new vehicles being designed to navigate the emerging information highways—but the Mac has also played a key role in making society comfortable with the central technology of the age.

"Macintosh was the crucial step, the turning point," writes Steven Levy in a book, *Insanely Great*, published to salute the machine's 10th anniversary. (The title comes from Jobs' hyperbolic claim for how great the Mac would be.) Levy, the author of *Hackers* and a columnist for *Macworld* magazine, believes the Mac set in motion a subtle intellectual process that is changing the way people think about information and, ultimately, thought itself. "In terms of our relationship with information," he writes, "Macintosh changed everything."

That overstates the case, but there is something to what Levy says. The crux of his argument is that the Mac moved computer users into the realm of metaphor. By making the workings of a machine as cozy as a living room, the Macintosh enabled people to feel at ease in cyberspace, "the place where information lives." The central metaphor of the Mac is the desktop. Like a typical office, the Macintosh screen is filled with folders, documents and stacks of paper. There is even a trash can for throwing things away. Rather than having to memorize abstract commands like A: INSTALL, Macintosh users simply point and click.

Buttressing the desktop are dozens of subsidiary metaphors. Overlapping "windows" let users peer into different areas within the computer without having to stop what they are doing. Pulldown menus drop like window shades from the top of the screen, eliminating the need to look up commands in a manual. Elevator bars "scroll" long documents up and down; "buttons" and "toggle switches" pop up when a decision must be made.

On the Macintosh, the medium is the metaphor, and users begin to think not in words but in symbols. Paint programs come equipped with electronic pencils, paint buckets, spray cans and erasers. Photographs are processed in electronic darkrooms; digital movies are spliced in electronic videotape editors.

These ideas did not, of course, spring fully formed from the mind of Jobs. Any good Mac historian can trace the machine's ancestry to Vannevar Bush (a White House science adviser who was dream-

Internet

The mother of all computer networks has thousands of "channels." Hackers navigating this sea of information have developed Mac-like guides to show how to get from A to Z.

ing about electronic desktops in 1945), Douglas Engelbart (who invented windows and the mouse) and Alan Kay's team at Xerox's Palo Alto Research Center in California (which put the ideas to work in a language called Smalltalk and a machine called the Alto). Levy re-creates in vivid detail the December 1979 "daylight raid" when the scrappy engineers from Apple, invited to see the Alto, walked into a Xerox demo room and walked out with something more valuable than gold bullion: a working paradigm for what a computer should be.

It is clear, however, that Apple significantly improved on Xerox's work. In Smalltalk, for example, all commands are executed through pop-up menus. On the Mac, users can reach right into cyberspace and manipulate documents directly, grabbing a file with a mouse, dragging it across the screen and dropping it into a folder. Much of the genius of the Mac is in the accumulation of such details: the pinstripes across the top of a window, the gray tint in the scroll bar, the way an icon "zooms" to fill the screen when a program is opened.

Despite all this, the Macintosh almost did not survive. Even worse than its initial hardware problems was the sneering contempt of "power users" reared on IBM machines, who made it clear that real men didn't use mice. Ironically, Microsoft's Bill Gates, whose company owned the operating system at the heart of the IBM PC, was plotting all the while to shift the entire market to the Mac way of doing things. Today, two-thirds of the computers that use Apple's desktop metaphor are made by the company's competitors.

As the information highway grows, people may find themselves relying more and more on their metaphors. The Macintosh interface has already been adapted by such network services as CompuServe and America Online (on which sending a message is like posting a note on a bulletin board). A similar Mac-like program, called Mosaic, is making the vast resources of the Internet increasingly accessible to general users.

Someday virtual-reality technology may enable people to put the screen icons behind them and "step" directly into the metaphor. In the future, says Levy, "we will cross the line between substance and cyberspace with increasing frequency, and think nothing of it." That's what Jobs would call a dent in the universe. ∎

Interactive TV

With 500 or more channels to choose from, how will anybody find out what's on? GTE displays the options using the metaphor of Main Street; Time Warner favors the shopping mall.

Virtual Reality

By donning eye-phone goggles, data gloves and other virtual-reality apparel, people will someday go beyond two-dimensional screen metaphors and step directly into cyberspace.

ARE MEN REALLY THAT BAD?

AFTER GOD CAST LUCIFER AND HIS FOLLOWERS into darkness, all the fallen angels came straggling together on the plains of hell—to recriminate, to console themselves and to discuss their new identities as devils.

It may be time for men to hold a convention for the same purpose.

Let all men be summoned to a gathering of the masculine tribes, like a jamboree of the Indian nations in Montana long ago—a Pandæmonium of the patriarchy, a sweat lodge of the Granphalloon, Le Tout Guyim: as if the entire male audience of the Super Bowl had been vacuumed through 100 million television tubes (*thuuuuppp!*) and reassembled in one vast bass- and baritone- and tenor-buzzing hive.

In would gather young and old, warriors and elders, turbulent adolescents, the sleek and paunchy middle-aged, the venerable and wheezing. Lawyers and truckers, body builders, Senators from Oregon, good husbands and wife beaters, Spur Posse mouth breathers, waiters, neurosurgeons, garbagemen and nerds, Tailhookers beastly and Kennedys innumerable, Bly drummers, sweet guys and feel-copping clerics, politicians, pillars of rectitude, forced-entry brutes, girlymen, stockbrokers, philosophers, sales reps, homeless ruins, ex-wife-drained alimoners, gangsta rappers, J. Crew preppies and gunrack bubbas, family-values Bobs and

THE BOBBITTS AS TARQUIN AND LUCREZIA

"The fantasy of the meek rising up and striking back stirs something deep inside us."
— Katie Roiphe, New York *Times*, 1933

SENATOR PACKWOOD
AS SATYR

"You monsters with firm and restless hands, white cuffs round the wrists."

— Ingeborg Bachman,
The Thirtieth Year, 1961

Herbs, whirlpooling cretins, introverts, fundamentalists, jocks, spazzes, fat boys and hunks and delicate blossoms, biologists, astronauts, alkies, Buddhist meditators, joggers, homeboys, bankers, skinheads, you few loathsome Lecters and Dahmerites, you libertarians, deer hunters, anchormen, bureaucrats, convicts, bleeding hearts, bikers, femsymps and harassers, Rotarians and punks. Welcome, overmortgaged yuppie. Welcome, beery lout in the gimme hat (MY BEST FRIEND RAN OFF WITH MY WIFE—AND I MISS HIM). Welcome, chunky Limbaugh ranter. Welcome, Mr. Justice Thomas.

(*Gavel bangs.*) Gentlemen: We meet at a moment when the prestige of maleness is in decline. It is time to talk. We must make an examination of conscience. They are saying terrible things about us. Masculinity is in disrepute.

Outbreak of mock sobbing, men sawing at imaginary violins.

In a sidelong and subliminal way, men have become the Evil Empire, or anyway the ancien regime. We are "They," "Them," "the Enemy." People come in two models: Women (good, nice) and Men (the heavier, hairier life form). The "manly" virtues (bravery, strength, discipline and, egad, machismo itself) remain admirable only by being quietly reassigned to women—to Janet Reno and Hillary Clinton, say.

Hiiiisssssssssss!

Perhaps I exaggerate. Anyway, we know the overt man bashing of recent years has now refined itself into a certain atmospheric snideness—has settled down to a vague male aversion, as if masculinity were a bad smell in the room. We have reached the point where the best a man can say for himself is that he is harmless.

The market economy has found that man bashing sells. Entrepreneurs have descended. Hallmark Cards' fast-selling line, Shoebox Greetings, traffics in whimsical male dissing. Simon & Schuster published *No Good Men*, 100 pages of cartoons about what slobs and fools men are. *No Good Women* could not find a publisher.

What is the larger significance? Allan Carlson, president of the Rockford Institute, a conservative think tank in Illinois, offers this analysis: "We are at the tail end of the deconstruction of patriarchy, which has been going on since the turn of the century. The last acceptable villain is the prototypical white male."

A surly silence in the hall. Men-devils nodding: Whud I tell you?

With masculinity under sustained assault, men have been slow to respond, to state their case, to articulate the rationale for something they regarded as self-evidently good: their manhood. Men should think more about their situation and their behavior. Women should as well. Both men and women have been oppressed by the other sex, in different ways. And both have been getting away with murder.

WHY—ASIDE FROM THE FACT THAT THEY ARE jerks—do men get angry? Does it have something to do with the fact that they die an average of seven years earlier than women do? Are they angry because they do society's dirty, dangerous work? (93% of people killed on the job are men.)

Actually, the real reason men get angry is that they feel unappreciated. Men are fairly simple creatures. Their quarrel lies not with feminism per se, but with feminism incompletely or dishonestly or opportunistically pursued. Women must do their share, not just take the share they find attractive. Equality must be equality in all things, not just in the professional opportunities that white middle- and upper-middle-class women wish to exploit. Equality is a matter of real responsibility and risk, of accepting the liabilities as well as claiming the assets.

Women now control the vast majority of consumer dollars in America, especially the discretionary dollars. If that is not power, and privilege, what is? When will women take full responsibility, fifty-fifty with men, for initiating sexual contacts, thereby assuming the risks of occasionally painful rejection? That risk of rejection often makes men, who usually must take the active part, look not only foolish but also like sexual harassers, when in fact they may be merely inept. A successful approach to a woman is called romance and courtship. An unsuccessful approach may be a crime.

JOEY BUTTAFUOCO AS
HENRY VIII

"The divine right of husbands, like the divine right of kings, may, it is hoped, be contested without danger."

— Mary Wollstonecraft,
A vindication of the Rights of Women, 1792

Feminist politics goes against the animal behaviorist's insight that females organize their lives around the getting of resources (food, shelter) while males organize themselves around the getting of females. The collision produces a dishonest configuration. Women elaborately manipulate and exploit men's natural sexual attraction to the female body, and then deny the manipulation and prosecute men for the attraction—if the attraction draws in the wrong man. Women cannot for long combine fiery indignation and continuing passivity, attempting to have the best of both worlds.

This leads us to the mystery that lies at the heart of the matter: Rape and the Antioch rules. More than any other factor, male violence against women animates the anger against men. That violence (murder, rape, battering) is in everyone's mind, an ambient viciousness that bewilders and angers and frightens even men—though never as much as it terrifies women.

What explains male violence toward women? The fact that men can get away with it so often? Some residual infantile anger at Mother? Inherent savagery? Or, more plausibly, men's sense of powerlessness? Whatever the deeper cause, violence against women has become a habit (though most men do not indulge) and has taken on a dark life of its own.

American men should build a culture of profound intolerance for violence against women, an almost (no condescension intended) knightly solicitude for the sake of women's safety (we know, we know, they can take care of themselves) and men's honor. Every rape and every battering of a woman is, among other things, a dishonor to men, and men should see it as such.

When the Antioch College rules went into effect in 1993, they provoked a week or two of whooping and snorting among columnists. Sexual Stalinism! How ridiculous for Antioch, that flawless little jewel of the correctness culture, to mandate that the boy must ask permission first before touching the girl, and then before advancing to each further stage of intimacy (the buttons, say, and all that lies beyond).

But the rules are an intelligent idea—a necessary first step in the rebuilding of a sexual self-discipline that was

hit by a nuclear device a generation ago, during the '60s. The smoking ruins of the '90s (the epidemic of date rape, for example) are the legacy of the "sexual revolution" 30 years ago.

During the derided '50s, any American past the age of 13 was not automatically thought to be "sexually active." A version of what have now become the Antioch rules was at that time a part of the adolescent's mental software. In the Pleistocene before the Pill and legal abortion (an era that most young feminists have been taught to consider barbaric), both boys and girls felt a terror that a mistake would lead to pregnancy, hence to unwanted, premature marriage or to an abortion nightmare. That terror enforced a certain discipline and formality. Everyone knew—as human beings understood from the dawn of time until the '60s—that sex was powerful, and that it had implications beyond the moment. The Antioch rules, which repeat that lesson, should be adopted on campuses throughout the country.

In the meantime, perhaps American men and women should face the fact that they are hopelessly at odds. Or anyway that they are a little sick of one another for the moment. Time to give gender a rest, to stop staring at life through the single monomaniacal lens of gender politics. Put on the other lenses.

If we were to leave off argument and think kindly for a moment, on the premise that men and women will go on mixing with one another in the current mindless and anarchic way, we might spin the thought that good can come of each sex's thinking the best of the other, and we might see the converse truth: that only bad can come of each one's thinking the worst. Tolerance and decency are creative, civilizing traits. A rising standard of expectation—a mutual hope, a sympathetic mingling of desires—will lift all boats. Quite a long time ago—remember?—we used to fall in love.

Rising uproar from outside the hall, angry women's voices shouting "Take back the night!" "Viva Lorena!" and "We know you're in there, rapists!"

That's it for now, boys. I was about to get sentimental. Time to break it up.

Go, and sin no more. ∎

FASHION FOLLIES

Over-the-top designers turned springtime in Paris into the silly season

DURING THE MARCH 1994 PARIS SHOWS FOR ready-to-wear fall clothing, director Robert Altman appeared with such stars as Sophia Loren and Julia Roberts to shoot scenes for his new film, *Pret-a-Porter* (Ready-to-Wear). At first the fashion community welcomed him: What a chance to show off! What free advertising! But a chill quickly set in. Banning the movie crew from his show, Chanel designer Karl Lagerfeld said, "I'm afraid Robert Altman will make fashion look like a nightmarish cartoon." Evidently Lagerfeld had not noticed that he and his colleagues had achieved that all by themselves. The depressing news of the 1994 fall collections, shown in Paris, Milan and New York in the spring, is that the nightmare is far from over.

An epidemic of cynicism passing for wit has overtaken fashion as designers work harder at being funny than at crafting beautiful clothes. There has always been a theatrical side to fashion, but lately the over-the-top gesture is usurping the real thing. A decent goal of female clothing design is to enhance a woman, but styles in the past few seasons have often made a grotesque distortion of the natural silhouette.

Interruption in the form of extravagant collars, peplums and other superfluous add-ons to skirts has replaced graceful flow. Having peaked several years ago, multiple layering was back in 1994, even bulkier and more intrusive than in its last incarnation. All the elements that make a great dress—materials, tailoring, imagination—seemed to have been degraded.

When the venerable house of Chanel shows a black fur hat the size and shape of Mickey Mouse's ears, as it did in the spring, something is clearly wrong. Lagerfeld's other japes included fuzzy fake-fur skirts shaped unmistakably like muffs that barely covered the buttocks. He has made the classic Chanel suit look tartier by the year, a crude parody of itself. At this point it would be preferable to retire it altogether; versions of the design go back to the '20s, so the suit may have run its course. Lagerfeld has also vulgarized the Chanel logo, plastering it large all over accessories and jacket backs.

Jean-Paul Gaultier first made a corsetlike bustier for Madonna four years ago, and it was a good joke. Now further variations of underwear as outerwear have overtaken the runways. So have other tired gambits that can only encourage a woman to stay out of the

stores and wear what she already has in the closet. The metallic look is suffering from fatigue, but it's still in favor. And nobody looks good in disheveled fake fur, now everywhere. The effect is to present a woman as an unclipped poodle who just swam a stream and had a good, vigorous shake.

Across the board—and the ocean—skirts were mostly very short. One wonders where designers spent the brutal winter of 1993-94 as they designed their collections for the following fall. (Not only were skirts scanty, but there were also plenty of bare midriffs.) Of course, the micromini phenomenon is partly phony, since clothes are shipped to stores at longer, more freeze-friendly proportions. Nonetheless, if one house shows short, others apparently feel obliged to be just as daring. A micromini with fancy tights or patterned, lace-topped hose looks glamorous when Claudia Schiffer sashays down the runway. But when she is in mufti, she can usually be seen wearing pants.

Lagerfeld was afflicted with the fuzzy-wuzzies, but he was not alone. In the U.S. several younger houses—Vivienne Tam, Isaac Mizrahi, Ghost—went fuzzy. Ralph Lauren, in a collection that relocated his country look to Sherwood Forest sometime in the Middle Ages, featured fuzz in rare long skirts. In his CK line, Calvin Klein raised the ante—and the hemline—with bunny minis in furry pastels.

When designers were not selling sex, they were kissing babies. Altman should have been at Milan's Blumarine show when model Carla Bruni rolled a baby carriage containing another model down the runway. High-waisted baby-doll dresses, started by New York's Anna Sui in 1993, were ubiquitous in 1994. Even Giorgio Armani, who should know better, had one. Going along with the fake-innocent look were—what else?—Peter Pan collars.

In New York some of the newer designers seemed to be talking only to one another. Sui, a smart stylist who is capable of authentic downtown chic, concentrated instead on jarring outfits that needed translation, either to fit the body or to decipher where they might possibly be worn. Britain's Tonya Sarne, who designs Ghost and was a big hit in 1993, seemed intent on damning British society rather than selling beautiful or interesting clothes.

When interviewed by the press, designers enjoy saying their efforts are for women who are much too busy with important things to have time for adornment. If that were true, they would be aiming at Hillary Clinton and other working women, and this is patently not the case. As the wise veteran Geoffrey Beene noted, "These are chaotic times, but that need not be reflected in chaotic clothing." Still, buyers shopping in 1994 had cause to be wary, for the reign of chaos was not yet over. ∎

DUDS OF 1994
From left, Chanel: riffing on midriffs. Ghost: underwear as outerwear. Chanel: boggles the goggles and muffs the purse. Sui: if in doubt, throw in everything. Bill Blass: a shocking display of restraint. *Above,* Geoffrey Beene: elegant costumes fit for the cold—and with the surprisingly homely virtue of looking like winter clothes. *Right,* Lacroix: a model wearing—what else?— her own image.

How Could She Do It?

A mother confesses she killed her two young boys

DEATH AND DECEIT: Susan Smith, with ex-husband David, pleaded for the "release" of Michael, 3, and Alex, 14 months.

THE DIVERS FINALLY FOUND THE BODIES, NEARLY 100 feet out in the man-made lake stocked full with catfish. The children were still securely strapped in, with the windows shut. The car had floated slowly out into the lake as it filled with water, then flipped over and settled into the silt. The divers had searched the lake before, but in the murky water it would have been impossible to find the car unless they knew where to look—as they did by then. Sweet Susan Smith—the mother America had seen crying for the return of her stolen children on television, pleading that the kidnapper care for them—had confessed to killing them.

These things don't happen in Union, South Carolina, a 200-year-old mill town where the Smiths, Susan and David, were well known and well liked. Susan was an honor student who met David while working at the local supermarket; they married in 1991 and had Michael seven months later. The marriage fell apart just one year after the birth of their second child Alex, but everyone said the split was amicable.

Susan's story, first related to police on October 25, rocked Union. She explained that she had been on her way to visit a friend when she stopped at a red light and encountered her attacker, a black man in his twenties who waved a gun, jumped into the passenger seat and said, "Shut up and drive, or I'll kill you!" Ten miles out of town, he ordered her out of the car. She begged him to let her take the kids. "I don't have time," she claimed he said as he drove off, "but I won't hurt them."

The town reared up in horror. Police, state troopers, FBI agents and thousands of volunteers fanned out through the county, searching for the car, the kids, any clue at all. But there were all sorts of irksome questions about Smith's story. No crimes had been reported in the area that night—so why would a suspect be fleeing? If he needed a car to make a getaway, why take the kids? Above all, where was the car?

Smith's initial image of innocence also faded as rumors surfaced of her suicide attempts and money problems. Moreover, she had recently begun a romance with Tom Findlay, son of the owner of the textile plant where Smith worked as a secretary. A week before the boys disappeared, he sent her an E-mail letter, saying that he wanted to be with her but was not prepared to be responsible for a ready-made family.

Smith's story had begun to crumble even before she failed the first of two lie-detector tests. Then, on the same day police called her in for another round of questioning, a team searched her home, dusting for fingerprints and removing several bags from the house. It was finally too much: Smith broke down under questioning and told police where the boys' bodies could be found. She was arrested and charged with two counts of murder.

The reaction was intense. Townspeople, feeling betrayed, railed against Smith. Union's African Americans were particularly bitter, having been tarred by Smith's racist lie. But soon, down by the lake, the first crosses appeared, and then the flowers, an improvised memorial for the boys whom everyone had wanted so desperately to find, anyplace else but there. ∎

Murder in Miniature

ROBERT ("YUMMY") SANDIFER, 11, GOT his nickname from his love of cookies and junk food. The 4-foot, 8-inch-tall Chicago boy ran with a gang called the Black Disciples, intimidating his neighborhood with his use of knives, matches and guns. Often accompanied by four other youths just as small, he would steal, sell drugs, set fires. In September "Yummy" was found under a South Side train viaduct, shot to death execution-style. Days before, apparently on gang orders, Yummy had opened fire with a 9-mm semiautomatic into a crowd of kids playing football, killing passerby Shavon Dean, 14. Two members of Yummy's gang—brothers ages 14 and 16—were charged with his death.

Whitestone didn't know she had won.

Breaking the Sound Barrier

THERE SHE IS—YOUR IDEAL. WHEN judges named ballet-dancing college junior Heather Whitestone, 21, as the new Miss America, she didn't realize she had won the tiara until her runner-up pointed to her. Whitestone, is completely deaf in one ear, 95% deaf in the other.

Babes in Byteland

NEARLY TWO DECADES after the birth of personal computers, millions of techno-shy Americans were finally discovering a reason to bring them home. Filled with hope that

Aesop meets multimedia.

The body of 11-year-old "Yummy" Sandifer was found in this train underpass.

their children would find learning as compelling as blasting aliens in a video game, parents bought more than $243 million worth of educational software in 1993, a 66% increase over 1992, with 1994 sales expected to continue the strong pace. The popularity of kidware made it not only the hottest segment of the $6.8 billion software industry, but also a driving force behind the rapid growth in hardware sales.

For Whom the Bell Curves

IT'S A RARE SOCIOLOGICAL TEXT THAT gets riffled for the dirty parts, but *The Bell Curve*, 845 pages and footnotes written by conservative social scientist Charles Murray and the late Harvard psychologist Richard Herrnstein, addressed two great taboos of American life: IQ differences between the races and the degree to which intelligence is hereditary. The authors claimed heredity plays a larger role than environment in intelligence and insisted that it is almost impossible to nudge the IQ upward by much after the earliest stages of life. *Bell Curve's* explosive contentions generated a firestorm of controversy; one critic described the theories as "indecent, philosophically shabby and politically ugly."

Disney Sounds Retreat

THE BATTLE BEGAN WHEN THE WALT Disney Co. announced plans for a $650 million American history and entertainment park to be built 35 miles west of Washington, site of the two Civil War battles of Manassas. Fearing desecration, residents teamed up with historians to oppose the project. In September Disney canceled its plans—and Mickey came marching home again. ∎

Whipping Boy

Despite pleas for clemency from his parents, the White House and U.S. Ambassador Ralph Boyce, authorities in Singapore carried out a sentence of caning on American Michael Fay, 18, who was found guilty of vandalism for spraypainting cars. Sentenced to six blows, Fay received a reduced—but severe—punishment: four strokes from a rattan cane soaked in water to prevent it from splitting while it lacerated his skin.

EMPIRE OF THE SPIRIT

In a time of moral confusion, John Paul II is resolute about his ideals and eager to impress them on a world that often differs with him

P EOPLE WHO SEE HIM—AND COUNTLESS MILLIONS HAVE—DO NOT FORGET HIM. HIS APPEAR-
ances generate an electricity unmatched by anyone else on earth. That explains, for instance,
why in rural Kenyan villages thousands of children are named John Paul, or why a CD fea-
turing him saying the rosary—in Latin—climbed the charts in Europe in 1994. Pope John
Paul II possesses, among many other things, the world's bully-est pulpit. Few of his predecessors over the past 2,000 years have spoken from it as often and as forcefully as he. When he talks,
it is not only to his flock of nearly a billion; he expects the world to listen. And the flock and the world
listen, not always liking what they hear. In 1994 he cast the net of his message wider than ever: *Crossing the Threshold of Hope*, his meditations on topics ranging from the existence of God to the mistreatment of women, became an immediate best seller in 12 countries. It was an unprecedented case
of mass proselytizing by a Pontiff—arcane but personal, expansive but resolute about its moral message.

John Paul can also impose his will, and there was no more formidable and controversial example of
this than the Vatican's intervention at the U.N.'s International Conference on Population and Development in Cairo in September. There the Pope's emissaries defeated a U.S.-backed proposition John
Paul feared would encourage abortions worldwide. The Pontiff was unfazed by the widespread op-
probrium this victory earned him. His popular book and his unpopular diplomacy, he explained to
TIME, share one philosophical core: "It always goes back to the sanctity of the human being." He added,
"The Pope *must* be a moral force." In a year when so many people lamented the decline in moral val-
ues, Pope John Paul II forcefully set forth his vision of the good life and urged the world to follow it.
For such rectitude—or recklessness, as his detractors would have it—he was TIME's Man of the Year.

Believing himself to be the direct successor of St. Peter, the rock on whom Jesus Christ built his
church, John Paul sees it as his duty to trouble the living stream of modernity. He stands solidly against
much that the secular world deems progressive: the notion, for example, that humans share with God
the right to determine who will and will not be born. He also lectures against much that the secular
world deems inevitable: the abysmal inequalities between the wealthy and the wretched of the earth,

This ceremony at the Hill of Crosses in Lithuania in 1993 displayed John Paul's continuing attention to Eastern Europe. He has long spoken of his wish to visit Moscow.

the sufferings of those condemned to lives of squalor, poverty and oppression. "He really has a will and a determination to help humanity through spirituality," says the Dalai Lama. "That is marvelous. That is good."

John Paul's impact on the world has already been enormous. He has covered more than half a million miles in his travels. Many believe his support of the trade union Solidarity in his native Poland was a precipitating event in the collapse of the Soviet bloc. His power rests in the word, not the sword. As he has demonstrated throughout the 16 years of his papacy, he needs no divisions. He is an army of one, and his empire is both as ethereal and as ubiquitous as the soul.

In 1994 the Pope's health visibly deteriorated. His left hand shakes, and he hobbles with a cane, the result of bone-replacement surgery after a fall. It is thus with increased urgency that John Paul has presented himself as a moral compass for believers and nonbelievers alike. He spread through every means at his disposal a message not of expedience or compromise but of right and wrong. He did not say what everyone wanted to hear, and many within and beyond his church took offense. But his fidelity to what he believes remained unwavering. "He'll go down in history as the greatest of our modern Popes," says the Reverend Billy Graham. "He's been the strong conscience of the whole Christian world."

John Paul was personally affected by the turmoil of 1994. He could not make planned visits to Beirut and Sarajevo because of vicious conflicts. The slaughter in Rwanda dealt him particular grief: an estimated 85% of Rwandans are Christians, and more than 60% of those Roman Catholics. But when circumstances allowed him to act, the Pope did so decisively. His major goals have been to clarify church doctrine and to reach out to the world, seek contacts with other faiths and proclaim to all the sanctity of the individual.

He made advances on all of these fronts in 1994. The new Catechism of the Catholic Church—the first such comprehensive document issued since the 16th century—appeared in English, having already been translated into several other languages. In June, John Paul oversaw the establishment of diplomatic relations between the Holy See and Israel, ending a long standoff. He tried to still debate on one issue by releasing an apostolic letter in which he said no, for the foreseeable future, to the ordination of women. The document disappointed and outraged many Catholic women and men, even some sympathetic to John Paul. But he was most strongly criticized for his opposition to Paragraph 8.25 of the 113-page plan proposed at the 185-nation population conference in Cairo. The passage, which had been strongly endorsed by the Clinton Administration, stated that "the United States believes access to

John Paul locates the source of the great schism between faith and logic in the writings of the 17th century French philosopher René Descartes, who was a major inspiration for the scientific revolution and the Enlightenment. In the Cartesian view, truth is a matter not of doctrine or received traditions but of something materially present on earth, accessible either through research or sound reasoning. The human intellect, thus liberated, has proved prodigious, its accomplishments tantalizingly seductive to the modern world.

John Paul is no fundamentalist who wants to repeal the Enlightenment and destroy the tools of technology. As the most traveled, most broadcast Pope in history, he knows the value of change. Instead he argues that rationalism, by itself, is not enough: "This world, which appears to be a great workshop in which knowledge is developed by man, which appears as progress and civilization ... this world is not capable of making man happy."

IN ESSENCE, THE POPE AND HIS CRITICS are talking at cross-purposes, about different universes. His reaffirmations of the church's doctrines on sexual matters actually form a small part of his teachings, but have drawn most of the attention of his critics. To the widespread conviction that sexual morality and conduct are private concerns alone, the Pope would ask, "Who guides those consciences?" While many population experts see a future tide of babies as a problem to be solved, the Pope sees these infants-in-waiting as precious lives, the gifts of God.

John Paul has never stepped back from difficulties, and he looked forward to an arduous 1995 agenda, including a 10-day trip to Asia and Australia and preparations for the 1995 U.N. Conference on Women in Beijing, which could be a replay of Cairo. In June, he planned to meet with Ecumenical Patriarch Bartholomew I, the leader of the Eastern Orthodox Church, with whom he hoped to mend the centuries-old breach between the Roman and Eastern churches.

The Man of the Year's ideas about what can be accomplished differ from those of most mortals. They are far grander, informed by a vision as vast as the human determination to bring them into being. After discovering the principle of the lever and the fulcrum in the 3rd century B.C., Archimedes wrote, "Give me where to stand, and I will move the earth." John Paul knows where he stands. ∎

safe, legal and voluntary abortion is a fundamental right of all women." Vatican spokesman Joaquín Navarro-Valls recalled the Pope's reaction: "He feared that for the first time in the history of humanity, abortion was being proposed as a means of population control." Vatican delegates filibustered against the paragraph, aided by Latin American and Islamic delegations. In the end, the Pope won. The conference inserted an explicit statement that "in no case should abortion be promoted as a method of family planning."

Cairo crystallized the problem of the Pope in the modern world and the problem the Pope has with the modern world.

He is Roman Pontiff and Polish priest, philosopher and autocrat, sovereign, servant, aging idealist

FOR 16 YEARS NOW, KAROL WOJTYLA—ONCE actor, then priest, then Archbishop and Cardinal—has been Pope John Paul II, the Supreme Pontiff, Bishop of Rome, leader of a church of nearly 1 billion souls. "It's curious," an Italian Archbishop has said, "you'd think he had always been Pope." And yet to understand the man and his papacy, one must look not only to the Vatican, from which he issues spiritual guidelines, but also to the almost mystical Poland he holds in his heart. Indeed, though the Pope's corner bedroom on the third floor of the Vatican's Apostolic Palace has a view of the baroque wonder of St. Peter's Square, it is almost as spare as a monk's. The room contains a single bed, two straight-backed upholstered chairs, a desk. The walls too are unembellished except for a few souvenirs, mostly icons. But these are eloquent by their very presence. They are from Poland.

The great paradox is that this most universal of Pontiffs, this most traveled and most global of Popes, is, at the same time, a loyal son of Poland. He is ever mindful of its painful legacies—repeated partition, Nazi occupation, communist oppression—and that vision suffuses his view of the church and its mission in the world. To some dissenting Catholics, of course, John Paul's Polish heritage is a mixed blessing. They see him as the product of a conservative, patriarchal church, who is increasingly autocratic and negative on such subjects as the ordination of women and artificial birth control. For all his manifest charisma and personal compassion, these critics charge, John Paul rules with an iron hand—and there is no velvet glove to soften it.

For a man of his age (74) and infirmities, the Pope follows a vigorous routine. He plows through daily scheduled meetings and audiences, prayers and Masses, engages with aides and visitors in deep philosophical discussions and continues to visit Rome's 320 parishes. All access to John Paul is controlled by his Polish secretary, Monsignor Stanislaw Dziwisz, 55, of Cracow. Utterly loyal and discreet, Dziwisz (pronounced *Gee*-vish) served as Wojtyla's secretary and chaplain when the future Pope was still Archbishop and Cardinal of Cracow. Today no one—neither papal friend nor foe—comes to the Holy Father save through the humble monsignor. Says a close papal aide: "Whoever the Pope is, he's going to be someone who feels very much alone. You need someone by your side, a kind of soul mate, and that's what Don Stanislaw is."

The Pope's day begins while Rome still sleeps, around 5:30, and does not end until 11:30 p.m. By 6:15 a.m. John Paul is in his private chapel, praying and meditating before its altar, over which hangs a large bronze crucifix. The testimony is universal that prayer, more than food or liquid, is the sustaining force of this Pope's life. He makes decisions "on his knees," says Monsignor Diarmuid Martin, secretary of the Vatican's Justice and Peace Commission. Sometimes John Paul will prostrate himself before the altar. At other times he will sit or kneel with eyes closed, his forehead cradled in his left hand, his face contorted intensely, as if in pain. At this time, too, he brings to his God the prayer requests of others. His prie-dieu, at the front center of the chapel, contains a couple of prayer books—and a big stack of people's intentions, written on yellow sheets.

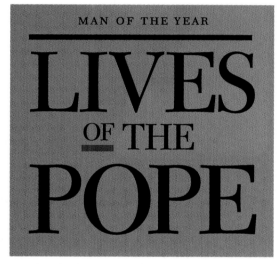

MAN OF THE YEAR

LIVES
OF THE
POPE

The prayers nowadays may also concern the decline of his own health, the result of age and the lingering effects of wounds suffered in the 1981 assassination attempt by Mehmet Ali Agca. John Paul has written an apostolic letter on the supernatural value of human suffering in which he teaches, "Each man, in his suffering, can also become a sharer in the redemptive suffering of Christ." Though he does not mortify his flesh with a hair shirt—as Paul VI sometimes did—he clearly sees his own physical ailments in this light.

Every morning, before his private and general audiences, John Paul devotes an hour or so to writing or—increasingly, as age and injuries have taken their toll—to dictation. He composes quickly, in Polish, with a neat, flowing hand, using a black felt-tipped pen. The Pope's literary output is staggering. His letters, sermons and speeches fill nearly 150 volumes. Besides 10 issued encyclicals, two are in the works, on ecumenism and the sanctity of life.

His goal, says his spokesman and intimate adviser Joaquín Navarro-Valls, is nothing less than the establishment of a completely Christian alternative to the humanistic

ADMINISTRATOR

The Pope's day usually begins at 5:30 a.m. and ends at 11:30 p.m. He spends much of his time in consultation, as here with aides in the corridors of the stately Loggia Raffaello.

philosophies of the 20th century—Marxism, structuralism, the atheistic ideas of the post-Enlightenment. Navarro-Valls notes: "They were simply among the tools of the age. Wojtyla said no, we have something new, we don't have to copy. Let us humbly build a new sociology, a new anthropology, that is based on something genuinely Christian."

So the Pope writes and thinks as well as discusses and debates—even through mealtimes. For John Paul, meals are occasions to bounce ideas off friends from Poland, bureaucrats and theologians who want to discuss policy and liturgy, young seminarians, a few people who are invited for his 7 a.m. Mass and breakfast. There is a kind of hierarchy of meals. Says Marek Skwarnicki, a Polish journalist and papal friend: "Lunch is for bishops, dinner is for friends." Fluent in eight languages, the Pope chooses his idiom to suit his dining companions. Says a Vatican aide: "He listens, talks directly, asks questions, puts you at ease. After five minutes you forget you are talking to the Pope."

The Pope's reading is eclectic: philosophy, history, sociology—all in the original languages. He will also take time for serious fiction and poetry: he knows Dostoyevsky and the other great Russians and has a special fondness for the poet Rainer Maria Rilke. He rarely watches TV—except for a brief glance at a soccer match—or reads a newspaper other than Cracow's weekly Catholic paper. He relies instead on a daily summary of the news prepared by aides to Angelo Cardinal Sodano, 67, the Vatican's Secretary of State.

Sodano is, in effect, the Pope's Prime Minister and the only curial official with instant access to John Paul. But there are other Cardinals the Pope confers with regularly. Every Friday evening, the Pontiff meets with Joseph Cardinal Ratzinger, 67, the austere German theologian whose title is prefect of the Congregation for the Doctrine of the Faith (once known as the Holy Office). On Saturday evenings, he has another standing appointment, with Bernardin Cardinal Gantin, 72, of Benin, the black chief of the Vatican's Congregation for Bishops, to discuss episcopal appointments. Naming heads of dioceses is one of the Pope's most effective weapons in maintaining doctrinal discipline within a church that he believes became dangerously fragmented after the Second Vatican Council.

The Pope has relied heavily for advice on the synod of bishops that meets in Rome every three years. He has attended all its sessions—including the most recent ones in October—listening with his usual intensity. But there is never a joint final communiqué. Indeed, the Pope may be advised, but to the private dismay of many bishops, any decision on issues is made by the Pope, and the Pope alone. As John Paul once told TIME's Wilton Wynn: "It is a mistake to apply American democratic procedures to the faith and the truth. You cannot take a vote on the truth. You must not confuse the *sensus fidei* [sense of the faith] with 'consensus.'"

AS FOR THOSE WHO DO NOT AGREE? JOHN Paul's most recent encyclical, *Veritatis Splendor*—The Splendor of Truth—makes it clear that clerics and theologians are bound to a "loyal assent." He has imposed the equivalent of ecclesiastical gag orders on those who, he feels, have challenged church teaching, including German theologian Hans Küng, American moral theologian Charles Curran and Brazil's Leonardo Boff, an exponent of Liberation Theology. John Paul can also be moved to wrath—and not just over theology. In 1985 he defrocked four Nicaraguan priests for not quitting the Sandinista government, including Minister of Culture Ernesto Cardenal, a onetime Trappist monk.

John Paul's dissatisfaction with some of the church's traditional priestly operatives—like the Je-

" It is a mistake to apply American democratic

COUNSELOR	PHILOSOPHER
John Paul, with Monsignor Dziwisz to his right, shares breakfast with guests, including Stephen Cardinal Kim of Seoul, facing the Pope.	*The papal schedule includes time for John Paul, an amazingly prolific writer, to work at a desk in the library of his private apartment.*

With so much less time to do what he believes must be accomplished, the Pope chafes under the burden of his infirmities. His image has always been that of a robust mountain climber, swimmer, skier, soccer goalkeeper. John Paul was skiing as recently as March of 1994, but he will never ski again. He now has an artificial femur and must walk with a cane. "He doesn't know how to use it," says Navarro. "He was operated on the right hip and holds the cane in his left hand. The recovery is not as fast as hoped, because he didn't spend enough time in physiotherapy." The appearance of weakness has prompted rumor and speculation: bone cancer, Parkinson's disease, a series of small strokes. All are denied by the Vatican.

What keeps John Paul on the move, despite his age and numerous injuries? A few Pope watchers believe that if he becomes immobilized by infirmity, he will resign the papacy and retire to a monastery in Poland. Others, though, are convinced that John Paul is determined to reign at least until the year 2000, which has immeasurable symbolic importance for him. According to a papal aide, "Stefan Cardinal Wyszynski [the late Archbishop of Warsaw] told John Paul he would lead the church into the 3rd millennium, and he believes it."

John Paul's ambitions for the millennial year are vast. He dreams of having a summit of all monotheistic religions at Mount Sinai and of concelebrating a Mass with Patriarch Aleksey II of Moscow to mark the reconciliation of Roman Catholicism with Russian Orthodoxy. In November the Pope issued an apostolic letter on preparing for the year 2000 in which he asked Catholics to "reflect on all those times in history when they departed from the spirit of Christ and his Gospel." Specifically, he suggested that the church needs to repent for its sometimes intolerant treatment of other faiths—thus shocking some bishops, who would have liked to emphasize the accomplishments of the church.

suits, whom he perceived until recently as having become too liberal—has led him to encourage lay Catholic movements such as Opus Dei. The Pope has also given warm encouragement to a new religious order, the Legionaries of Christ, which some conservatives see as a replacement for the Jesuits of old. With more than 300 priests and nearly 3,000 more in training, the Legionaries are on track to become a major force in the Catholic Church.

The Pope has two modes of decision making: quick and slow. On large strategic issues, he can be instantly decisive, since he has invariably thought through what he wants to do beforehand. But if he is unhappy with options proposed by the bureaucrat-heavy, 2,300-member Roman Curia on a tricky problem, he will put the issue aside for weeks or even months. When he brings up the problem again, startled aides have discovered, he will not have forgotten a detail. His aides attest that John Paul has immense powers of concentration and a virtually photographic memory for names and details.

As time erodes his physical powers and numbers the days of his pontificate, John Paul seeks strength from the friends of his youth. Several times a year, he dines with Jerzy Kluger, a Jewish classmate from Poland who is a businessman in Rome. John Paul until recently liked to spend his vacations hiking with Father Tadeusz Styczen, the Polish philosopher who succeeded to Wojtyla's chair at the University of Lublin and plays a key role in the shaping of his encyclicals.

A major, driving force in the Pope's waning years is the injunction of St. Paul in *I Corinthians*: "Woe to me if I do not preach the gospel!" It is this single imperative, more than anything, that accounts for the impact of John Paul II on the world. From it proceeds all the hope—and all the controversy—that surrounds the fascinating papacy of the man from Cracow. ∎

procedures to the faith and the truth. " —JOHN PAUL II

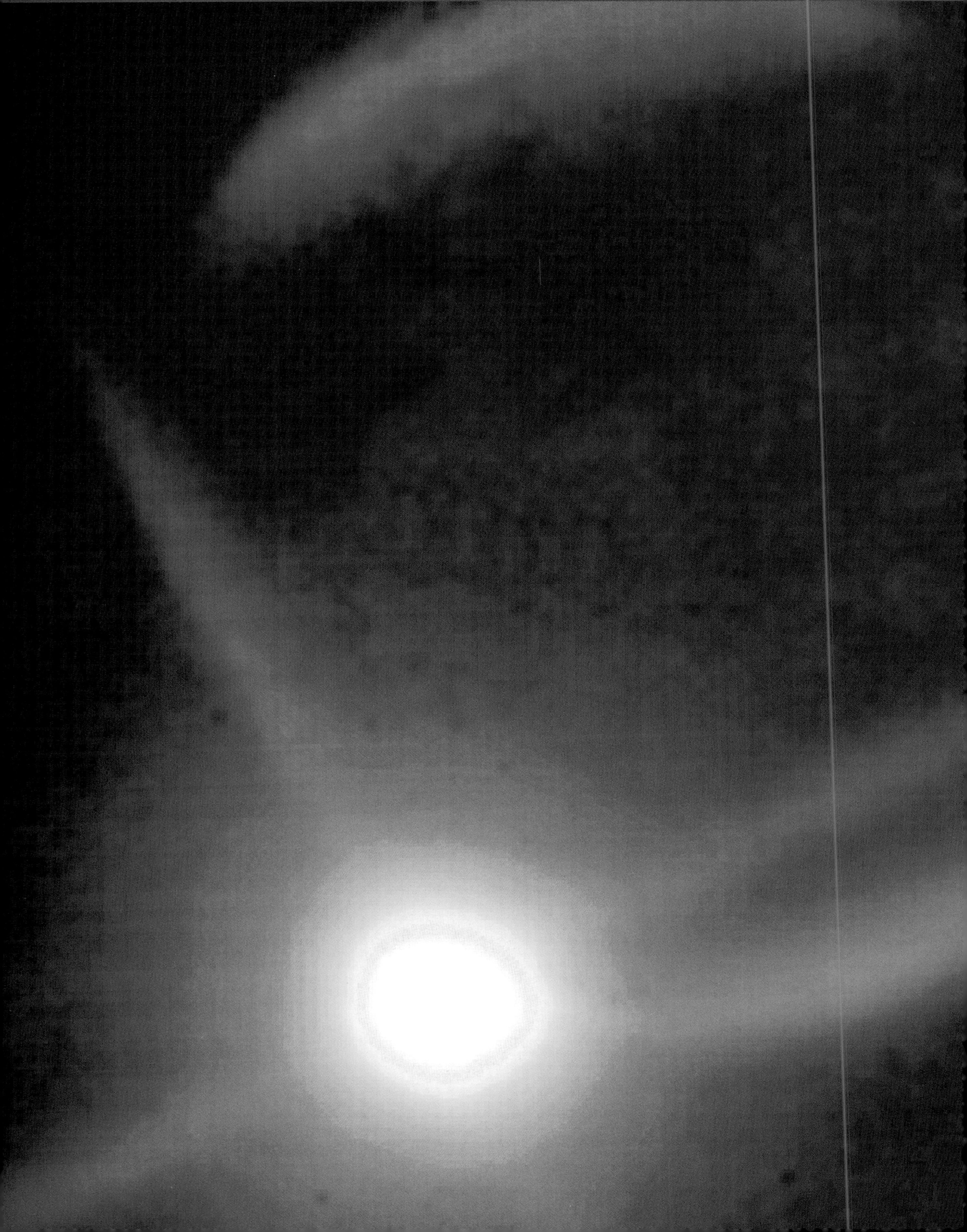

Cosmic Crash

It was the greatest show off earth: the largest planet in the solar system was bombarded by a comet shattered into a celestial "string of pearls"

O N JULY 16 A CHUNK OF INTERPLANETARY DEBRIS THE SIZE OF A MOUNtain smashed into the largest planet in the solar system. That was only the beginning of one of the most violent encounters mankind has ever witnessed. Over the following six days, more chunks—some perhaps 2½ miles in diameter—smacked into Jupiter, one after another, in a barrage as predictable as a burst of automatic gunfire. The agent of destruction was an icy comet (or, as some scientists came to believe, an asteroid), long held captive by Jupiter's gravity, that had broken up into a fleet of 21 natural megabombs.

The resulting explosions defied comprehension. While the largest hydrogen bomb ever detonated in the earth's atmosphere was the Soviet Union's 58-megaton blast in 1961, the combined energy of the 21 explosions on Jupiter reached 40 million megatons. The comet, named Shoemaker-Levy 9 for its discoverers, dazzled stargazers and thrilled astronomers around the world. As the first images from the Hubble telescope came into the Space Telescope Science Institute in Baltimore, Maryland, the assembled astronomers looked at the video screen for a second in silent disbelief— then began cheering and toasting one another with swigs from champagne bottles. Despite their sober warnings that the Great Comet Crash of 1994 might be an uneventful dud, the first chunk plowed into Jupiter's atmosphere with the force of perhaps a million hydrogen bombs, lofting a mushroom cloud of hot gas nearly 1,000 miles out into space and leaving a dark scar on the planet's familiar, brightly colored clouds.

The comet circled Jupiter until July 7, 1992, when it broke into pieces during its closest approach to the giant planet

Joining in the celebration in Baltimore were three visitors who had a special stake in the Hubble results: the discoverers of the comet. A graduate of Caltech and Princeton, and a winner of the National Medal of Science, Eugene Shoemaker, 66 in 1994, had made a career out of tracking down asteroids and comets while working for the U.S. Geological Survey. In 1982 his wife Carolyn, 64, had joined him as an unpaid partner. She had proved to be particularly adept at the painstaking process of examining the tiny dots of light in a telescopic picture. Using analytical techniques devised by her husband, she had already discovered 28 comets, the world record. David Levy, 45, was no slouch either, even though he was sometimes patronized as an amateur. An author and columnist for *Sky & Telescope*, he was credited with discovering eight comets and co-discovering 13 others—many with the modest 8-in. Schmidt telescope in his Tucson, Arizona, backyard.

Around midnight on March 23, 1993, the three skygazers stood outside the

BIGGEST BLAST In this view, a vast fireball becomes visible 12 minutes after Jupiter is hit by the largest of 21 pieces of comet Shoemaker-Levy 9, which bombarded the planet between July 16 and July 22.

KAMIKAZE COMET

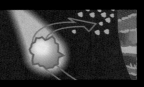

On July 7, 1992, the fragile comet passed very close, about 16,000 mi. (25,000 km) above Jupiter's cloud tops, and was shattered into at least 21 pieces.

JUPITER'S ORBIT VIEWED FROM THE SUN

IMPACT The major comet fragments, from about ½ mi. to 2½ mi. (1 km to 4 km) in size, struck Jupiter between July 16 and July 22, 1994, on the night side of the planet.

great telescope at Palomar Observatory near San Diego, California, looking disconsolately at the cloudy sky. Through January and February they had been skunked in their search for undiscovered comets and asteroids. Briefly, the clouds seemed to thin, and Levy, ever the optimist, wondered aloud whether there were a few more sheets of the damaged film that had been slightly exposed by accident back at the Shoemakers' home base in Flagstaff, Arizona. In a mom-and-pop operation like their Mount Palomar Asteroid and Comet Survey, the Shoemakers had to watch the bottom line. Good film like theirs cost $4 a sheet. Reluctantly the Shoemakers

indulged the enthusiastic Levy and took a few shots through the clouds.

Later, peering through her stereomicroscope at the damaged film, Carolyn thankfully observed that it was blurred only slightly around the edges. As she moved methodically across sections of sky, 60 square miles each, something bizarre and exotic suddenly appeared in a region of space not far from Jupiter. Not a dot but a streak, seeming to levitate out of the picture. "It looks like a squashed comet!" she exclaimed, calling Gene over. With his first glimpse, the geologist was uncharacteristically silent. The object

July 1

GAS GIANT It would take 11 Earths to span Jupiter's 90,000-mile diameter and more than 300 to equal its mass. Yet aside from an Earth-size core of iron and rock, the largest planet in the solar system is mainly gas.

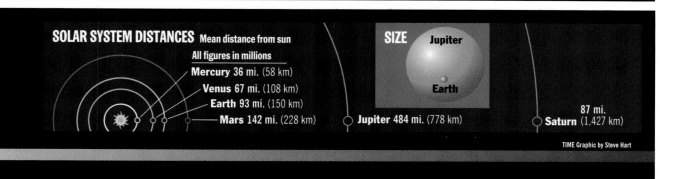

was unique. Bar-shaped, a faint line with a dense tail, it gave Shoemaker an eerie feeling.

To confirm their find, an excited David Levy called Jim Scotti, an astronomer in Tucson, Arizona, who scans the skies from a telescope on Kitt Peak. Sometime after midnight, in the course of his own search for asteroids, Scotti moved his telescope to the spot Levy had specified. Alone on the mountain peak, he watched as an amazing image scrolled onto his computer screen. For 15 minutes Scotti tried to collect his thoughts as he waited for Levy to return his call.

"Well, do we have a comet?" Levy demanded from his distant mountain. "Do you have a comet!" Scotti replied. "I've been trying to pick my jaw up off the floor!" Scotti's observations supported Gene Shoemaker's hunch: the object was composed of at least 21 fragments forming a "string of pearls." They were remnants of a single "mother" comet that had been torn

apart a year earlier by Jupiter's gravity— and they would all crash into **April 1, 1994** the planet between July 16 and July 22.

Astronomers could not agree, though, on how big the pieces were, and thus how explosive the impacts would actually be. But when the news of the first massive impact—and the champagne—arrived, a beaming Gene Shoemaker said, "This is just the best possible news. And remember, this isn't even the biggest piece." In fact, it was on the small side, and in the following days the bigger chunks created even more vast fireballs upon hitting the surface of Jupiter, the most prominent features ever seen on the giant planet.

The cosmic show provoked a question few had anticipated: Was Shoemaker-Levy 9 really a comet, or was it an asteroid instead? Comets tend to be a mixture of ice, rock and dust, along with substances like carbon monoxide that evaporate easily to form a halo and a tail. Scientists studying the chemical composition of the

spots on Jupiter where S-L 9 hit thought they might see evidence of water and oxygen, two of the expected products when an icy comet vaporizes. But except for one unconfirmed report, they found only ammonia, hydrogen sulfide and sulfur gas.

Asteroids are rockier than comets. Yet it is possible for an asteroid to have a halo or a tail, made mostly of dust. Said Hal Weaver of the Space Telescope Institute: "The only real evidence that [S-L 9] was a comet is that it broke apart, and we've never seen that in an asteroid. But maybe this was a fragile asteroid." However, as discoverer Levy was quick to point out, comets were originally distinguished by their appearance. He argued that comets are objects that look like fuzzy stars with tails, and in any previous century astronomers would have called this discovery a comet. Therefore, he claimed, "Shoemaker-Levy 9 is a comet, period."

> **The impacts left an unexpected puzzle that may never be solved: Was Shoemaker-Levy 9 a comet— or an asteroid?**

The apparent absence of water at the impact site provided a clue about how far the S-L 9 fragments penetrated the Jovian atmosphere before exploding. Theorists think that a layer of water vapor lies some 60 miles below the visible cloud tops; above the vapor layer, about 30 miles down, are clouds believed to consist of ammonium hydrosulfide, a sulfur compound. Since no water seems to have been stirred up, the explosions probably took place in the presumed sulfide layer. If researchers confirm that the sulfur rose up from Jupiter, it will be "a major discovery," said University of Arizona astronomer Roger Yelle. For scientists, perhaps. But for skygazers around the world, the mighty collision of the "string of pearls" with the largest planet had already created a sense of discovery—one that had much to do with wonder, and little to do with sulfide. ■

March 25, 1993 Comet discovered

Jan. 1, 1994

Oct. 1, 1993

July 16, 1993 Farthest point: 31 million miles (50 million km)

STOPPING CANCER

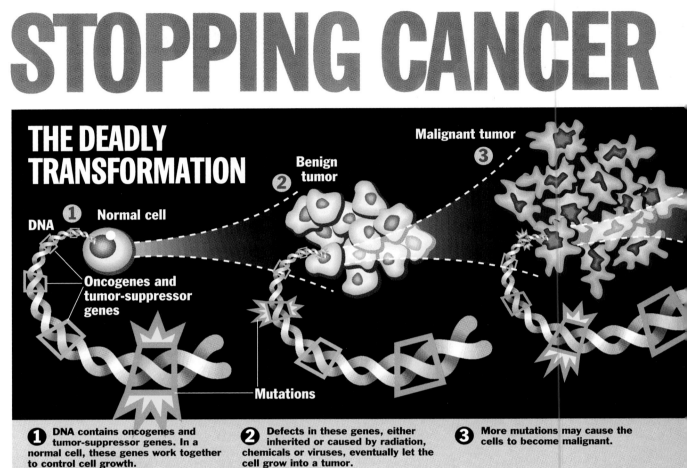

THE DEADLY TRANSFORMATION

DNA
① Normal cell
Oncogenes and tumor-suppressor genes

② Benign tumor

Malignant tumor
③

Mutations

① DNA contains oncogenes and tumor-suppressor genes. In a normal cell, these genes work together to control cell growth.

② Defects in these genes, either inherited or caused by radiation, chemicals or viruses, eventually let the cell grow into a tumor.

③ More mutations may cause the cells to become malignant.

TIME Diagram by Joe Lertola

TEALTHY AS A PIRATE SLIPPING FROM A COVE, the cell severs the moorings that attach it to surrounding tissue. Slowly it extends finger-like probes and begins to move. Then it detects the pulsating presence of a nearby capillary and darts between the cells that compose the blood-vessel wall. It dives into the red river that courses through lung and liver, breast and brain. An hour or so later, it surfaces on some tranquil shore, settles down and—at the expense of its neighbors—begins to prosper. Gradually it invades the area occupied by its normal counterparts, killing those in its path. It tricks its neighbors into forming food-bearing blood vessels, then compels them to churn out growth-spurring chemicals. To shield itself from patrolling immune cells, this cancer cell sprouts spiny armor like a sea urchin's. Is there any way to fight such a foe?

Until now medicine has tried to overwhelm cells that have become cancerous, like this one, with brute force—slicing them out with surgery, zapping them with radi-ation or poisoning them with chemotherapy. All too often, however, a few manage to survive and germinate into tumors that are impervious to treatment. The result: more than 500,000 Americans succumbed to cancer in 1994, making it the nation's second leading killer, after cardiovascular disease.

Yet despite the continuing casualties, there is reason to believe the war against cancer has reached a turning point. During the past two decades, a series of stunning discoveries has revealed the innermost secrets of the cancer cell. Now these insights are being translated into novel approaches to cancer therapy. The task of eradicating malignant cells continues to be a major challenge, but scientists are exploring ways to tame them and thus greatly prolong the lives of people with the disease. The new therapies carry the promise of being not only more effective than the current slash-and-burn strategy but also gentler to patients.

Early in 1994, encouraging news poured out of several labs all at once. From Thomas Jefferson University in

New discoveries show how cells become malignant, offering hope

IN ITS TRACKS

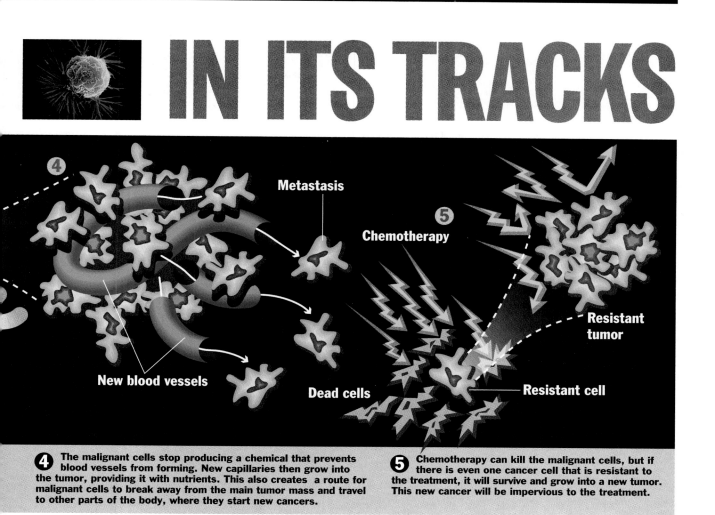

4 The malignant cells stop producing a chemical that prevents blood vessels from forming. New capillaries then grow into the tumor, providing it with nutrients. This also creates a route for malignant cells to break away from the main tumor mass and travel to other parts of the body, where they start new cancers.

5 Chemotherapy can kill the malignant cells, but if there is even one cancer cell that is resistant to the treatment, it will survive and grow into a new tumor. This new cancer will be impervious to the treatment.

Philadelphia came word that an experimental vaccine had given patients unusually long remissions from advanced melanoma, a deadly form of skin cancer. From Canada's McMaster University emerged a report identifying a telltale enzyme found in cancer cells—but conspicuously absent from most normal cells. If cancer researchers can find a way to deactivate this enzyme, telomerase, they may at last have the magic bullet they have long been seeking. Equally tantalizing was an article published in *Science* by molecular biologist Alexander Kamb and his colleagues at Myriad Genetics, a Salt Lake City, Utah firm. A majority of cancer cells, they found, lack functioning copies of a gene that in healthy cells shuts down the abnormal growth that causes malignancy. Already Kamb is dreaming up ways to fix this seemingly simple glitch. "The route to therapy," he says, "seems surprisingly clear."

The conceptual revolution that is just now sweeping into the clinic began in the 1960s, when researchers started to realize that cancer is a disease of DNA, the master molecule that encodes the genetic script of life.

One of DNA's most important jobs is to govern cell division, the process by which a cell makes a copy of itself and splits in two. Ordinarily cell division is tightly regulated, but a cancer cell divides uncontrollably, pushing into surrounding tissue.

Researchers have found perhaps 100 cancer genes, at least three dozen of them important in human tumors. Some, known as oncogenes, activate cell division, whereas others, called tumor-suppressor genes, are responsible for switching the process off. In their normal form, both kinds of genes work as a team, enabling the body to perform such vital tasks as replacing dead cells or repairing defective ones. But mutations in the chemical makeup of these genes, whether inherited or acquired later in life, can disrupt this finely tuned balance. A cell containing a faulty oncogene is often likened to a car with a stuck accelerator, a cell with a damaged tumor-suppressor gene to a car with no brakes.

The tumor-suppressor gene p53 is often described as "the guardian of the genome," because it keeps watch

that cancer may not be cured so much as placed under control

IMMORTALITY

Calvin Harley has found how cancer stops these glowing telomeres from timing a cell's natural death

over DNA during cell division. When damage occurs, p53 commands other genes to bring cell division to a halt. If repairs are made, then p53 allows the division cycle to continue. But in some cases, if the damage is too serious to be patched up, p53 activates other genes that cause the cell to self-destruct. Mutations in p53, which have been detected in more than 50% of all human cancers, are thus extremely dangerous.

Healthy cells apparently have a precise system for ensuring their mortality: short strips of DNA known as telomeres seem to provide a molecular clock. When a cell is young, it has more than a thousand telomeres strung along the ends of chromosomes like beads in a necklace. Each time a cell divides, 10 to 20 telomeres are lost, and the necklace grows shorter. Eventually, after many cell divisions, the necklace becomes so short that the cell fails an internal health check designed to keep old, possibly damaged cells from reproducing. Result: cell division stops, the cell begins to age rapidly, and eventually it dies.

C ANCER CELLS, BY CONTRAST, HAVE LEARNED to stop the ticking of the telomere clock. According to research published in April in the *Proceedings of the National Academy of Science* by Calvin Harley and colleagues at McMaster University in Hamilton, Ontario, malignant cells foil the clock by producing an enzyme—telomerase—that protects the length of the telomere chains. In essence, telomerase makes the cancer cell immortal.

Perhaps the most critical stage in the life of a tumor comes after it expands to about a million cells. At this point, it is "much smaller than a BB," says Dr. Judah

Folkman of Harvard Medical School. This tiny mass—known as a carcinoma in situ, literally cancer in place—is malignant, but not yet dangerous, because the cells at the center of the tumor are too far from the bloodstream to obtain essential nutrients. Months, years, even decades may pass. Then an ominous transition may occur. Some cells in the tumor begin secreting chemicals that attract endothelial cells, the key components of blood vessels. These cells form capillaries that grow into the tumor. They also produce molecular messengers called growth factors that stimulate the cells in the tumor to divide more quickly.

What triggers blood-vessel formation, or angiogenesis? A major factor, scientists believe, is a sudden drop in the cancer cell's production of thrombospondin, a protein that inhibits the growth of new blood vessels. At a scientific conference in November 1993, Noel Bouck, a molecular biologist from Northwestern University Medical School, stunned her colleagues by presenting data suggesting that thrombospondin production may be regulated by that ubiquitous gene p53.

Until early 1994, p53, the subject of some 1,000 scientific papers in 1993 alone, was considered the most important cancer gene. The journal *Science* even named it Molecule of the Year. But there is a new contender for notoriety—MTS1, for multiple tumor-suppressor gene—discovered by Alexander Kamb and his colleagues. "Multiple" refers to the fact that a defect in this gene can cause many kinds of cancer. In fact, functional copies of MTS1 may be missing in more than 50% of all human cancers.

What makes MTS1 significant is its clear role in the

Researchers no longer speak of slaughtering the cancer cell, but of

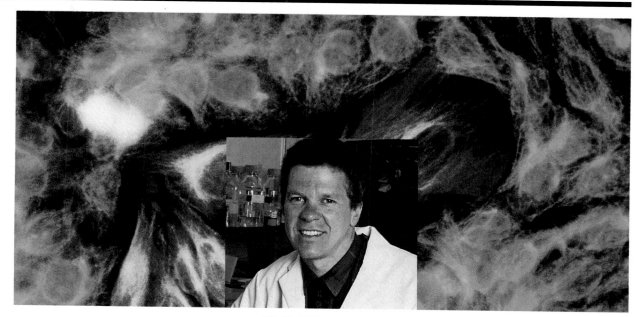

cell-division cycle. A cell divides not at will but in response to specific signals passed along by proteins in the cell to a master "on" switch positioned deep in the nucleus. Many oncogenes are involved in this type of signaling pathway. But there are other molecules that determine whether the cell should heed these signals. And the small protein produced by MTS1 appears to be among the most important inhibitors of cell division. In 1993 researchers at New York's Cold Spring Harbor Laboratory discovered that a protein they called p16 stifled an enzyme that is a growth promoter. A year later it became clear that p16 and the MTS1 protein are one and the same. "In terms of therapeutic potential," declares Kamb, "MTS1 may be the most important tumor-suppressor gene yet discovered."

T HESE DISCOVERIES ARE SUGGESTING NEW approaches to therapy. Among the possibilities are anticancer vaccines designed to stimulate the immune system to combat tumors. Currently being tested in the U.S. and Canada is a vaccine that spurs an assault on the weirdly configured carbohydrates that protrude from tumor cells like sea urchin spikes. At the meeting of the American Association for Cancer Research last April, Dr. David Berd of Thomas Jefferson University presented the most encouraging evidence to date that the vaccine strategy may work. Berd told of inoculating 47 melanoma patients with a vaccine made of their own tumor cells, inactivated by radiation. Three years later, 60% remained tumor free, compared with 20% in the unvaccinated control group.

MALFUNCTION

Alexander Kamb discovered the gene that may explain why these melanoma cells first went astray

The discovery that cancer cells rely on the enzyme telomerase to stay alive opens up a different attack strategy. Calvin Harley and the McMaster University team are trying to craft a drug that will block the action of telomerase without serious side effects. "If we can inhibit telomerase," explains Harley, "we might cause the tumor to die after a few doublings."

Another promising development: clinical trials have begun on several compounds that interfere with the formation of blood vessels in a tumor. One such compound comes from a fungus that was accidentally discovered in 1989 when it contaminated cultures of endothelial cells in Judah Folkman's Harvard laboratory, dramatically curtailing their growth. This drug, says Folkman, is aimed not at curing cancer but at prolonging the period of time that colonies of tumor cells missed by conventional therapy will remain in place without spreading. "Suppose we prolong this period of dormancy for 10 years, and then another 10 years," muses Folkman. "Why, now we're beginning to compete with the normal life span."

Indeed, what seems most significant about all the new therapies is the seismic shift in strategy they represent. Increasingly researchers speak not of slaughtering the cancer cell but of tricking it into dying naturally, as other cells do. They also talk of reining in the cancer cell, even rehabilitating it. The model for cancer therapy of the future already exists. "After all, we don't cure diseases like diabetes and hypertension," says Dr. Lance Liotta, the National Cancer Institute's leading metastasis expert. "We control them. Why can't we look at cancer that way?" ∎

tricking it into dying naturally, perhaps of old age, as other cells do

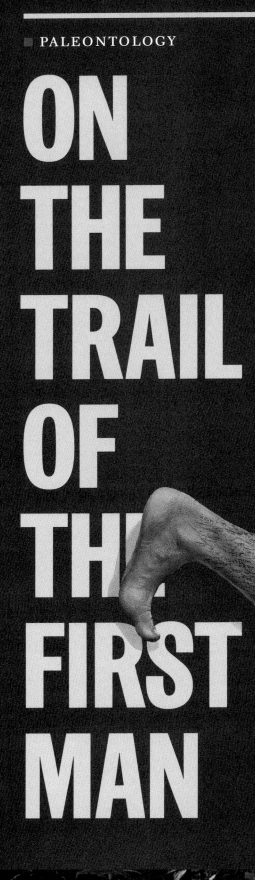

ON THE TRAIL OF THE FIRST MAN

Did the first men begin wandering out of Africa earlier than we once thought—or did man evolve in many places at once?

ALONE AMONG ANIMALS, HUMANS WONDER, endlessly, about their origin—when, where and how did the human race arise? Despite more than a century of digging by archaeologists and anthropologists, the fossil record remains sparse. A single bone that doesn't fit into the picture can force scientists to concoct new theories, amid furious debate.

In 1994 that seemed to be happening once again. Findings announced in early spring and in September rattled the foundations of anthropology. It turned out that humanity's ancestors may have departed Africa, the cradle of mankind, ages earlier than scientists had assumed; that humans may have evolved not just in a single place but in many places around the world; that a previously unknown species apparently walked the earth 4.4 million years ago—half a million years earlier than the oldest human ancestors hitherto identified; and that our own species, *Homo sapiens*, may be much older than we had suspected. If even portions of these claims prove true, they will herald fundamental changes in man's saga.

One shocker came in the March 3, 1994 issue of the science journal *Nature*, in which Chinese scientists contended that the skull of a modern-looking human, found in their country a decade ago, is at least 200,000 years old—more than twice as old as any *Homo sapiens* specimen ever before found in that part of the world. Moreover, the skull had features resembling those of today's Asians. The controversial implication was that modern humans may have evolved just in Africa, as most scientists believe, but emerged simultaneously in several regions of the globe.

The *Nature* article came only a week after an even more surprising article in the competing journal *Science*. There, U.S. and Indonesian researchers reported that they had redated fossil skull fragments of *Homo erectus*, the first primate to look anything like modern humans, found at two sites on Java. Instead of being 1 million years old, as earlier analysis had suggested, the fossils appeared to date back nearly 2 million years. If the evidence holds up, it means that protohumans left their African homeland hundreds of thousands of years earlier than anyone had believed, long before the invention of the advanced stone tools that, according to current textbooks, made the exodus possible. It would also mean that *Homo erectus* had plenty of time to evolve into two different species, one African and one Asian. Most researchers believe that the African branch of the family evolved into modern humans. But what about the Asian branch? Did it die out? Or did it also give rise to *Homo sapiens,* as the new Chinese evidence suggests?

Answering such questions requires convincing evidence—and the 200,000-year-old Chinese skull in particular was received cautiously by most scientists. In part that was because the dating technique used is still experimental. Confidence was much stronger in the ages put on the Javanese *Homo erectus* fossils. The leaders of the team that performed the analysis, Carl Swisher and Garniss Curtis, then of the Institute of Human Origins in Berkeley, California, are acknowledged masters of the art of geochronology, the dating of things from the past.

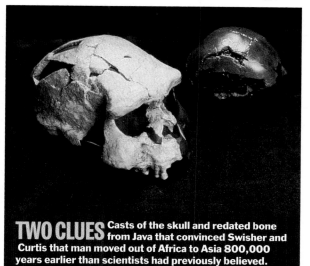

TWO CLUES Casts of the skull and redated bone from Java that convinced Swisher and Curtis that man moved out of Africa to Asia 800,000 years earlier than scientists had previously believed.

The inescapable conclusion of their re-dating, Swisher maintained, is that *Homo erectus* left Africa nearly a million years earlier than previously thought.

Experts are now scrambling to decide how this discovery changes the complicated saga of humanity's origins. Scientists are increasingly convinced that *Homo sapiens* was clearly not the inevitable design for an intelligent being. The species seems to have been just one of several product lines in the evolutionary marketplace, though the only one successful today.

Until September 1994, the story of that survivor began in Africa's lush forests nearly 4 million years ago. The warm climate was right, animal life was abundant, and that was where the oldest hominid fossils that had been uncovered came from. The crucial piece of evidence came in 1974, when an expedition to Ethiopia led by Donald Johanson, now president of IHO, painstakingly pieced together a remarkable ancient primate skeleton. Although the animal stood only 3 feet 6 inches tall, seemingly too short for a hominid, it had an all-important human characteristic: this creature walked fully upright. As Johanson and other scientists discovered more fragments of the species—the first specimen was famously dubbed Lucy, then formally classified as *Australopithecus afarensis*—the pieces began to resemble a creature much more apelike than human, with a forward-thrust jaw and chimp-size braincase. These short creatures were probably no smarter than the average ape. Their upright stance and bipedal locomotion, however, may have given them an advantage by freeing their hands, making them more efficient food gatherers. Some of the specimens date from about 3.9 million years B.P. (before the present), making them the oldest hominid fossils ever discovered—until the stunning September announcement that bone fragments unearthed in Ethiopia were those of a new hominid species dating back to 4.4 million years ago.

This discovery, announced in *Nature*, stretched man's family tree back another half a million years. The new species was given the name *Australopithecus ramidus*. Like Lucy, *ramidus* had teeth with some apelike and some human characteristics. Some scientists hailed the discovery as the fabled "missing link" between ape and man; others argued that other intermediate species might yet be found.

Following *ramidus, afarensis* and *africanus,* the next character in the human drama was a species called *Homo habilis,* or "handy man." Appearing about 2.5 million years B.P., the new hominids probably did not look terribly different from their predecessors, but they had a somewhat larger brain and figured out for the first time how to make tools. The adaptations made by *H. habilis* enabled it to survive the rigors of prehistoric African life for 500,000 years or more, and at least one group of them apparently evolved, around 2 million years B.P., into a taller, stronger, smarter variety of human: *Homo erectus.*

TANDING ON AVERAGE 5 FEET 6 INCHES tall, *H. erectus* had a flattened forehead, prominent brow ridges and nothing resembling a chin. The first of this species probably had a brain no larger than that of a modern four-year-old. Even so, they constituted a successful, mobile group, so well traveled, in fact, that their fossils were first found in the 1890s thousands of miles away from their original home in Africa. Dutch physician Eugène Dubois, who found the fossils, called his creature *Anthropopithecus erectus;* its popular name was Java man. Over the next several decades, comparable bones were found in China (Peking man) and finally, starting in the 1950s, in Africa.

Gradually anthropologists realized that all these fossils were so similar that they could be assigned to a single species: *Homo erectus.* The African bones went back at least 1.8 million years, while the most primitive Asian fossils were considered to be a million years old at most. The relative ages, plus the fact that *H. erectus'* ancestors were found exclusively in Africa, led scientists to conclude that the species first emerged on that continent and then left sometime later.

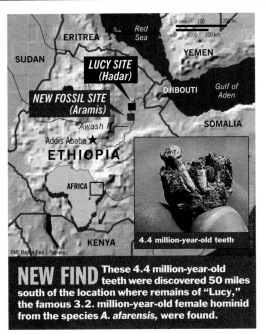

NEW FIND These 4.4 million-year-old teeth were discovered 50 miles south of the location where remains of "Lucy," the famous 3.2. million-year-old female hominid from the species *A. afarensis,* were found.

When and why did this footloose species take off from Africa? Excavations of sites dating back to 1.4 million years B.P., 400,000 years after *H. erectus* first appeared, uncovered a major technological advance: multifaceted hand axes and cleavers much more finely fashioned than the simple stone tools used before. With better tools, goes the theory, *H. erectus* would have had an easier time gathering food. And within a few hundred thousand years, the species moved beyond Africa, spreading first into the Middle East, then into Europe, and finally to the Pacific.

The most direct evidence of the time *H. erectus* arrived in Asia is obviously the age of the fossils found there. But accurate dates are elusive in Java, where much of the underground record of geological history is buried under rice paddies. The result: scientists have traditionally dated Javan hominids by determining the age of fossilized extinct mammals that crop up nearby. The two fossils cited in the new *Science* paper had originally been dated that way. The "Mojokerto child," a skullcap found in 1936, was estimated to be about 1 million years old. A crushed face and partial cranium from Sangiran were judged a bit younger.

In 1970 the IHO's Curtis, a scientific maverick, applied a radioactive-dating technique to bits of volcanic pumice from the fossil-bearing sediments at Mojokerto. His conclusion: the child's skullcap was not 1 million years old but closer to 2 million. Yet his dates would remain uncertain for more than two decades, until he and Swisher could apply a new, far more accurate method that ended up validating his claim. The Mojokerto child

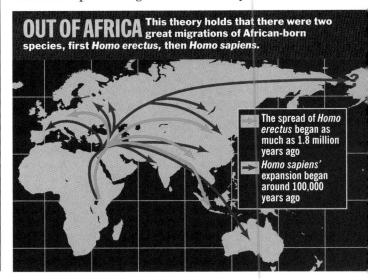

OUT OF AFRICA This theory holds that there were two great migrations of African-born species, first *Homo erectus,* then *Homo sapiens.*

The spread of *Homo erectus* began as much as 1.8 million years ago

Homo sapiens' expansion began around 100,000 years ago

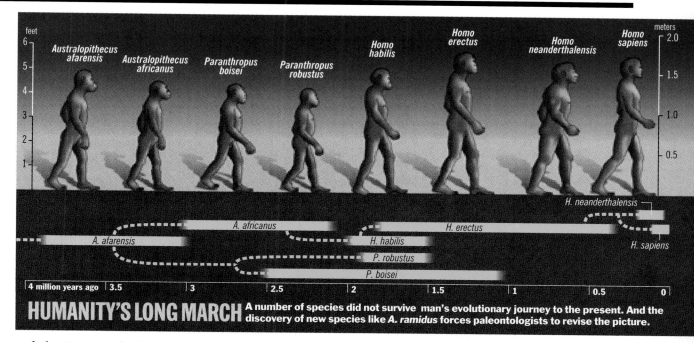

HUMANITY'S LONG MARCH
A number of species did not survive man's evolutionary journey to the present. And the discovery of new species like *A. ramidus* forces paleontologists to revise the picture.

and the Sangiran fossils were about 1.8 million and 1.7 million years old, respectively, comparable in age to the oldest *Homo erectus* from Africa. Here, then, was a likely solution to one of the great mysteries of human evolution. Says Swisher: "We've always wondered why it would take so long for hominids to get out of Africa." The evident answer: it didn't take them much time at all, at least by prehistoric standards—probably no more than 100,000 years, instead of nearly a million.

If that is true, the notion that *H. erectus* needed specialized tools to venture from Africa may be completely superseded. Some scientists believe climate spurred the exodus. An ice age about 2.5 million to 2.7 million years ago converted moist African woodland into much drier savanna, prompting forest-dwelling chimpanzees to yield to bipedal creatures better adapted to living in the open. *H. erectus*, finally, was equipped to spread throughout the Old World.

MULTIREGIONAL
This theory says that complex movements allowed interbreeding, enabling *H. sapiens* to evolve in a number of places at once.

Regional populations of *Homo erectus* may have evolved into *Homo sapiens* while intermingling with one another

The big question now: How does the apparent quick exit from Africa affect one of the most heated debates in the field of human evolution? On one side of the debate are anthropologists who hold to the "out of Africa" theory—the idea that *Homo sapiens* first arose only in Africa. Their opponents champion the "multiregional hypothesis"—the notion that modern humans evolved in several parts of the world.

Swisher and his colleagues believe their discovery bolsters the out-of-Africa side. If African and Asian *H. erectus* were separate for almost a million years, the reasoning goes, they could have evolved into two distinct species. But it would have been virtually impossible for these isolated groups to evolve into one species, *H. sapiens*. Swisher therefore thinks that the Asian *H. erectus* died off, leaving the African *H. erectus* the sole progenitor of *H. sapiens* in Asia and around the world.

Christopher Stringer of Britain's Natural History Museum agrees: "If we look at the fossil record for the past half a million years, Africa is the only region that has continuity of evolution from primitive to modern humans." Not necessarily, says multiregionalist Alan Thorne of the Australian National University in Canberra. Whenever *H. erectus* left Africa, he argues, the result would have been the same: populations evolved not in isolation but in concert, trading genetic material by inbreeding with neighboring groups. And, say the multiregionalists, what about the new report of the 200,000-year-old human skull in China? Stringer thinks that claim will not stand up to close scrutiny. If it does, he and his colleagues will have some explaining to do.

This, after all, is the arena of human evolution, where no bit of new evidence is ever interpreted the same way. The only certainty in this data-poor, imagination-rich, endlessly fascinating field is that there are plenty of surprises left to come. ∎

Tracking Killer Genes

Scientists gave hope to millions in 1994 when they succeeded in finding three long-sought genes that cause deadly disorders:

● **OBESITY:** Researchers in New York City said they had discovered a gene that, when defective, triggers obesity in mice. The gene apparently works by helping the body regulate appetite and metabolism. The team found a similar gene in humans, and hopes the finding could someday lead to more effective medical treatments for obesity—though development may take a decade.

● **OSTEOPOROSIS:** Australian researchers reported that they had discovered two versions of a specific gene associated with bone density that could lead to osteoporosis, the progressive disease that leaves bones thin and brittle. Its hallmark, the curving spines of elderly women, is a haunting symbol of old age.

● **BREAST CANCER:** An international team of researchers based in Utah located the errant gene that causes a hereditary form of breast cancer. Though this particular type is responsible for only about 5% of all breast-cancer cases, the discovery was hailed as a major step toward understanding the origins of a cancer that kills 46,000 women each year in the U.S. alone.

Polio Returns

FORTY YEARS AFTER THE GREAT POlio epidemic of the 1940s and '50s swept across the U.S., infecting millions and leaving some 640,000 (mostly children) with varying degrees of paralysis, survivors were being revisited by a degenerative muscle condition that has precisely the same symptoms as a mild case of polio. Postpolio syndrome was expected to strike 40% to 50% of the polio survivors, forcing many in their 50s, 60s and 70s to relive childhood pain and suffering.

Fertility with Less Fuss

MAKING BABIES: IT'S just no fun the test-tube way, especially for the mother. In-vitro fertilization requires a regimen of painful drug injections, daily blood tests and ultrasound

TROUNSON

exams. But a team in Australia led by Dr. Alan Trounson devised a new approach that is cheaper, simpler and easier on the mother. Instead of priming the woman with fertility drugs so the eggs will mature, doctors simply remove immature eggs. Success hinges on two new techniques: locating the immature eggs and then stimulating them to mature outside the ovary before placing one of them in the womb.

Brain Bane

THE SUBTLE COGNITIVE DISABILITY called dyslexia can prevent even intelligent and motivated children from learning to read. In the 1970s scientists began to suspect that people with dyslexia have some fundamental problem with their vision or hearing, since children verbalize words when learning to read. Now scientists in Boston believe they may have pinpointed a spot on the brain cortex associated with hearing where dyslexia originates. The size of neurons in this area of the cortex was smaller in the left hemisphere than in the right—perhaps just enough to confuse the brain.

You Are What You Read

IN MAY, NEW NUTRItion labels appeared on most American food products. Gone was the hodgepodge of information in tiny type that seemed to serve U.S. foodmakers rather than consumers. In its place:

Nutrition Facts	
Serving Size 1 Package (258g)	
Servings Per Container 1	
Amount Per Serving	
Calories 270 Calories from Fat 70	
	% Daily Value
Total Fat 8g	12%
Saturated Fat 3.5g	15%
Polyunsaturated Fat .5g	
Monounsaturated Fat 1.5g	
Cholesterol 30mg	9%
Sodium 500mg	20%
Total Carbohydrate 28mg	9%
Dietary Fiber 3g	13%
Sugars 5g	
Protein 21g	
Vitamin A 8% ● Vitamin C 20%	
Calcium 35% ● Iron 6%	

a legible bulletin developed by the FDA that steers shoppers toward foods labeled with clearer guidelines in such areas as the size, calories from fat and percentage of "daily value" of specific servings.

Trigger for Diabetes?

SCIENTISTS HAVE LONG SUSPECTED that people who develop the most severe form of diabetes harbor a genetic predisposition to the disease. In September, researchers announced they had discovered compelling evidence that a viral infection leads to the onset of Type I, or what used to be called juvenile diabetes. If confirmed, the finding could eventually lead to a vaccine for people with a family history of diabetes. ∎

An Eye on Alzheimer's

Following a hunch, doctors found that victims of the degenerative brain disorder Alzheimer's disease are very sensitive to tropicamide, a drug used to enlarge the pupils during eye exams. Now a group of researchers claims the eye test can help detect Alzheimer's more simply, quickly and at an earlier stage than current exams.

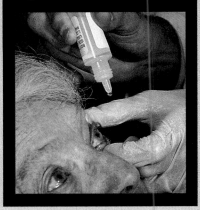

Out of danger but still off limits.

Winged Victory

DOWN TO A FEW HUNDRED BREEDING pairs in the lower 48 states when named an endangered species in 1978, the bald eagle has come back. Now there are 4,000-plus pairs of America's national emblem, redesignated "threatened"—out of grave danger but still off limits to hunters.

Scientists believe the rings are gases illuminated by a supernova explosion.

Hoop Stars

IN MAY ASTRONOMERS RELEASED pictures from the Hubble Space Telescope that prompted veteran sky watchers to chatter like awestruck kids. In one image, two huge hoops, each a few light-years in diameter, join a brighter, smaller ring surrounding the site of a supernova, an exploding star whose violent death was recorded in 1987. Though marveling astronomers offered hypotheses to explain the phenomenon, they could not reach consensus on the origin of what one called "the neatest thing I've ever seen."

The Top Quark: Gotcha!

PHYSICISTS THINK SIX TYPES OF quarks are the building blocks of all the particles within atomic nuclei. Scientists found the bottom quark, the last of the first five, in 1977. After a 17-year search, the top quark, the sixth and heaviest, was found in April at Fermilab, near Chicago. It took 440 scientists to spot the top quark, which disintegrates in an infinitesimal fraction of a second.

Microscopic Mass Murderers

THE WAR AGAINST INFECTIOUS DISeases is nowhere near over. That was made clear by outbreaks in 1994 of cholera, tuberculosis, Legionnaire's disease, hantavirus, plague, a new virus from Brazil called Sabiá, and—yes—the flesh-eating version of streptococcus bacteria, a particularly gruesome germ that reappeared in Gloucestershire, England. In fact, because of drug-resistant bacteria and newly emerging viruses, medical science actually seems to be losing ground in the struggle to tame infectious killers.

Oops ... Wrong Answer

NEW CALCULATIONS BASED ON SIGHTings by the Hubble Space Telescope seemed to answer one of the most profound questions of science: the universe is between 8 billion and 12 billion years old. But the news left scientists more puzzled than satisfied: our own galaxy has stars long believed to be as much as 16 billion years old.

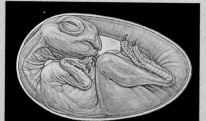

Dino Mites

Children raised on *Jurassic Park* may think they were only mean and bloodthirsty, but such favorite dinosaur bad guys as *Tyrannosaurus rex* may well have had a more caring side. The clue is the discovery of a fossilized embryo from a carnivorous dinosaur, an oviraptor found in Mongolia. The embryo was lodged in a nest that also contained bones from other tiny dinosaurs, which the mother oviraptor might have eaten while watching over her sharptoothed darlings. Apparently even prehistoric monsters knew how to parent—and cocoon.

Super Rice

PLANET EARTH'S FARMERS ARE HARD pressed to feed 5.7 billion mouths—not to mention the nearly 100 million newborns each year brings. So it was more than welcome news when the Philippines-based International Rice Institute announced a new strain of rice that yields as much as 25% more grain per acre than existing plants. Once disease and insect resistance have been bred into the rice, a process expected to take about five years, the grain will be set to join the worldwide fight against malnutrition. ■

Ancient Creatures in a Lost World

After a two-year survey in the remote mountains between Vietnam and Laos, biologist John MacKinnon announced the discovery of what appear to be three entirely new mammal species: *from left,* the giant, deerlike muntjac; the Vu Quang ox, a strange relative of cattle; and the slow-running deer.

The Great White Circus

At the Lillehammer Games, dreams came true
and the Olympic spirit triumphed over thuggery

The battles on ice transformed idyllic

Lillehammer into a backdrop for soap opera

FOR TWO WEEKS THE WHOLE world is young and strong and fearless, sporting and peaceful and clean. That is the Olympic myth and the wellspring of the Games' enduring appeal. The Games are like a patriotic day for the globe, a day when flags wave and people march and grim realities are forgotten in a worldwide surge of pride and unity. But as the 1994 Winter Games began in bucolic Lillehammer, in serene Norway, they seemed painfully ill-starred.

Over everything loomed the sorry spectacle of figure skaters Tonya Harding and Nancy Kerrigan (*see following story*). The brutal attack on Kerrigan by members of Harding's camp was a living metaphor for the tarnished ideals of sport, and for a while the attendant publicity threatened to overshadow the Games. Elsewhere skiers mourned the great Austrian Ulrike Maier, twice a world champion, who broke her neck in a routine downhill race only weeks before the Games began. And lurking in the background was the haunting presence of Sarajevo, home to a wonderful series of Winter Games 10 years before but now a besieged city, its bare ruined stadium a reminder of the impotence of Olympic promises.

But by the time the Games were over, the Olympic ideal seemed to have been swept clean in the snows of Norway. The tabloid scandals of Tonya and Nancy had given way to the real-life fairy tale of Oksana Baiul, the orphan who became an ice princess. The good guys seemed to be winning the gold medals—from the long-suffering Dan Jansen to bright new stars like the scrappy young skier Tommy Moe. There were also graceful curtain calls by great names

WE THREE QUEENS followed their star to the serene village of Lillehammer, where they waged a tabloid-ready showdown in figure skating. Though the spotlight focused on the rivalry between Americans Tonya Harding and Nancy Kerrigan, the gold went to the lyrical young Ukrainian Oksana Baiul—who had been left an orphan at 13 when her mother died of cancer.

from Olympics past: Torvill and Dean, Alberto Tomba, Katarina Witt.

At the striking opening ceremonies of the Games, the Olympic torch seemed to descend from the heavens: it was ski-jumped into the darkened arena at Lillehammer. The pageant evoked royalty, as Norway's amiable King Harald and Queen Sonja arrived in a regal sleigh. It summoned beauty in the form of actress Liv Ullmann, and grand adventure in the presence of Thor Heyerdahl of the raft *Kon-Tiki.*

Royalty, beauty, adventure: these

were the hallmarks of Lillehammer. Among the adventurers were America's skiers: Tommy Moe's go-for-broke style brought him a gold in the downhill and a silver in the super-G, while Diann Roffe-Steinrotter also won the super-G and Picabo Street took silver in the downhill.

The beauty was provided in the ice-skating arena at Hamar, dubbed "the Viking ship" for its unusual shape. The Russians once again dominated; Torvill and Dean once again dazzled; and the slight young Baiul—costumed as the Black Swan from Tchaikovsky's *Swan Lake*—gracefully stole away with the gold medal.

For royalty of a kind, there was

MEDALISTS IN MOTION: *Clockwise from top left:* silver bullet Georg Hackl of Germany won gold in the one-man luge; surprising Tommy Moe of the U.S. took two medals; in his last Games, Dan Jansen finally got his gold; Norway's homeboy Johann Olav Koss was the dominant figure of the Games, setting three world records; Russian husband-and-wife team Sergei Grinkov and Ekaterina Gordeeva triumphed in pairs figure skating; German jumper Jens Weissflog followed his skis to a gold medal.

THRONG OF NORWAY: *Clockwise from above:* Norwegian fans sweatered it out; Diann Roffe-Steinrotter schussed to Super-G gold; the home crowd cheered on Thomas Alsgaard in cross-country skiing; Austria's two-man bobsled team got off to a running start; Sweden upset Canada for hockey gold; veteran Bonnie Blair nabbed her fifth gold medal; ice dancers Torvill and Dean won the hearts of the world, if not the minds of the judges.

Norway's own Johann Olav Koss, the single most dominant athlete of the games. The 25-year-old medical student sped to three gold medals and set three world records—then pledged his $30,000 bonus from the Norwegian Olympic Committee to relief for Sarajevo. America's reigning Olympian, Bonnie Blair, won her fifth gold medal.

No competitor showed more nobility of spirit than Dan Jansen, the unlucky American. For a decade he had dominated men's speed skating, yet he had never won an Olympic medal. In 1988 in Calgary, news of his sister's death reached him just before he skated, and he fell in two events. In 1992 in Albertville he lost his balance and finished fourth in the 500. Now misfortune struck again in the 500: Jansen lost his balance and finished eighth, though he had set a new world record in the event only weeks before. He offered no excuses. In his final Olympic race, the 1,000-meter, he once again lost his balance briefly, then regained control and flashed to the gold. When he took a victory lap, he carried a hitchhiker: his nine-month-old daughter Jane, namesake of his sister. In Lillehammer, Olympic dreams really did come true. ∎

Vendetta on Ice

A vicious attack maimed a skater—and a sport

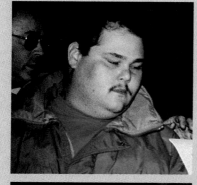

ROGUES' GALLERY: *From top,* Harding's husband Jeff Gillooly helped hatch the plot; bodyguard Shawn Eckardt took care of details; Derrick Smith drove the getaway car; Shane Stant hit Kerrigan with the baton.

P
OOR TONYA HARDING. THE WOULD-BE QUEEN OF FIGURE SKATING was the bead of raw sweat in a field of dainty perspirers, the pool-playing, drag-racing, trash-talking bad girl in a sport that thrives on illusion. While rivals floated through their programs, she bullied gravity, fighting it off like a mugger. Harding wanted gold at the Olympics, and the rewards of fame. "To be perfectly honest," she said, "what I'm really thinking about is dollar signs." She worked so hard, tried for so long, wanted so bad. But one rival in particular kept crossing her path—Nancy Kerrigan, 24, the slender, photogenic Massachusetts woman who won the hearts of fans as Harding never could and became America's favorite to win the Olympic gold medal.

On January 6 Kerrigan had just finished a practice session for the national championships in Detroit when a man approached her from behind. Wordlessly, without warning, he delivered a violent blow to her right leg with a retractable black police baton. The assailant vanished as her father carried the hysterical skater from the arena in his arms. Kerrigan withdrew from the competition with an aching, bloated knee; Harding skated to victory.

Shortly after the attack, the rumblings began: Harding, her husband Jeff Gillooly and her entourage might somehow be involved. Within 10 days, police had arrested Harding's hulking bodyguard, Shawn

TOO CLOSE FOR COMFORT: The rivals warm up—though not to each other— before they compete at Lillehammer.

Eckardt, 26, and Derrick Smith, 29, another bruiser. A day later, Shane Stant, 22, surrendered to authorities. Eckardt had helped plan the assault; Smith drove the getaway car; and Stant was the hit man. The trio's stories led police to Gillooly; in early February he pleaded guilty to his role in the plot and was sentenced to two years in prison and a $100,000 fine. He also claimed that Harding knew of the plan and approved its final form. Harding confessed only to failing to report her knowledge that people close to her were involved in the attack. The U.S. Olympic Committee threatened to expel Harding from the Games for complicity, but she struck back, filing a $25 million lawsuit accusing the U.S.O.C. of violating her right to participate. Shaken, the U.S.O.C. agreed to let her compete in exchange for her dropping the suit. At Lillehammer, Harding finished eighth and Kerrigan second to Oksana Baiul. In March, Harding pleaded guilty to conspiracy in the attack; she was fined $100,000 and sentenced to 500 hours of community service. In June she was stripped of the national championship and banned for life from the U.S.F.S.A. ∎

The Gold Medalists

Winners of selected Olympic events

BONNIE BLAIR

DAN JANSEN

BOBSLED			
Two-Man	Weder/Acklin, *Switzerland*		
Four-Man	*Germany*		

ICE HOCKEY	*Sweden*

LUGE	
Men's	Hackl, *Germany*
Men's Double	Brugger/Huber, *Italy*
Women's	Weissensteiner, *Italy*

FIGURE SKATING	
Men's	Urmanov, *Russia*
Women's	Baiul, *Ukraine*
Pairs	Gordeeva/Grinkov, *Russia*
Ice Dancing	Grichtchuk/Platov, *Russia*

SKI JUMP	
90K	Bredesen, *Norway*
120K	Weissflog, *Germany*
Team 120K	*Germany*

SPEED SKATING	Men	Women
500-m	Golubev, *Russia*	Blair, *U.S.A.*
1,000-m	Jansen, *U.S.A.*	Blair, *U.S.A.*
1,500-m	Koss, *Norway*	Hunyady, *Austria*
3,000-m		Bazhanova, *Russia*
5,000-m	Koss, *Norway*	Pechstein, *Germany*
10,000-m	Koss, *Norway*	

SHORT TRACK SPEED SKATING	Men	Women
500-m	Chae, *South Korea*	Turner, *U.S.A.*
1,000-m	Kim, *South Korea*	Chun, *South Korea*

SKIING	Men	Women
Downhill	Moe, *U.S.A.*	Seizinger, *Germany*
Combined	Kjus, *Norway*	Wiberg, *Sweden*
Giant Slalom	Wasmeier, *Germany*	Compagnoni, *Italy*
Slalom	Stangassinger, *Austria*	Schneider, *Switzerland*
Super G	Wasmeier, *Germany*	Roffe-Steinrotter, *U.S.A.*

YEAR OF THE
GUMP

Go figure: this movie sensation featured no sex, no careening cars, and a slow-witted hero with fast-moving feet

ALL SUMMER LONG, IT SEEMED, YOU COULD see them—folks of all ages and both genders—floating out of the movie theater on waves of honorable sentiment. The kids looked thoughtful, the grownups wistful. Couples were holding hands. This wasn't a *Speed* crowd; these people had completed an upbeat encounter session with America's recent past. No question: one more audience had been Gumped.

Forrest Gump, a romantic epic starring Tom Hanks as a slow but sweet-souled Alabama boy who lucks into nearly every headline event of the past 40 years, was a summer sensation: a popular hit and an instant cultural touchstone. As the film's director, Robert Zemeckis, said, *Gump* had "no typical storytelling devices: no villain, no ticking clock, no burning fuse." Maybe so, but it exploded at the North American box office. In its second week of release, when ticket sales for even the most robust hits drop 20%, *Gump* held even. After four weeks in release it topped the $100 million mark; by the end of the year, the movie had taken in a staggering $300 million at the box office.

Gump warmed the collective heart of moviegoers; they spread the word, commanded their friends to go. They stormed music stores for the two-CD album. They snapped up copies of Winston Groom's 1986 novel, on which the film was based, and copies of *Gumpisms: The Wit and Wisdom of Forrest Gump,* a pocket-size book of aphorisms from the novel. Then they ran back to the theater to relive the experience.

In the film, Forrest Gump's odd odyssey begins

> **Gump celebrated innocence and good manners— set in an age when Americans misplaced these virtues**

when he is born with a 75 IQ and deemed an embarrassment by everyone except his loving mother (Sally Field). The young Gump discovers two things: he can run like a gale-force wind, and he will always love his neighbor Jenny (Robin Wright). He goes to Vietnam with one friend, a young black man (Mykelti Williamson), and comes home with another, career soldier Dan Taylor (Gary Sinise). And wherever he is, he bumps into famous people: George Wallace and Richard Nixon, J.F.K. and L.B.J., Elvis and John Lennon (all integrated onscreen with Hanks through ingenious special effects). Almost everyone Forrest knows dies. He survives, through his goodness and the miracle of idiot grace.

The movie was a smart, easygoing fable, a social tragedy sanitized for a *Saturday Evening Post* cover. It celebrated innocence, acceptance and, not least, good manners in a tale set in the very era when Americans were supposed to have misplaced these virtues. The movie offered a cheerful alternative history—a Golden Book version—of the Vietnam War: it was all about the emotional triumphs of these nice American soldiers, and hardly a Vietnamese appeared. For younger viewers, *Forrest Gump* served as a gentle introduction to the '60s: baptism not by fire but by sound track. And to those who raged, suffered or sinned through that insane decade, the movie offered cheap absolution with a love pat. Did *Forrest Gump* make you think? No, it made you feel—or at its best, it made you think about what you feel, and about how long it had been since a movie found those remote corners of sympathy and sentiment. ■

Tim at the Top

Who's on first? Tim Allen was No. 1 at the movies, on TV and in bookstores

STAND-UP COMIC, TOOL LOVER, REGULAR GUY, EX-con (ex-con?)—Tim Allen pulled off an unheard-of triple play in 1994. *Home Improvement*, his ABC sitcom, was TV's top-rated show. His jokey auto-biographical book, *Don't Stand Too Close to a Naked Man*, reached No. 1 on the New York *Times* best-seller list in October, and though he trailed the Pope's tome briefly, he regained the top spot by Christmas. *The Santa Clause*, his first movie, was the surprise hit of the Christmas season, earning $71 million at the box office in its first 17 days and leaving Tom Cruise's fangs, Arnold Schwarzenegger's pregnancy and both generations of *Star Trek* in its dust.

Allen, 41, was hardly the most brilliant comedy star of this generation, though some might call him its most brilliant example of multimedia Hollywood marketing. But few superstars seemed less inflated by their success. Allen still kept a home in an unpretentious neighborhood in suburban Birmingham, Michigan, where he retreat-ed for holidays and other family gatherings. He had been married for 10 years to his college sweetheart, who had waited for him while he served more than two years in a federal penitentiary on drug charges. And when he threw temper tantrums on the set of his TV show—"My set! My camera! My props!" he'd been heard to shout—everybody knew it was really a joke.

With *The Santa Clause*, Allen joined the tiny frater-nity of stars who have suc-cessfully made the leap from TV to movies. But Al-len's entire life had been a study in clearing hurdles. He was born in Denver, one of six children of Gerald and Martha Dick. His last name was the occasion for a thousand playground taunts, teaching him how to steel himself with humor. At age 11, Allen faced a far more serious trauma: his father

Regular guy Allen went from stand-up comic to America's hottest multimedia star—thanks to a stop in the cooler.

was killed in a car accident. His mother remarried about two years later, and the family moved to the Detroit sub-urbs, where Allen struggled through high school and barely made it through Western Michigan University with a degree in TV production. Not long after, he fell in with a hard-partying crowd and started selling cocaine. In 1979 he was arrested; he was later sentenced to eight years in a minimum-security prison in Minnesota.

Allen served just over two years there, and it was a transforming experience. He occupied himself by reading books and writing letters, and slowly he faced the real-ization that he had messed up his life. He found humor useful in prison, making the meanest guards laugh and staging comedy shows for the other inmates. Returning to Detroit after his parole, he worked in advertising while developing a stand-up comedy act at night. Even-tually he hit on the macho-tool-guy persona that be-came his trademark.

The novice comedian began shuttling to Los An-geles and eventually broke into the big-time comedy clubs. After a few TV ap-pearances and cable spe-cials, he was discovered by The Walt Disney Company, which offered to develop a sitcom with him. After turning down three of Dis-ney's ideas for the show, Allen came up with his own idea: a series about the host of a TV handyman show. The result, *Home Improve-ment*, turned into TV's biggest family-show hit of the '90s. The movie and the book were icing on Al-len's—and Disney's—cake.

"I think what people see in Tim Allen," said his TV producer Matt Williams, "is a man-child. He's attractive, sensitive and strong, and he's a little impish 12-year-old boy. You feel like he could be you." And he could be—if for one month you were Ameri-ca's favorite movie star, No. 1 television personality and best-selling writer. ■

Ready for Her Close-Up

Glenn Close triumphed in Andrew Lloyd Webber's latest extravaganza

EW SHOWS EVER ARRIVED ON BROAD-way hauling as much excess baggage as *Sunset Boulevard,* the Andrew Lloyd Webber megamusical that opened in November. Having already conquered London and Los Angeles, *Sunset,* based on the Billy Wilder film, generated enormous expectations—reflected in a record advance sale of $38 million. There had been backstage drama aplenty, as the mercurial composer sacked not one but two leading ladies, and snubbed New York by opening the $13 million production in Los Angeles in 1993. No doubt, legions of Lloyd Webber haters would have loved to see the infuriatingly successful British interloper have another flop like his last Broadway outing, *Aspects of Love.*

The actress's strong vocals wowed audiences.

Sorry, folks, but the show was a hit—thanks in large part to its star, Glenn Close. The actress projected authentic glamour as Norma Desmond, the demented former silent-screen star who wins her final close-up on a police blotter. Close starred in the L.A. production and won the Broadway part after Lloyd Webber reneged on a contract with Patti LuPone, the creator of the role in London; it cost him $1 million to buy LuPone out. Faye Dunaway, meanwhile, was engaged as Close's successor in L.A., only to be fired when Lloyd Webber decided her voice was not up to the part; her $6 million lawsuit was pending. Close, her mobile face and twitching hands working overtime, captured all the character's narcissistic neuroticism, and she sang in a clear soprano that, though unschooled, was nevertheless a welcome relief from LuPone's raw edge.

The radiant *Sunset* might not be Lloyd Webber's best score, but it is his most seamlessly and artfully constructed thus far. The show resembled *The Phantom of the Opera*—reclusive mad protagonist conceives passion for young member of the opposite sex—but that was merely plot. Musically, *Sunset's* real forebear was *Evita.* The angular, chromatic recitatives for Norma explicitly recalled Eva Perón's egocentric ravings. If the music of the new show lacked *Aspect's* delicious subtleties and *Phantom's* gothic flamboyance, it still offered two of Lloyd Webber's best songs yet: *With One Look* and *As If We Never Said Goodbye.*

Director Trevor Nunn and designer John Napier, the *Cats* team, fashioned one *coup de théâtre* after another, reprising Wilder's opening, with the newly deceased hero (Alan Campbell as Joe Gillis) facedown in a swimming pool, and working up to a levitating mansion. This larger-than-larger-than-life approach had doomed the gentle *Aspects,* but it suited the more histrionic material of *Sunset.* And though the lavish stage machinery might have dwarfed another actress, the stellar Close easily fought the scenery to a draw. ■

Reaching new heights in Broadway spectacle, set designer John Napier's mansion actually levitated on the stage.

The Way She Is

Peddling memories—and mementos—Barbra Streisand comes back

BARBRA STREISAND IS NOT HAPPY. HERE SHE IS, a pop superstar revered by millions, newly embarked on her first paid concert tour in 28 years. Yet all she hears is complaints. Take those ticket prices. With a top fee of $350 a seat, the Streisand show far surpasses even the priciest predecessors in the can-you-top-this field of concert extravaganzas. But Streisand doesn't see a problem. "I think this price is fair," she says. "If you amortize the money over 28 years, it's $12.50 a year. So is it worth $12.50 a year to hear me sing live? I'm not going to do it again."

Then there is the TelePrompTer. During her show, a video screen hangs high above the audience, displaying for Barbra not only the lyrics to her songs but also most of the patter in between them. Critics who caught her first concerts in London were derisive. Streisand claims that she hardly ever looks at the prompter but needs it to relieve the stage fright that has kept her away from touring since a 1967 concert in New York City, when she forgot some lyrics.

Yet her biggest peeve of all is the nosy, mean-spirited press. Usually Streisand tries to avoid reporters. But in a rare interview with TIME before the tour began, she had all the recent slights at her fingertips: a British tabloid had claimed she arrived in London toting her own trash can (it was actually a hatbox); a New York *Times* op-ed piece had criticized the dress she wore at the Inaugural gala; a story in TIME had listed her alleged tantrums. And when, at a dinner honoring Hillary Clinton, she had given a speech about American society's view of women, nobody had covered it.

Powerful, complex, frightened—all might fairly be applied to Streisand. She is the most popular and enduring pop singer of her generation, a filmmaker with more clout than any other woman in Hollywood, a political activist with the money to back her beliefs. Yet stories of her rampaging ego, of fights with co-stars and directors, of her obsessive perfectionism, are legion. More recently, she was knocked for being first among Hollywood's Clinton groupies. "On a clear day in Washington," a catty New York *Times* story put it, "you can see Barbra Streisand forever."

After all the posturing and behind-the-scenes brouhahas, it is a relief to encounter Streisand where she belongs—onstage. Her show, previewed in Las Vegas

> "I've been around 33 years. When I hear my own overture play, I say, 'My God! You mean I sang all those songs?'"

over New Year's 1994 and launched in London in April, is a sleek, impressive showcase. Appearing on a lavishly appointed living-room set (Greek columns, flowing sheer drapery), Streisand glides through most of her big hits (*People, Evergreen*), the standards she has made her own (*My Man, Happy Days Are Here Again*) and a few recent additions to her canon (*As If We Never Said Goodbye*, from *Sunset Boulevard*). The voice, still strong and supple, is too polished and self-conscious to convey much real emotion anymore, but for sheer musicality it is as thrilling as ever.

Between numbers, Streisand introduces some film clips, reminisces about her childhood, pokes fun at her obsession with psychotherapy. The only thing missing (and the TelePrompTer is at least partly to blame) is any sense of free-flowing interaction with the crowd. It is not so much a concert as a well-oiled Broadway tribute—or maybe an *American Masters* TV special, presented by the Master herself.

For Streisand, 52, the concert is both a career capstone and a personal milestone. "I enjoy the privacy of the creative process when I make films and when I record, " she says. "There's a certain kind of perfection that you attain when you're doing it privately. [But] being on the stage now is the acceptance of all imperfections."

Streisand accepting imperfection? It's hard to swallow. A musician who played in her Las Vegas show logged in 60 hours of rehearsal time, and says that Streisand, unlike most singers, was present for almost every minute. Lyricist Marilyn Bergman, who helped write the script for the stage show, acknowledges Streisand's intensity, but scoffs at her reputation as a difficult diva. "Barbra never says, 'That's good enough.' People who don't understand this process might find it threatening or tiresome. But she is indefatigable."

Streisand approaches her tour in a mellow, almost wistful new mood. "I felt it was time to give back something to the people who have wanted me to sing live all these years," she says. "I've been around 33 years. When I hear my own overture play, I say, 'My God! You mean I sang all those songs?' People talk to me, and they say, 'I remember, the birth of my child was when you sang that song.' I used to never let that stuff in. Now it's kind of a wonderful thing, to appreciate my own career." ■

ROYALTY? In London, Streisand joked about marrying Prince Charles to become "the first real Jewish princess."

The Greatest Show On Earth

Go-o-o-a-a-l-l! The fans were as colorful as the players when soccer's World Cup invaded America

FORGET THE SUPER BOWL AND WORLD SERIES. THE WORLD CUP IS THE most eagerly anticipated event on the sporting calendar for most people on earth. Held every four years, the tournament decides the world championship of football—the kind of football actually played with the feet. In December 1991, 143 nations signed up to compete in the qualifying rounds for the 1994 World Cup. It took two years and 491 matches to whittle the field down to two dozen finalists, who in early summer played 52 games in nine cities in the U.S. By July 17, when Brazil faced Italy in Pasadena's Rose Bowl for the championship, more than 30 billion television viewers around the globe had tuned in to the action.

And how did the host country—notoriously soccerphobic America—react to the invasion? Just about everyone enjoyed the crazed devotion of the fans, whose modes of cheering favored lots of body paint and unusual headgear. But depending on your point of view, the Cup was either a subtle, riveting drama or a soporific bore. Even the least interested Americans woke up, however, when the underdog U.S. team, coached by the mystical Serb Bora Milutinovic, tied Switzerland 1-1, then defeated mighty but flighty Colombia 2-1. "It's been such a long road getting here," said Michigan-born Alexi Lalas, the team's redheaded, dreadlocked, rock 'n' rolling defenseman. "Being American soccer players, half the time we don't know where our next job is coming from. We're all road warriors."

The Americans' luck ran out when they lost to the dazzling Brazilians—on the Fourth of July, no less. Then it was on to the final, (*right*) where the great quest for the Cup ended—not with a bang, but with a whimper: Brazil defeated Italy not on a brilliant breakaway but on penalty kicks in overtime. Purists howled for a rules change to guarantee the Cup would never be decided in such anti-climactic fashion again. Still, for those who gave it a chance, the World Cup was a refreshing breather from standard summer sports fare. Soccer as a profitable spectator sport in America may have to wait for a decade or two. But those who became addicted to the World Cup in 1994 would have to wait only until 1996 for the elimination rounds to begin again. ■

U.S.A.
WELCOMES
WORLD CUP
SOCCER
"94"

HEARD ANY GOOD

No time to read? For millions, recorded books are giving literature a new aural tradition

The Way Things Ought to Be
By Rush Limbaugh
Read by Rush Limbaugh
A BETTER DEAL: The tape is $17; Limbaugh is on the radio for free

THE HOTSHOT COLUMNIST-AUTHOR PLAYED by Nick Nolte in the 1994 movie *I Love Trouble* runs into a lawyer friend, played by Saul Rubinek. "I'm dying to read your book, man," says the lawyer. "When is it coming out on tape?" It is hardly a surprise that Rubinek's character turns out to be the movie's chief sleazebag. What kind of shallow, no-time-for-anything '90s philistine confuses listening to books with actually reading them?

A lot of people, as it happens. Books on tape are steadily encroaching on those old-fashioned cloth-and-paper-bound items that used to be the main purveyors of literature in our culture. Most of the credit—or blame—goes to a pair of ubiquitous electronic devices: the Walkman and the car cassette player. Just as they have increased sales of music cassettes, they have made audiotapes practical: now you can "read" while you're on the rowing machine or making that long drive to the beach. Your choices range from self-help books to celebrity biographies, from John Grisham thrillers to the works of Dickens and Shakespeare, most of them narrated by well-known actors (Sam Waterston, Whoopi Goldberg, Glenda Jackson, Michael York). They are compressed into easy-listening chunks of three or four hours "because," as one audio publisher's blurb puts it, "books are long and life is short."

Retail sales of audio books (which typically cost around $17 for a two-cassette package) reached $1.2 billion in 1993, up 40% from the year before. Titles and celebrity readers are proliferating. Sharon Stone has just been signed to narrate *The Scarlet Letter. Gone With the Wind* is about to be released on tape for the first time, unabridged on 30 cassettes. "Nine years ago only 8% of the population had heard a book on tape; now it's close to 25%," says Michael Viner, co-founder of Dove Audio, a Los Angeles company that helped pioneer the field.

Bidding wars for the audio rights to potential best sellers are becoming nearly as heated as those waged over movie rights. Tom Clancy's newest novel, *Debt of Honor,* was picked up by Random House Audio for a then record sum—supposedly $1 million. Though sales of a typical book on tape still represent only a fraction of the hardcover sales (usually 10% or less), the numbers are climbing. *The Bridges of Madison County,* read by author Robert James Waller, sold 163,000 audio copies. Some 250,000 tapes of John Grisham's 1994 novel, *The Chamber,* were initially shipped to bookstores. And Rush Limbaugh has sold 300,000 tapes of *The Way Things Ought To Be*—not bad for a $17 version of his daily radio show.

> **"The text is not an amputee. I thought it represented the essence of the thing very well."**
>
> —THOMAS KENEALLY
> Novelist

On the retail front, the racks of audio books that have sprouted in bookshops are appearing in video and record stores as well. Inevitably, specialty stores have begun to crop up. Houston's BookTronics is one of the largest to carry nothing but audio—with 8,000 titles for sale or rent. "We call ourselves the bookstores of the future," says co-owner Alan Livingston.

And what sort of future is it? Literary purists wince at the prospect of tapes undermining the printed page. Yet listening to a book is not an experience to be sneered at. Storytelling began as an oral art, after all, and there can be something profoundly satisfying about hearing a book

The Crossing
By Cormac McCarthy
Read by Brad Pitt
A BOY AND HIS WOLF: Pitt finds just the right tone for the novel's hardscrabble prose

BOOKS LATELY?

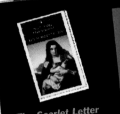

The Scarlet Letter
By Nathaniel Hawthorne
To be read by Sharon Stone
SO HOLLYWOOD: Another adultery story

44 Anything that offers language and the sound of words and literate thought is a good thing. 77

—E.L. DOCTOROW
Novelist

read aloud. In some ways an audio book demands more concentration than a printed one. Reading allows freedom—the freedom to proceed at one's own pace, to stop and savor a passage, to pause and re-read or jump ahead and skim. With an audio book, the pace is steady and unyielding; if a moment's distraction causes you to miss a key passage, you can return to the exact place only with difficulty.

The greatest drawback of audio books, of course, is that they are usually heavily abridged. (Unabridged versions are available for many books, both in stores and through mail order, but they represent a relatively small segment of the market.) Most mass-market audio books are boiled down to a length of three to six hours. Even at a relatively brisk reading pace of a minute-and-a-half per page, that typically means more than half the author's prose is left on the cutting-room floor. To the detriment of some writers, editors generally delete fine shading while retaining passages that carry the narrative forward.

Most audiotape narrators are well chosen, easy on the ear and fully engaged in their work. Sometimes too engaged. The problem with moonlighting actors is that they can't help, well, acting. In reading *Disclosure*, Michael Crichton's best seller about a man who sues his female boss for sexual harassment, John Lithgow hams it up with overripe accents—the protagonist's Hispanic lawyer seems to come from somewhere near Transylvania. But on the other hand, Brad Pitt delivers Cormac McCarthy's hardscrabble prose in *The Crossing* with a twangy stoicism that perfectly reflects its tone.

Authors who read their own work are generally less polished but often more effective than actors. Winston Groom reads his novel *Forrest Gump* in a husky Alabama drawl, delivering a lot more salt and a lot less sappiness than there is in the hit movie. Historian and TIME art critic Robert Hughes intones his searing saga of the founding of Australia, *The Fatal Shore*, with a robust Aussie accent that charges the narrative with vitality. Hearing Stephen King read the beautifully modulated opening chapter of *Needful Things* is almost enough to convince you to stick around for the rest of the 24-hour tape. Almost, but not quite: one odd aspect of the audio-book market is that King, perhaps the contemporary author who could most benefit from trimming, is the one whose books are never abridged.

How do writers regard the cutting of their books for the tape format? After refusing to allow audio condensations of his previous novels, E.L. Doctorow permitted his latest, *The Waterworks*, to be cut to four audio hours. "I have changed my position on this," he says. "It is pretty clear to

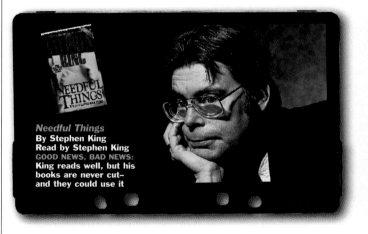

Needful Things
By Stephen King
Read by Stephen King
GOOD NEWS, BAD NEWS: King reads well, but his books are never cut– and they could use it

me that print culture is under enormous assault today. I take the position now that anything that offers language and the sound of words and literate thought is a good thing."

Doctorow's dilemma reflects the conflict between purists and realists. Will the popularity of books on tape further erode the interest in reading? Or should we welcome any new literary medium—even a slightly degraded one like books on tape? One hopeful sign is that, despite the boom in audio books, sales of hardcovers and paperbacks have not fallen. Just as Hollywood once feared the advent of videocassettes but later discovered they fed rather than discouraged interest in movies, books on tape may actually promote the cause of literature. Four hours of Doctorow or McCarthy is better than nothing, especially when the alternative is to stare at the brake lights ahead of you. ∎

THE ONLY GAME IN TOWN

With baseball on strike, Ken Burns pinch hit with an 18-hour TV film

IN 1990 FILMMAKER KEN BURNS garnered all-time viewing records for public television with his epic documentary, *The Civil War*. Burns managed to tell the story of America's bloodiest, most traumatic war in 11½ hours. In 1994 Burns returned to public television with *Baseball*, an eagerly awaited history of the national pastime: it took up 18 hours. The series was not just a history of the game but also a slice of Americana that spanned 150 years. It covered the impact of the Depression and two World Wars, player-owner conflicts that go back more than a century, and the long struggle to achieve racial integration. For baseball lovers it was the World Series, All-Star Game and Fan Appreciation Day rolled into one—and, with a strike shutting down the Major Leagues and scratching the World Series, Burns gave fans their only trip to the ballpark of the fall.

Baseball put a wealth of material into intelligent order. There were vivid sketches of greats both ancient (Christy Mathewson, a model of rectitude during the game's early, roughhousing years) and more recent (the ornery but incomparable Ted Williams). But even though it was the only game in town, *Baseball* was also a bit much. The show's dogged, decade-by-decade approach was a little rigid, the format a shade precious.

As in *The Civil War*, Burns filled his narrative with evocative anecdotes and fascinating trivia. Yet the series' bulging length and rhapsodic tone became wearying. Burns mixed his archival footage with commentary from assorted experts—sportswriters, ex-players and other students of the game. These box-seat philosophers, shot in dreamy-eyed close-up, treated the sport as something like a religion. But it is, after all, a game—and a game of finesse. *Baseball* swung for the fences on every pitch. ■

HOMER EPIC: Clockwise from top left, Jackie Robinson—by integrating the Dodgers in 1947, he made the game a truly national pastime; the Pittsburgh Crawfords of the Negro Leagues; a svelte Babe Ruth, baseball's greatest hero; filmmaker Burns; the classic swing of Joe DiMaggio.

THE FIRST DAY OF SPRING • 1929

■ ART

Poses, Plans and Provocations

How the young Salvador Dali invented his greatest creation: himself

WAS ANY PAINTER A WORSE EMBARRASSMENT than Salvador Dali? Not even Andy Warhol. Long before his physical death in 1989, old Avida Dollars—Andre Breton's anagram of his name—had collapsed into wretched exhibitionism. Genius. Shocker. Lip-Topiarist. Though he once turned down an American businessman's proposal to open a string of what would be called Dalicatessens, there was little else he refused to endorse, from chocolates to perfumes. He was surrounded by fakes and crooks and married to a false muse, the greedy Gala, who made him the indentured servant of his lost talent.

Nevertheless, Dali was an important artist for about 10 years, starting in the late 1920s. Nothing can take that away from him. Other Surrealists—especially Max Ernst and Joan Miro—were greater magicians, but Dali's sharp, glaring, enameled visions of death, sexual failure and deliquescence, of displaced religious mania and creepy organic delight, left an ineradicable mark on our century when it, and he, were young. Dali turned "retrograde" technique—the kind of dazzlingly detailed illusionism that made irreality concrete, as in *The First Days of Spring, 1929*—toward subversive ends. His soft watches will never cease to tick, not as long as the world has adolescent dandies and boy rebels in it.

But what of Dali's own clockwork? What wound him up? This was the theme of "Salvador Dali: The Early Years," an exhibition that opened in June at New York City's Metropolitan Museum of Art. The show brought together a mass of Dali's juvenilia, starting at age 12; it ended in 1929 with Dali in Paris, already the 25-year-old darling of both Left and Right Banks.

In art, the fledgling Dali believed he could do anything—including what other artists had done, which became "Dalinian" by virtue of being redone by him. The exhibition shows him running through the styles, with slowly increasing calculation, trying them on for fit. He was a 15-year-old Impressionist and then a 16-year-old Symbolist. He does Fauve blotches and combines them with elements of the classicizing movement, with "timeless" peasant figures, olive trees and old arches.

"I'll be a genius," the young Dali wrote in his diary. "Perhaps I'll be despised and misunderstood, but I'll be a genius, a great genius." Cold and diligent, he figured out all his poses and provocations in advance. Though he eventually became an archconservative, he was a vehement parlor red in his youth. There was, however, nothing particularly revolutionary about his painting. It is an easy matter to go through this early work identifying, here and there, what would grow and what would not. Perhaps the most important imaginative relationships in young Dali's life were with people, not paintings: the poet Federico Garcia Lorca and the future filmmaker Luis Bunuel. The crystalline and extravagant beauty of Lorca's imagery helped release similar qualities in Dali's work. It was the poet's baroque character, his preoccupation with death, sex and the morbidity of flesh—his extreme Spanishness—that encouraged the younger artist's imagination. That is why Dali's best work has lasted. ■

VIEW FROM MOUNT HOLYOKE, NORTHAMPTON, MASSACHUSETTS, AFTER A THUNDERSTORM • 1836

Storm Warnings in Arcadia

The landscapes of Thomas Cole gave America a new national image

DURING HIS SHORT LIFE—HE DIED IN 1848, AT the age of 47—Thomas Cole became something of a national cultural hero: a young one for a young nation. He was esteemed as the founder of national landscape painting in the U.S., the so-called Hudson River School. His death, opined a newspaper editorial, was "a public and national calamity." Why did a painter inspire such sentiments? That question was answered by "Thomas Cole: Landscape into History," a show of more than 75 paintings on view at the National Museum of American Art in Washington in the summer of 1994.

Unlike his predecessors Benjamin West and John Singleton Copley, Cole was the first boy wonder of American painting to prove himself entirely on native ground. He learned about landscape painting from theoretical tracts and the early 19th century equivalent of how-to manuals, backed up by attentive looking. He couldn't draw the human figure; wisely, he kept his Indians and woodsmen and saints in the far distance.

The outline of his life seems a fable of what emigration could inspire. The young artist—Cole was the son of a small trader from Lancashire—arrives in the æsthetically uncharted wilderness, where, self-taught by dint of "natural vision," he begins to create a new, true and specifically American picturesqueness out of rocks, gorges, sunsets, trees and distant Indians. He is taken up by the plutocrats of his day, from patricians like Stephen van Rensselaer III to the more recently arrived, like the grocery millionaire Luman Reed. Old

money wanted to show that taste was not a monopoly of Europeans. New money hoped to prove that it too had refinement and a stake in forming the American national image.

For Americans of the late 18th century, this national image dwelt in the faces of founder-heroes like Washington. But from 1820 on the desire to symbolize America was to pour, in a veritable cataract, into the great repository of American difference from Europe, the landscape itself. Cole's painting of the Hudson River and its environs is often suffused with doubt and nostalgia, a sense that the America of early settlement and cooperative virtue was passing away, to be replaced by a more competitive, get-and-spend society. His work keeps circling around the image of pastoral America as an imperiled Arcadia, beset by storms that pass by, connoting disturbances in the social fabric.

His most famous image of this kind is *View from Mount Holyoke, Northampton, Massachusetts, After a Thunderstorm, 1836*—"The Oxbow," for short. On the right, the serene bend in the river, the golden light; on the left, a storm blotting out the distance; in the foreground, the artist's painting kit, including a parasol—the frail equipment of a witness to immense forces. Cole later expanded this theme in grandiloquent allegorical paintings like *The Course of Empire*. In these corny yet convincing views of the rise and fall of an imaginary state—by inference, the U.S.—Cole embodied the same peculiarly American anxiety of an imperiled Arcadia. ■

FERRAGOSTO IV • 1961

The Graffiti of Loss

In nuanced abstractions, Cy Twombly shores up fragments against the ruins

BY NOW, WITH RECORDED AUCTION PRICES OF $3 million and up, Cy Twombly must be the most fashionable abstract painter alive. But you didn't have to be an all-out fan of Twombly's—though he certainly has them—to have welcomed the show of his paintings and drawings that opened at New York City's Museum of Modern Art in September 1994. Born in Lexington, Virginia, in 1928, Twombly belongs to the generation of American artists that followed Abstract Expressionism and had to contend, Oedipus-like, with its influence. He is the Third Man, a shadowy figure beside the vivid duumvirate of his friends Jasper Johns and Robert Rauschenberg. But unlike them, he made his life in Europe. After some gestation in one of the wombs of the postwar American avant-garde, Black Mountain College in North Carolina, he went to Italy in 1957 and has lived there ever since.

His work is cryptic, devoted to nuance and practically impossible to reproduce. No color plate conveys the way those little scribbles and blots can keep the whitish-blond surface of a big Twombly in coherent tension. His American reputation bottomed out in 1964 with a show of nine florid paintings called *Discourse on Commodus.* They were trashed as a fiasco, in print and by word of mouth. Twombly was repatriated to America 20 years later through the enthusiasm that younger European artists and collectors felt for him.

Twombly was one of the first American artists to interest himself in graffiti. Forty years ago, the term didn't suggest city kids spraying their aggressive colored tags all over subway cars and buildings. It wasn't bound up with the seizure and degradation of public space. It was, so to speak, more muted and pastoral: harmless scratches, small obscenities, chalk on Roman distemper. To adopt graffiti to the painted canvas was to pay homage to European *art informel*—Fautrier, Wols and especially Jean Dubuffet. Their influence plays on Twombly's earliest paintings of the 1950s, with their lumpish glandular forms, the movement of the paint slowed up by mixing it with earth but then accelerated by a nervous, hairy scratching around the edges.

Through Twombley's paintings trickles a current of double nostalgia—on the one hand for the closed-off "heroic" possibilities of Modernism and on the other for the ancient Mediterranean world, experienced at a remove by his living in modern Italy. Love (or its facsimile) among the ruins. In sum, Twombly is a textbook case of High and Low in one parcel: an Alexandrian painter in love with entropy and yet capable of toughness. The phrases he writes on the canvas are place names and snatches of poetry; done in a faint cursive script that is always on the point of trailing off into illegibility, they suggest fatigue and forgetting. These skittering, affectless quotations—a shoring up of fragments against the ruins—are written all over Twombly's work. But the structure of the paintings themselves, the placement of the marks on the big field, is energetic and often brilliant. Behind the current fashion for Twombly, behind the hyperbole of his admirers, one senses the artist's own hand. But he is still a considerable painter. ∎

THE BEST BOOKS OF 1994

FICTION

❷ The Afterlife and Other Stories *by John Updike* (Knopf). Elder writesman Updike proves his durability by turning out yet another fine collection of elegant short stories about—stay with him—Wasp geezers who golf. Now and then, unblocked metaphors rise up shrieking: one duffer is resigned "to a golfing mediocrity that would poke its way down the sloping dogleg of decrepitude to the level green of death." Fore? Sure, but Lord, how that senior citizen can write!

❸ The Bird Artist *by Howard Norman* (Farrar, Straus & Giroux). Here's a marvelously operatic novel, roiling with outrageous men and women and with jealousy, revenge, gunfire, deadly sea swells and lust in a lighthouse, all set in the tiny Newfoundland community of Witless Bay (one

❶ In the Lake of the Woods *by Tim O'Brien* (Houghton Mifflin). A boyish politician, spooked by memories of Vietnam, retreats to a Minnesota lake to sort things out. He and his wife, who has spooks of her own, slip separately into a subterranean world of the mind where morality, evil and reality itself are shifting phantoms.

store, one restaurant, a sawmill and a drydock) just after the turn of the century. The author writes well against this florid grain, producing extravagant melodrama in language that is strict, laconic and evocative.

❹ The Waterworks *by E.L. Doctorow* (Random House). This Poe-esque tale of murky doings in 1871 Manhattan offers the surreptitious exhumation of a corpse while, sure enough, fog swirls in the phosphorescent light of early dawn. What it can't supply, for all the author's huffing and puffing, is social significance. But with a ghostly white stagecoach whose passengers are supposedly deceased rich men, significance (which closes on Saturday night anyway) shouldn't be an issue.

❺ Open Secrets *by Alice Munro* (Knopf). Once more the Canadian writer supplies rich, daring and satisfying short stories, all rooted in rural Ontario, most of them about women who find themselves balanced uneasily between a conventional past and a present that tips them in new and strange directions. The constants in Munro's relevatory stories are remorseless time, blind fate and the author's wry sense of the bizarre hidden in the ordinary.

NONFICTION

❷ Last Train to Memphis: The Rise of Elvis Presley *by Peter Guralnick* (Little, Brown). The author, a music critic, follows the self-created rock hero as he is borne to platinum paradise on a great celebrity updraft. Guralnick writes evocatively and sympathetically of Presley's first wild fame—his first recording, *That's All Right, Mama,* made him a millionaire—and tracks the star through the shattering death of his mother Gladys and his entry into the Army.

❸ South Wind Changing *by Ngoc Quang Huynh* (Graywolf Press). A Vietnamese refugee to the U.S. tells movingly of surviving a Marxist re-education camp and escaping Vietnam by boat. His adventures in the U.S. include learning the rhythms of English well enough to write

❶ Winchell: Gossip, Power and the Culture of Celebrity *by Neal Gabler* (Knopf). Walter Winchell would have sent the likes of Rush Limbaugh out for coffee. Doubters among today's uninstructed young are invited to read biographer Gabler's superb, richly detailed portrait of the grade-school dropout and vainglorious, third-rate ex-hoofer who, more than any other gossipist, invented the modern celebrity industry. Almost forgotten today, Winchell's syndicated "colyums" and brassy, red-baiting broadcasts to "Mr. and Mrs. America and all the ships at sea" shaped America's lowbrow culture for the 1930s and '40s.

this haunting, oddly pastoral memoir.

❹ Family *by Ian Frazier* (Farrar, Straus & Giroux). A long, moody rummage in time's attic. Frazier began to gather material about his near and distant family after the death of his parents, searching, he says, for the meaning of life, for "a meaning that would defeat death." The result of this painstaking process adds up to a remarkable demonstration of Frazier's ability to write with rare, pure love and to make his feelings meaningful to casual passersby—his readers.

❺ My Own Country *by Abraham Verghese* (Simon & Schuster). When the physician-author arrived in the Appalachian town of Johnson City, Tennessee, in 1985, AIDS was an alien, virtually unknown, something that happened only to gays in New York City. But now the virus was beginning to kill in this isolated, staunchly religious community, and Verghese had to deal with it. At the same time he had to fight the ignorance and prejudice of townspeople. An Indian Christian who was born in Ethiopia, Verghese brings strength and humility to his agonizing story. Fatigue and burnout are detectable here too, but his compassion and sorrow are a gift to his country, and to ours. ■

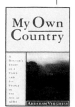

❷ Red Rock West

Film noir is more than a lighting style. It's a seedy, cynical world view: people are motivated by greed, stupidity and sexual avarice. Director John Dahl gets it all right in his mean, hilarious tale of a drifter (Nicolas Cage) mistaken for a contract killer. The title town is off all the moral maps, and so—deliriously, invigoratingly—is this lowbrow, low-budget assault.

❸ Heavenly Creatures

Pauline and Juliet, two love-struck teenagers in 1950s New Zealand, created a voluptuous fantasy world and moved into it. Director Peter Jackson moves in with them; his fevered camera style communicates the rapture and peril of adolescent hysteria. This hurtling, upsetting film, based on a true murder case, has a thrillingly nervy performance by Melanie Lynskey as the darker, needier Pauline.

❹ The Shawshank Redemption

Jailbirds and moviegoers both do time—and depending on the picture, two hours can

seem like a life sentence. Time is the preoccupation of Frank Darabont's deeply satisfying prison drama about a man wrongly convicted of murder who plots revenge and escape. Tim Robbins and Morgan Freeman are tough, smart, patient. So is the film.

❶ **Pulp Fiction. Now here's a *movie*. Three stories that begin as clichés but soon go wild and wily. A gallery of tough guys who minor in philosophy. Career-defining turns by John Travolta, Samuel L. Jackson and Uma Thurman. Peppery dialogue that brings macho swank into the '90s. Quentin Tarantino's adrenaline rush of a melodrama is a brash dare to timid Hollywood filmmakers. Let's see, he says, if you can be this smart about going this far.**

❺ Hoop Dreams

At 14, William Gates and Arthur Agee are sports heroes and working stiffs—magicians on the high school basketball court who stagger under the burden of producing wins (and glory and revenue) for their team. Documentarians Steve James, Fred Marx and Peter Gilbert have produced an epic of love, betrayal, heartbreak, true grit.

❻ Bullets over Broadway

Woody Allen rounds up the usual show-biz subjects—egomaniacal star (Dianne Wiest in a great, bold comic performance), earnest young playwright, desperate producer—and an underworld hit man (Chazz Palminteri) who has what none of them has: theatrical genius. He teaches them all a thing or two about art and life in Allen's happiest, most assured comedy in many years.

❼ The Lion King

Primal Disney on the African plains: a lion cub survives banishment and his father's death. This cartoon feature (directed by Roger Allers and Rob Minkoff) has the glories of

narrative savvy, voicemanship, lively songs and scenic splendor—familiar Disney virtues but still fresh and fine.

❽ Little Women

The March sisters navigate the passage from girlhood to womanhood with grace, spirit and infinite appeal in Gillian Armstrong's passionate realization of the 19th century children's classic. Winona Ryder leads an entrancing cast in a family film that interrupts our pious pratings about "family values" to say something truthful and unsentimental on the subject.

❾ White

A Polish nebbish gets even with the nasty Frenchwoman of his dreams. In this dark comedy (second episode in the wonderful *Blue-White-Red* trilogy), director Krzysztof

Kieslowski cannily observes the flourishing of capitalism and the festering of emotion in his wayward homeland.

❿ Clerks

In a Jersey mini-mall, the convenience-store guy and his pal from the video store talk dirty but think long and wistfully about the life that is passing them by. Their customers and girlfriends are just as lost, goofy and irrelevant. The budget for Kevin Smith's movie was $27,575, but he's the Chekhov of slacker life—and maybe of America's secret life. ∎

...AND THE WORST

Female Trouble. Remember when popular movies had *women* in them? In 1994's top films, the ladies were lucky if the guys let them even drive a bus. The typical female role was a captive or a pinup, wounded faun (*Forrest Gump*) or ditsy wife (*True Lies*). For its Best Actress prize, the New York Film Critics had to go to a TV movie (*The Last Seduction's* Linda Fiorentino). Affirmative action is démodé these days, but Hollywood needs some spur to bring women into full partnership with the Toms and Arnolds and Simbas.

1 **Various Artists,** *Stolen Moments: Red Hot + Cool* **(GRP). The goal: to raise money for the fight against AIDS. The high concept: to match some of the most exciting performers in hip-hop (the bands Digable Planets and Us3, bassist-rapper Me'Shell NdegéOcello and others) with some of the finest performers in jazz (including saxophonist Joshua Redman, trumpeter Donald Byrd and keyboardist Herbie Hancock) and create a benefit CD of jazz-rap songs. The result: a landmark album that brilliantly harnesses the fire of rap and the cool of jazz, transcending genres and generations.**

2 **John Eliot Gardiner** *Beethoven: The Nine Symphonies* (Archiv). What did Ludwig van Beethoven's symphonies sound like in Beethoven's day?

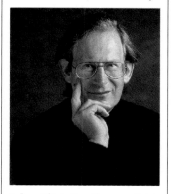

John Eliot Gardiner and his Orchestre Revolutionnaire et Romantique try to show us by using gut-stringed fiddles, valveless horns and other period instruments, and by adopting brisk tempos. To listen to this electrifying set is to rediscover these revolutionary compositions in all their terror and wonder.

3 **Green Day** *Dookie* (Reprise). Do you like playing your car stereo so loud that cars in back of you flash their

lights? If the answer is yes, then Green Day is for you. If no, then here's a CD you can give to your younger relations that will make them all think you're incredibly cool. While the raucous, cathartic songs of this Berkeley-based punk band are adolescent and snotty, they're always laughing with you, not at you ... or are they? The best rock CD of the year.

4 **Nanci Griffith** *Flyer* (Elektra). This wide-eyed, waiflike folk singer from Texas—picture Emily Dickinson with a guitar—has long been a cult favorite. She breaks into the mainstream with this moving, semiautobiographical cycle of lost loves and missed opportunities, all the while smiling through her tears.

5 **Sviatoslav Richter** *The Authorised Recordings* (Philips). In an era of cookie-cutter virtuosos, the Ukrainian-born Richter is the the last of the larger-than-life pianists, brilliant and willful. This magnificent 21-CD collection, culled from unreleased tapes covering a span of 25 years, proves he is one of the great artists of the age.

6 **Hootie & the Blowfish** *Cracked Rear View* (Atlantic). Charged by rock 'n' roll but grounded in the blues, this quartet, based in Columbia,

South Carolina, makes music with frat-party swagger, but the band's lyrics address such serious topics as the death of a parent and the racial implications of flying the Confederate flag. The rough, commanding voice of lead singer Darius Rucker, at left, makes it all work.

7 **Wynton Marsalis and Cassandra Wilson** *Blood on the Fields.* Marsalis' lush, undulating jazz composition, performed at Lincoln Center in April and broadcast on National Public Radio, captured the pain of American slavery in piercing trumpet peals and the joy of liberation in the playful bleats of trombones. The three-hour big-band piece featured singer Cassandra Wilson, who, with her performance in *Fields* and the success of her transcendent album *Blue Light 'Til Dawn*, came into her own this year as the reigning queen of jazz.

8 **The Cranberries** *No Need to Argue* (Island). A wondrous collection of crunching rock and dreamy ballads, heartfelt confessionals and political declarations. There's no arguing that this youthful band of Irish rockers, led by singer Dolores O'Riordan, is maturing gracefully.

9 **Witold Lutoslawski** *Symphonies Nos. 3 and 4* (Sony). Krzysztof Penderecki may be better known, but Lutoslawski, a composer of uncompromising integrity, was the dean of contemporary Polish composers. He died in February, but his work lives on in these splendid readings by Esa-Pekka Salonen and the Los Angeles Philharmonic. Particularly noteworthy is the Fourth Symphony, Lutoslawski's last and most moving orchestral essay.

10 **TLC** *CrazySexyCool* (LaFace). The producer known to all as Babyface was everywhere this year, producing

and writing hit songs for Boyz II Men, Madonna and Aretha Franklin, among others. But he's done some of his finest work with the vocal trio TLC and their latest collection of slinky, saucy R&B tunes. ■

...AND THE WORST

The Three Tenors II. To vary Marx's formulation slightly, history repeats itself—the first time as an enchanting evening of song, the second time as an example of extreme bad taste and lazy greed. What was wonderful in Rome in 1990 was awful in L.A. as Luciano Pavarotti, Placido Domingo and José Carreras sight-read their way through arias and show tunes on a set that included a waterfall. And no, the Brindisi from *La Traviata*—the sequel's intended *Nessun dorma*—did not fly to the top of the charts.

1 **O.J. on the Run. On a Friday night in June, two-thirds of America's TV households tuned in to the oddest car chase in TV history: O.J. Simpson's slow-speed flight along the Los Angeles freeways, ending with his surrender in the driveway of his Brentwood home. The courtroom drama that** followed has grown increasingly tedious (anybody know what Judge Ito's *right* profile looks like?). But that evening-long episode of The Fugitive, with play-by-play from Barbara Walters, Tom Brokaw and seemingly every local newscaster in Los Angeles, was the daffiest media spectacle of the year.

2 **Watergate (Discovery)**
Liddy, Magruder, Dean and the rest of them were back, 20 years older, to tell what they knew and when they knew it. The BBC interviewers elicited candor, several fresh revelations and, in five compelling hours, a definitive account of the scandal that brought down Richard Nixon's presidency.

3 **To Play the King (PBS)**
Francis Urquhart (Ian Richardson), the Tory party whip who had schemed his way to the prime ministry in *House of Cards*, returned to battle a reformist King of England (Michael Kitchen) in a sequel that nearly matched the original in savage wit.

4 **ER (NBC)**
Michael Crichton drew on his experiences as a medical student and ignored the usual formulas of TV drama to reinvent the doctor show for the 1990s—and create the season's surprise hit. The emergency-room action is better than the sometimes-soapy personal stories, but no hour on TV is more gripping.

5 **Fatherland (HBO)**
In an alternate world where Hitler has won World War II, an SS officer (Rutger Hauer) and an American reporter (Miranda Richardson) stumble on the Nazis' terrible secret, in this suspenseful, well-paced adaptation of Robert Harris' best seller.

6 **Baseball (PBS)**
Granted it was too sanctimonious and too long, but Ken Burns' 18-hour paean to America's national pastime was a gigantic achievement nonetheless, packed with history, nostalgia and, yes, poetry. Burns (*The Civil War*) was too much in love with his subject, but could anyone else have got this made, or made it so well?

7 **She TV (ABC)**
ER showed that quality drama could still make it in prime time; this short-lived summer series showed that quality comedy could not. An hour of satire from a female point of view, the program skewered everyone from Rush Limbaugh to Barbra Streisand, as well as the way real men and women miscommunicate.

8 **David's Mother (CBS)**
Kirstie Alley played the overprotective mother of an autistic teenager (Michael Goorjian) in this surprisingly affecting TV movie. Directed by Robert Allan Ackerman from Bob Randall's script, the film avoided sentimentality as it told the story of a woman who must learn the difference between love and selfishness.

9 **My So-Called Life (ABC)**
Teenage angst is all over the television dial, from sitcoms to *Beverly Hills, 90210*, but this new series from the creators of *thirtysomething* is the only one that seems to get it right. Claire Danes is super as the introspective 15-year-old who makes us remember what it was really like to be, like, a kid.

10 **Tales from the Far Side (CBS)**
Just after announcing that he was retiring his daily syndicated cartoon, Gary Larson brought his mordant wit to television for the first time in this weird, wordless animated special. Highlight: a sentimental wolf weeps over home movies. Unearthly and wonderful. ∎

Madonna. The Material Girl, rapidly running out of material, tried pouty intransigence and four-letter words on David Letterman's *Late Show*, an appearance that proved you *can* turn your head away from a train wreck. By the end of her bleepathon, even the studio audience was hooting her off the stage. She tried to salvage the p.r. disaster by acting like Little Bo Peep on Jay Leno's show and cooing with Dave at the MTV awards. No sale. Terumi Matthews in *Madonna: Innocence Lost* was more fun.

① **Three Tall Women.** This is Edward Albee's comeback drama: it signals his triumphant return to New York theater and to the acclaim that was his 30 years ago. But in this poignant, formally exciting memory play he also comes back to the issue of family, which energized *Who's Afraid of Virginia Woolf?* Albee faces his demon—his adoptive mother—in a dazzling act of exorcism and forgiveness.

② **Love! Valour! Compassion!**
Eight gay men on three summer weekends: a simple device for Terrence McNally's elegant meditations on manhood and friendship, maturity and mortality. This witty, generous, intimate epic (in a pristine off-Broadway production directed by Joe Mantello) follows McNally's *Lips Together, Teeth Apart* and *A Perfect Ganesh.* By now he has to be rated our most consistently satisfying playwright.

③ **As You Like It**
Adventurous directors love to bend and spindle Shakespeare to make contemporary points. Declan Donnellan, of Britain's Cheek by Jowl company (on display in Brooklyn last fall), uses the most traditional means—a bare stage, an all-male cast—for radical ends.

Does cross dressing lead to tatty camp? No, it's an apt way of addressing the crises of eros and identity at the heart of the play, where comic ingenuity escalates into poetic rapture.

④ **Broken Glass**
She (Amy Irving) is crippled with obsession over Hitler's mistreatment of Jews. He (Ron Rifkin) is a raging, gelded bull. And Arthur Miller, in a scalding play that brought him back to Broadway 50 years after his debut, is still pursuing his theme: that connecting with other people is at once our most destructive and redemptive condition. Brilliant, remorseless drama.

⑤ **Mystère**
Broadway isn't the only place for grand spectacle. At the Treasure Island hotel in Las Vegas, that Mecca of excess, the Montreal troupe Cirque du Soleil has created a gorgeously surreal, thrillingly theatrical pageant. Acrobats mingle with Adam and Eve, spaceship Earth and a giant snail in a fantasy of rebirth. It plays like the fever dream of some millennial impresario. Call him Siegfried Roy Webber.

⑥ **Show Boat**
Jerome Kern and Oscar Hammerstein II put Edna Ferber's panoramic novel onstage in 1927. It keeps on rollin' in Harold Prince's vigorous Broadway version of the old paddlewheel musical. The story still works, the great score is well sung, and Lonette McKee makes for a lustrous, heartbreaking Julie.

⑦ **All in the Timing**
Even with a mountaineer's ax stuck in his head, Leon Trotsky (Philip Hoffman) can find nine ways to muse on life and death. And even in a 10-minute sketch, playwright David Ives can find a dozen ways to aerobicize the playgoer's brain. Six pieces in one dazzling off-Broadway evening display Ives' verbal gifts and humanist brooding. These are breathless sprints that the heart makes over the high hurdles of language.

⑧ **Communicating Doors**
Play is a verb to Alan Ayckbourn, the consummate games player among modern writers for the theater. This time (in a production that brought his

Scarborough company to Chicago) the stage is a time machine, carrying women 20 years forward or backward in their hectic lives. But beneath the formal ingenuity, Ayckbourn finds depth, despair and, finally, redemption. A serious farce from a man who takes comedy into the shadows.

⑨ **The Glass Menagerie**
Director Frank Galati's Broadway revival brings Tennessee Williams' great early play bracingly back to life. Zeljko Ivanek is inspired as Williams' alter ego; Julie Harris is fine as Amanda, the matriarch who doesn't realize that her glass family is at the breaking point.

⑩ **Poor Super Man**
Thank the Cincinnati, Ohio, bluenoses for this one. When the vice squad stopped by for a look at Brad Fraser's incendiary new work, which contains some nudity and naughty words, it guaranteed the media's attention. But this Canadian author always offers more than shock value. What he gives us here is a witty, moving slice of urban life—gay and straight, gay and sad. ∎

...AND THE WORST

The Tonys. Each June, Broadway throws itself a party called the Tony Awards. It's a celebration of high prices, geriatric shows and a paucity of competition—the very things that keep young, adventurous artists and audiences away. The Tonys are not about the quality of theater in America, but about real estate: the rules say it's not a Broadway show unless it plays in a (pricey) midtown house. Until they are opened at least to vital off-Broadway theater, the awards will remain a posh wake. The tombstone could read BROADWAY.

NOBLE ROT

Britain's royal farce festered, with Charles playing Prince of Wails and Diana's honor besmirched

P RINCE CHARLES A HERO? YES, FOR ONE BRIEF shining moment in 1994, the heir to the British throne was actually hailed by his loyal subjects as a paragon of courage. It took an attack by an Australian youth angry about his country's treatment of Cambodian boat people to do the trick. On January 26, greeting 10,000 Australia Day celebrators in Sydney, the prince remained imperturbable when a student leaped from the crowd, aimed a gun at him and fired two blanks. The assailant was immediately seized by police. The day after the event, Britain's cruel and unforgiving press universally praised Charles for his sangfroid.

But that would be the sole moment of glory for the prince in 1994. A series of damaging revelations—including his admission that he had committed adultery during his marriage to Diana, the Princess of Wales—was capped by the fall release of his authorized biography, in which he claimed that he had never loved Diana and had agreed to marry her only when pressured by his father, Prince Philip.

Diana's year also began on a high note. In May, as she was passing a London park, she saw a vagrant drowning in a pond and had her chauffeur call for help. She later visited the man twice in the hospital. But, like Charles, her year went immediately downhill; she was accused of making a series of crank phone calls, and a new book charged her with carrying on a five-year affair with her riding instructor during her marriage to Charles. The continuing troubles of the separated-but-not-yet-divorced royal couple left Britons apprehensive about the future of the monarchy, and particularly about the prince's fitness to assume the throne.

Buckingham Palace must have hoped that the prince's stiff-upper-lip display in Australia would mark the beginning of a comeback in public esteem for the troubled royal. But in late June, the prince managed once again to grasp public-relations defeat from the

"Whoever is trying to destroy me is inevitably damaging the institution of the monarchy."

–PRINCESS DIANA

> **"[I was faithful and honorable to my wife] until the marriage became irretrievably broken down."**
>
> —PRINCE CHARLES

jaws of victory. The occasion was a 2½-hour documentary on his life broadcast on Britain's ITV network. The documentary was intended to impress the public with images of the prince's tireless toil in support of worthwhile projects. To that end, TV journalist Jonathan Dimbleby had been given unusual access to Charles for more than a year. And the film did show that attractive side of the prince in great detail. But the scenes of the prince's charitable work were completely overshadowed by two grave missteps by the heir.

The moment everyone had been waiting for came halfway through the program. Dimbleby was asking Charles about his relationship with Camilla Parker Bowles, the woman long rumored to be his mistress. The prince's face assumed the pained intensity of one suffering from an acute intestinal disorder. Speaking in his characteristically elliptical sentences, Charles stammered that Parker Bowles was an old friend who was "helpful and understanding" during his marriage crisis.

Dimbleby persisted: "Were you faithful and honorable to your wife when you took the vow of marriage?" "Yes," Charles answered, then paused before adding, "until it became irretrievably broken down." There it was: the confession. Charles, the Prince of Wales, the heir to the British throne, was by his own admission an adulterer. Charles provoked further controversy with his statements involving the Church of England. Noting that all great religions contain common elements of truth and that his subjects follow a variety of faiths, he suggested that when he did become King he should be called "Defender of Faith" rather than "Defender of the Faith." Since this would mark a historic break between the monarchy and the Church of England, the remark set off alarm bells for many Anglicans.

The House of Windsor once again was forced to raise the drawbridge and fill the moat against a barrage of criticism, including renewed discussion of the prince's suitability to be King. The press, long criticized by the prince for its assaults on his privacy, took the occasion to gloat. The tabloids reveled in his admission of adultery, while the more serious papers zeroed in on his political indiscretions. Meanwhile, Diana scored a coup, upstaging Charles the evening of his telecast by attending a charity dinner wearing a smashing ink-blue silk crepe off-the-shoulder cocktail dress. It was her picture, not the prince's, that was featured on the front pages in Britain the next day.

The royal tag-team farce continued in August; this time it was Diana's turn on center stage. The tabloid *News of the World* claimed Diana had made some 300 hang-up calls to a well-connected London art dealer, Oliver Hoare, 48. Hoare feared the calls were the work of terrorists who knew his business was in Middle Eastern art. But according to the tabloid, a police investigation showed the calls were made from phones in Kensington Palace, where Diana lived; from pay phones near the palace; from Diana's car phone; and from the home of her sister, Lady Sarah McCorquodale.

Just as with the Squidgy tapes and Camillagate—already part of the language—the Waleses were undone by the telephone. To deny the charges, mysteriously leaked to the paper, Diana produced her diary, which showed that she was sometimes out on appointments when she was supposedly at home conducting phone war. "I don't even know how to use a parking meter, let alone a phone box," she cried, noting quite shrewdly that "whoever is trying to destroy me is inevitably damaging the institution of the monarchy."

Diana was in an increasingly vulnerable situation. In 1992 she had been the wronged woman; by the summer of 1994 she was portrayed as selfish, a spendthrift and maybe crazy. The tabloids charged that the high-maintenance royal spent $240,000 a year on hairdressers, clothes, skincare products and New Age treatments like aromatherapy.

PAWNS: Perhaps the most sympathetic characters in the tug-of-war were the young princes—William, 12, and Harry, 10.

Worse was to come. In the fall, Anna Pasternak's *Princess in Love* recounted in 192 pages the salacious details of Di's alleged five-year affair with her riding instructor, army officer James Hewitt. According to the book, the two were instantly captivated with each other when they met at a party in 1986 and subsequently engaged in sleep-overs at the princess's Kensington Palace residence when Prince Charles was traveling. The book was based entirely on Hewitt's account of the relationship. While the publisher claimed the handsome cavalry officer received no payment for his story, the tabloids reported that he indeed made millions of dollars as a result of his conversations with Pasternak. Hewitt kept mum, busy with the purchase of a $387,000 Georgian house on 70 acres of land. "Tawdry," "worthless" and "grubby" were the words Buckingham Palace used to describe *Princess in Love.* The *Daily Mirror* branded Hewitt a "revolting creep" who deserved a "horsewhipping."

With Diana reeling from the accusations, only one man could save her—and Prince Charles obliged, committing yet another massive misjudgment with the publication of serialized portions of his approved biography, *The Prince of Wales,* in the Sunday *Times.* Like the ill-fated television interview of the summer, the book was the work of Jonathan Dimbleby, who had not only the long television interviews to draw on, but also access to diaries, letters and other records.

The portrait Dimbleby presented was shocking. Charles, it appeared, was never in love with Diana. He claimed to have entered the mar-

HE DIDN'T KEEP MUM: But dashing cad James Hewitt claimed he did keep pupil Diana as his mistress for five years.

riage under severe pressure from Prince Philip, who was depicted as a bully with a scathing tongue, easily capable, when Charles was a child, of reducing him to tears. In having a bride thrust upon him, Charles felt "ill-used and impotent." His mother was remote and passive, usually leaving family matters to her husband. Along the way, institutions came in for criticism: Gordonstoun School—picked, of course, by Philip—was for Charles a hell of hazing and teasing. And the media never knew their place.

In fact the prince seemed eager to blame anyone at all for his problems. It was bad enough to reveal to the world—including his sons William, 12, and Harry, 10—accounts of his wife's mood swings and depression. It was clear that Charles somehow thought if he besmirched Diana's name often enough, he would be rinsed in the process. It seemed lost on the prince and his advisers that the princess's popularity was genuine, not something Charles could bestow or withdraw.

But Charles' resentment of his wife's success was familiar. What was new was his willingness to disparage his parents. Prince Philip had a ready retort, sheathed in a brusque politesse of understatement that seemed totally beyond Charles: "I've never discussed private matters, and I don't think the Queen has. Very few members of the family have." So there.

Once again, the question seemed to be whether Charles' judgment was too flawed for him to be an effective King. To wage the image battle, at once vengeful and quixotic, was to endanger the fragile institution he served. If he needed a reminder, it came in the Establishment weekly *The Economist,* which called for Britain to become a republic.

Polls showed that 75% of Britons support the continuation of the monarchy (down 10% from a decade ago). That is enough for the Windsors to work with if they can establish some decorum within their ranks. Writer Auberon Waugh, always a mischiefmaker, thanked the royals in the *Telegraph* for "the diversion they bring into our humdrum lives as we follow their ups and downs, triumphs and disasters ... we can honestly say we love them all, each in a different way." He had a point. The appeal of this unscripted soap opera should not be ignored. But in the long run, the royals would lose out by counting on it. ∎

Hollywood Green

With his bartender good looks, **DAVID CARUSO**, the star of *NYPD Blue,* became television's reigning Everyguy sex symbol. But his dreams were grander: Caruso shocked fans when he left the show after just one season to pursue stardom in the movies. For a beginner at top billing, the carrot-topped heartthrob didn't do too badly: his paycheck for his first film was $2 million—about half the cost of the palimony suit filed against him by a former masseuse with whom he broke off a four-year relationship.

Foreman KO's Father Time

An inspiration to middle-aged men—and pleasingly plump individuals of both genders—boxer **GEORGE FOREMAN**, 45, won the heavyweight crown for the second time, defeating Michael Moorer. Said the new/old champ: "If any of those young guys out there think I ought to retire, I might just give them a chance to fight me and see." His first choice for his next opponent: former champ Mike Tyson, expected to remain a prisoner in Indiana until May of 1995.

Big Merger: Graceland Marries Neverland

Despite formidable odds, LISA MARIE PRESLEY managed to find a man like her father: a popular singer who possessed terrifying celebrity, a fashion plate who dressed as an acolyte of Liberace, a star who, if not the King, called himself the "King of Pop." Yes, in a secret May wedding, Elvis' daughter married MICHAEL JACKSON, claiming "We both look forward to raising a family." In September the couple caused an uproar at the MTV Music Video Awards when they—gasp!—kissed onstage. Newlywed Michael had more good news later: when the 13-year-old who had accused him of molestation (and whose family had received an undisclosed settlement) refused to testify against him, the Los Angeles district attorney decided not to press charges.

Next: A Flannel Tux?

Without covering a single Pearl Jam number, 67-year-old crooner **TONY BENNETT** has become a decidedly hip alternative-rock act. Bennett first won a following among the nose-ring set when he served as a presenter at the 1993 MTV Video Music Awards. In 1994 he starred in his own *MTV Unplugged* special, where he was joined by such unlikely fellow lounge lizards as Elvis Costello, k. d. lang and J Mascis of Dinosaur Jr. "It's funny," Bennett mused, "because I've always been unplugged."

Bus Dude: Fame Ensued

Who says American schools aren't demanding enough, when a California art college was offering a course called "Films of **KEANU REEVES**"? Five years ago Reeves was primarily known as one of the two eponymous heroes of the teenage-wasteland comedy *Bill and Ted's Excellent Adventure.* But in 1994 he rode to fame in a new role: action hero. Starring in the bomb-on-a-bus summer smash *Speed,* he-man Reeves skated on a mechanic's dolly under a runaway bus, survived plummeting elevators and subway crashes, and even faced down Hollywood's scariest special effect: Dennis Hopper doing his psychopath routine.

Dumb and Richer

What Robin Williams does with his mind—kick it around, bend it and blend it, find witty twists at lightning speed—**JIM CARREY** does with his body. He can freeze into an exclamation point

or go all loose and noodley. A veteran of the TV skitcom *In Living Color,* Carrey stunned Hollywood in 1994 with an incredible hat trick: the surprise smash *Ace Ventura: Pet Detective* was topped by two more box-office bonanzas: the special effects–driven *The Mask* and the holiday hit *Dumb and Dumber.*

The "Condom Queen" Returns to Private Life

Bill Clinton's Surgeon General **DR. JOYCELYN ELDERS** had been a lightning rod for criticism since assuming office, but finally she went too far. In December she resigned at the President's request, eight days after she remarked that schoolchildren should perhaps be taught about masturbation as a measure to prevent sexually transmitted diseases. A White House desperately seeking the center after the November elections cited the growing list of areas in which the President and Elders disagreed—from possible legalization of drugs to distribution of condoms in the schools—as the reason for the President's action. Earlier in the year, the Surgeon General had stated, "If I could be the 'condom queen' and get every young person who is engaging in sex to use a condom, I would wear a crown on my head with a condom on it. I would!"

Martina's Last Serve

After nine Wimbledon championships, 167 tournament titles overall, $20 million in prize money and—most important—22 years of grinding, competitive tennis, **MARTINA NAVRATILOVA**, 38, decided it was time to hang up her racquet. The final tournament for the onetime defector from communist Czechoslovakia was the Virginia Slims at Madison Square Garden. Navratilova vowed to spend more time catching up on "life," claiming "I'm not dead, but this year my tennis almost has been."

Jordan Strikes Out

When the world's greatest basketball player, **MICHAEL JORDAN,** 31, left the court in 1993 to pursue a baseball career, observers groped for explanations. His father's murder? Burnout? A profound desire to hit under .200 playing for the Birmingham Barons? None of the above. In a newspaper interview, Jordan revealed the primary reason: lack of gratitude among his Chicago Bulls teammates. "They had no idea how much pressure and grief I had to put up with off the court while carrying them on the court," said the would-be slugger.

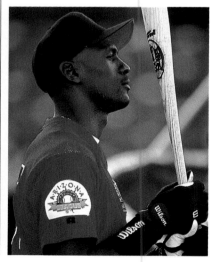

A Voice in the Wilderness

In a country where the idols and ideals of the past have been shattered, **ALEKSANDR SOLZHENITSYN** at 75 remains a moral authority for millions of Russians: a man who stood up against the totalitarian state and survived. In May the Nobel-prizewinning novelist returned to his homeland from two decades of exile in Vermont. Fittingly, he spent his first days traveling through the lands of the Gulag that he had chronicled, where millions of victims of Stalin's purges perished in forced-labor camps. Received as a prophet by many—though declared ready for mothballs by urban sophisticates in Moscow—he preached a simple message: Repent! His oft stated belief is that Russia cannot move into the future until it has exorcised its communist past.

Four Weddings and a Star

Hollywood leading man roll call: Clint Eastwood, Arnold Schwarzenegger, Harrison Ford, Sylvester Stallone, Hugh Grant ... **HUGH GRANT?** Yes, the male star of the moment, thanks to the surprise success of the bright British comedy *Four Weddings and a Funeral*, was a 33-year-old Londoner, all beguiling smile and self-deprecating wit. "He's found something that's gone from the movies: the intelligent comic leading man," said *Four Weddings* producer Duncan Kenworthy. The Oxford man and onetime satirical revue performer dripped his patented brand of charm in two other films, Roman Polanski's *Bitter Moon* and the Australian erotic romp *Sirens*.

Into the Sunset

He seemed invincible—after all, he had survived falls off horses, colon and skin cancer, prostate problems, even an assassin's bullet in the chest. But now he was fighting his toughest foe: former President **RONALD REAGAN** announced he was suffering from Alzheimer's disease, the mysterious malady that attacks brain cells, causing memory loss and confusion. In a handwritten note to the nation, he said, "I have recently been told that I am one of the millions of Americans who will be afflicted with Alzheimer's disease. [Nancy and I] feel it is important to share [this information] with you." Health officials applauded Reagan's candor, saying it would help build awareness of a dread malady.

The Perils of Pamela

Democratic Party power hostess, former wife of Winston Churchill's son, former wife of millionaire statesman Averell Harriman, former wife of legendary theatrical producer Leland Hayward and current U.S. ambassador to France, **PAMELA HARRIMAN** has had many good years. But 1994 was not among them. A best-selling biography painted her as a money-hungry, man-crazy transcontinental gadabout. More distressing, the descendants of Averell Harriman sued her for wasting the $30 million he left them in his trust fund, leaving them with a paltry $3 million.

Life Imitates Tattoo

Gangsta rapper **TUPAC SHAKUR,** 23, whose tattoo reads THUG LIFE, was shot five times at a recording studio and robbed of $45,000 in cash and jewels— two days before he was convicted of sexually assaulting a young woman.

TWO BY TWO GOD MADE THEM—AND IT'S BEEN DOWNHILL EVER SINCE

"For what do we live, but to make sport for our neighbors, and laugh at them in our turn?" mused Jane Austen in *Pride and Prejudice.* Doing their part in 1994 were several famed couples. ● Slacker actor **JOHNNY DEPP** hooked up with wonder waif **KATE MOSS,** then went into his Edward Scissorhands mode and trashed a New York hotel suite—keeping room smasher emeritus Roger Daltrey of the Who awake next door. ● Millionaire magician **DAVID COPPERFIELD** be-

came the envy of Everyman when he revealed he'd soon marry the 23-year-old German übermodel **CLAUDIA SCHIFFER.** ● When the long-running soap opera contrived by comics **TOM** and **ROSEANNE ARNOLD** ended in an acrimonious divorce, the sitcom heavyweight put her billing on a diet, vowing to use only her first name as her professional moniker in the future.

● Calling it quits in classier fashion were Piano Man **BILLY JOEL** and his former Uptown Girl, **CHRISTIE BRINKLEY;** they divorced amicably after nine years of marriage and one child. ● Much less friendly were the year's most unusual couple, **DAVID LETTERMAN** and **MADONNA.** When the king of late night welcomed the queen of the calculated shocker to his show, she uttered a verboten vulgarism 13 times. For her pains, she was upbraided by her Midwestern-bred host, but romantics rejoiced when they billed, cooed, and made up at the MTV awards show. ● Model-with-mole **CINDY CRAWFORD** and her husband, Holly-

wood's **RICHARD GERE,** said at year's end that they would be divorcing—as everyone had known they would since they took out a full-page ad in a London newspaper to say they wouldn't.

America's First Lady

The most private of public persons, Jacqueline Kennedy Onassis
radiated grace, restraint and strength

O N MAY 19, 1994, JACQUELINE BOUVIER Kennedy Onassis died as she had lived: the most private of public persons, a delicate glow in the harshly lit landscape of American celebrity, a figure who radiated courage and restraint, glamour and conspicuous shyness. In the public eye, her heroism was imprinted through indelible images: at L.B.J.'s side, gazing into space as he took the oath of office; gripping Robert Kennedy's hand and then her children's; receiving the flag that covered J.F.K.'s coffin. Yet what she thought about her crowded life no one knows, for she never spoke publicly about her experiences after the President's assassination.

Jacqueline Bouvier's world was one of manicured lawns, the fox hunt and the ballet. The Bouviers were an old Catholic family entrenched in New York society; her father, known as "Black Jack" because of his dark good looks, lived recklessly both in the stock market and in his dashing private life. He was an exuberant but careless investor, and the Wall Street crash of 1929 finished his market ride. Thereafter, his marriage began to falter, and it ended when Jackie was nine. Her mother, Janet, then married into one of the richer branches of the vast Auchincloss clan.

Her stepfather, Hugh Auchincloss, was generous; she headed off to Miss Porter's School, an ultra-posh boarding school, with her own horse. Two years at Vassar followed, but Jackie was too restless to thrive in the leafy confines of the Poughkeepsie, New York, campus. She finished college at George Washington University, then landed a job as the Inquiring Photographer for the Washington *Times-Herald.*

The next year she met her fate at a Washington dinner party: Jack Kennedy, then 34, was a handsome, ambitious Congressman from Massachusetts. They dated, and he proposed by telephone to London, where

AN INNER LIGHT: Though she knew privilege and married into great wealth, her style came from within. At left, she dazzles in a $59 off-the-rack gown at her coming-out party.

she was snapping the coronation of Elizabeth II.

From the start, marriage to Jack was not easy for Jackie. There were problems—his wandering eye, her clothing bills—but mostly the trouble was that he was constantly running for President. Jackie got what she wanted in that her husband was wealthy but, rather than living a life of comfort and perfection in a private world, she found herself immersed in the public rough-and-tumble of politics. She wanted children, and suffered through a miscarriage and the birth of a stillborn baby before daughter Caroline was born in 1957. By 1960, when she gave birth to John Jr., there were visible cracks in the marriage and gossip about J.F.K.'s supposed affairs.

At one point Joseph Kennedy offered Jackie a million dollars not to leave Jack, and reportedly she took it.

The presidency did not initially improve matters; for one thing, she disliked the White House. But she made peace with the problem by asserting her own aesthetic. She had a stage built and invited in performers like cellist Pablo Casals and dancers from the American Ballet Theatre—a glamorization of politics that was unprecedented. More important, she redid the place, replacing routine reproductions with authentic period pieces and fabrics. The redecoration was a triumph, and Jackie showed it off to the American public on a breathless TV tour.

In time, Jackie's marriage grew more stable; Kennedy gained new admiration for his wife just by watching the world's reaction to her grace and beauty. In August 1963 a third child, Patrick, was born to the Kennedys, but he lived only two days. His father went down to the hospital boiler room and wept. But, howev-

STARTING OUT: From their wedding day in 1953, she had few illusions about J.F.K. She learned when to look away.

er briefly, they were a real family now. In November the Kennedys went to Dallas to mend political fences; the shots rang out as they endured a hot motorcade trip. Afterward Jackie refused to take tranquilizers, fearing they would blunt her reactions and interfere with her planning—and personally plan the funeral was just what she did. The riderless horse, the eternal flame, the wailing Irish bagpipe—all were her idea. When the hearse rumbled past, she asked little John to salute his father.

She moved to a house in Georgetown, but tour buses were soon belching smoke in her windows. She sought out the relative anonymity and familiarity of New York City, buying an apartment on upper fifth Avenue across from Central Park. Then, not long after the assassination of Bobby Kennedy, which stunned and depressed her, Jackie shocked the world by marrying Aristotle Onassis, the Greek shipping tycoon 29 years her senior. Soon she was seen in all the trite celebrity camera shots: cruising the Mediterranean behind her trademark shades, sunbathing on a Greek isle, smiling

broadly in nightclubs. Onassis had magnetism, but money was probably Jackie's largest motivation. She had no intention of not living very well.

The union was not a success. Though he and Jackie were sometimes happy and at peace, the pair would quarrel over her spending, and Onassis took to calling his wife "the widow." Following his death in 1975, Christina Onassis, the shipper's daughter and his only major heir, reportedly decided to get her hated stepmother out of her life with a settlement of $20 million.

And so Jackie was back in New York. Instead of endorsing a cause, as many ex–first Ladies have done, she took a job. She became an editor, working three days a week. Until shortly before she died, she was responsible for a dozen books a year, and she gets straight A's from everyone who worked with her. In the last 10 years of her life, Onassis kept company with a married financier and diamond merchant, Maurice Tempelsman, who eventually moved into her flat.

BEARING GIFTS: At J.F.K.'s side, she brought glamour to U.S. public life; at his death, she brought courage and dignity.

They spent summers at her spread on Martha's Vineyard.

Fortunate in her close relations with her children Caroline and John Jr., in three young grandchildren, a history of good health, a job she loved and a congenial companion, Jackie had seemed set for a happy old age. But it was not to be. Friends say Onassis, who had prided herself on her fitness, was shocked to discover in January 1994 that she had non-Hodgkin's lymphoma, a form of cancer that often strikes people in their 60s and 70s. She announced the following month that she was undergoing treatment. But the cancer spread quickly. The day before her death, when doctors decided that further treatment would be fruitless, she went home. She died the next evening and, after a private funeral Mass, was buried in Arlington National Cemetery beside her husband and her son Patrick. Later, John Kennedy Jr. said that his mother had died "surrounded by her friends and her family and her books. She did it in her own way and on her own terms." He might well have said the same of her entire life. ∎

"Better to Burn Out"

Kurt Cobain, guru of grunge, takes his life

H E BLEW HIS MIND OUT IN his home. On April 8, Kurt Cobain, leader of the pioneering Seattle grunge band Nirvana, took his life with a shotgun blast to his head. His body was discovered by an electrician working at the home of Cobain and his wife, fellow musician Courtney Love. He left a suicide note

mind, released in 1991, contained a series of crunching, screaming songs that also had catchy melodies, part punk, part Beatles. Selling almost 10 million copies and knocking Michael Jackson's *Dangerous* from the top of the charts, the album fibrillated the psyche of a generation. It also launched the commercial vogue for grunge, helped turn equally abrasive

depression and suicide. He even began joking about death; a song called *I Hate Myself and I Want to Die* was recorded but dropped from the last album. "It was totally satirical, making fun of ourselves," Cobain said. "I'm thought of as this pissy, complaining, freaked-out schizophrenic who wants to kill himself all the time. I thought it was a funny title."

Growing up in the depressed logging town of Aberdeen on Washington's Pacific coast, Cobain had, by his account, a relatively happy childhood until his parents, a cocktail waitress and an auto mechanic, got divorced. He was only eight, and he later claimed that the traumatic split fueled the anguish in Nirvana's music. He shuttled back and forth among various relatives, even finding himself homeless at one point and living under a bridge. His budding artistry and iconoclastic attitude didn't win him many fans in high school; instead he attracted beatings from "jocks and moron dudes," as an old friend once put it. Cobain formed and reformed a series of bands before Nirvana finally coalesced in 1986 as an uneasy alliance among guitarist Cobain, bassist Krist Novoselic (a hometown friend) and eventually drummer Dave Grohl.

Cobain married Love in 1992, when the band was first peaking on the charts and she was already pregnant with daughter Frances Bean. But success, marriage and fatherhood did not remove his characteristic unease. Nirvana's unexpected stardom seemed to eat at him. He suffered the usual torments of the underground poet moving into the mainstream, and he was worried that his band had sold out, that it was attracting the wrong kind of fans (i.e., the guys who used to beat him up). Cobain's subject was the same, perennial, youthful fury captured by the Sex Pistols and the Who before him. Youthful nihilism may not be new, but Cobain wrote great rock songs as he explored a familiar theme with genius. ■

RELUCTANT ICON: Cobain was "bewildered" by his instant fame.

"I'm thought of as this pissy, complaining, freaked-out schizophrenic who wants to kill himself all the time."

that quoted a defiant line from veteran rocker Neil Young's anthem *Rust Never Sleeps*: "Better to burn out than to fade away."

Kurt Cobain, dead at 27. The news came as a shock to millions of rock fans, and MTV pre-empted its usual programming for hours of J.F.K.-like mourning. Given Cobain's talent and influence as a songwriter and bandleader, the reaction was understandable. Nirvana came from the music-industry equivalent of nowhere, with a rough-edged first album recorded for a chiselly $606. The next, *Never-*

local bands like Pearl Jam into stars and made Seattle famous for something other than cappuccino, rain and bad professional sports. The New Liverpool, *Rolling Stone* called the city. Cobain was at the center of it all, the John Lennon of the swinging Northwest, a songwriter with a gift for searing lyrics and seductive hooks, an edgy and complicated performer.

If the loss of an oddly magnetic musician was jolting, though, the manner of his death was not unexpected. Cobain admitted to using heroin and spoke openly about drugs,

His Own Man

Confident and charismatic, Burt Lancaster reinvented stardom

WE'LL REMEMBER HIM for the laugh. His muscular head would snap back, and out would come three bold, staccato barks: "Ha. Ha. Ha." That laugh helped define Burt Lancaster's personality and gave amiable employment to a generation of mimics. But the mystery of the Lancaster laugh was that it could mean anything: it might express amusement or a jolly contempt. His smile, a Cinema-Scope revelation of perfect teeth, had the same enigmatic edge to it. Was it benediction or absolution? Was it seductive or—perhaps—a predatory baring of fangs?

This mystique made Lancaster, who died on October 20 of a heart attack at 80, the first modernist movie hunk. He sprang to prominence in the emotional chaos after World War II and was a star in his first role, as the doomed Swede in *The Killers* (1946). Immediately viewers could spot a gritty urban charm, brooding good looks, a handsome physique. He made the most of this charisma in *The Crimson Pirate*, an ebullient homage to Douglas Fairbanks that drew on Lancaster's own acrobatic skills, and later as the consummate con man in both *Elmer Gantry* (for which he won an Oscar in 1961) and *The Rainmaker*. Before hitting it big at 33, Lancaster had been a salesman, and these performances suggested that here was a man who could peddle any dream to anyone.

He was the dishy, tough-talking sergeant in *From Here to Eternity*, in which he took a roll on the beach with Deborah Kerr and made himself a pinup idol. But unlike most earlier male stars, who were straitjacketed in heroic roles, Lancaster could be his own man, choose parts and not worry whether audiences would like him. He always had that measure of confidence in himself: as a young man he left New York University, where he had a basketball scholarship, to join the circus. What showed through was the will not to *be* somebody, but to *do* something.

Without making a big deal about

HUNK: He radiated urban charm and brooding good looks.

"Before hitting it big, he had been a salesman; here was a man who could peddle any dream to anyone."

it, Lancaster had artistic ambitions. Early on he smartly inhabited characters created by prestige dramatists: the returning soldier in Arthur Miller's *All My Sons*, the drunken husband in William Inge's *Come Back, Little Sheba*, the buffoonish Italian suitor (a terrific turn) in Tennessee Williams' *The Rose Tattoo*.

Lancaster was an ingenious manager of his career. In a group of films made between 1962 and 1964 that included *Birdman of Alcatraz, Seven Days in May* and *The Train*, he shepherded young John Frankenheimer toward the top rank of Hollywood directors. His itch for artistic adventure led him to work with two great Italians: Luchino Visconti, for whom he played the put-upon prince in *The Leopard*, and Bernardo Bertolucci, for whom he played another Italian squire, grandfather to Robert De Niro in *1900*. In Bill Forsyth's *Local Hero*, Lancaster was the Texas oil tycoon—and the Hollywood imprimatur for a small, beguiling film. Even when playing a failure, as in Louis Malle's *Atlantic City* or as the elderly ballplayer in *Field of Dreams*, he was majestic in his convictions.

Lancaster was also an imposing presence offscreen. One of the first actors to create an independent production company, he had a rangy entrepreneurial curiosity. In some of the films he produced, such as Paddy Chayefsky's *Marty* (an Oscar winner in 1955) and *The Catered Affair*, the star did not make an appearance. But he got the pictures made, and they set the mood for other sympathetic dramas about little people—Hollywood's neatly scrubbed version of Italian neorealism.

In an important way, Burt Lancaster put a brash face on post-studio Hollywood, on the industry-cum-art that wanted to retain its old magic while venturing to faraway places and into man's dark heart. But he was never a Hollywood tabloid star; he stayed away from scandal. He will be remembered not for his sins but for his achievements. And that's a grand legacy for a mysterious, hard-working man. ■

Sir Harold Acton, 89, historian, writer and art collector. A "dandy aesthete" in 1920s England, Acton inspired the character Anthony Blanche in his friend Evelyn Waugh's *Brideshead Revisited*.

George Wildman Ball, 84, State Department official under Presidents Kennedy and Johnson. Ball is best remembered for advice he gave that was tragically ignored. As Kennedy's No. 2 man in the State Department in 1961, Ball urged the new U.S. leader not to send 15,000 soldiers to Vietnam, arguing that the move would lead to even greater troop commitments.

Ezra Taft Benson, 94, President of the Church of Jesus Christ of Latter-Day Saints. Benson was a controversial figure when he became head of the Mormon Church in 1985. Agriculture Secretary under Eisenhower, Benson was a John Birch Society sympathizer who once called the civil-rights movement "a communist program." But once in office, he focused on church matters; during his tenure, membership increased from 5.9 million to nearly 9 million.

Baron Marcel Bich, 79, father of the Bic pen and other disposable yet classic examples of modern design. He invented his breakthrough product in the early 1950s: a cheap, plastic pen (the *h* in Bich's name was apparently just as impermanent). The same use-it-and-lose-it philosophy created disposable razors and disposable lighters.

Charles Bukowski, 73, writer. A lifetime of poems, novels and screenplays reflected Bukowski's boozy, gritty, carnal view of the universe—including his screenplay for the critically praised 1987 film *Barfly*, starring Mickey Rourke and Faye Dunaway as a pair of joined-at-the-neurosis alcoholics.

Cabell ("Cab") Calloway, 86, Big Band leader. The ultimate hepcat, Calloway led an orchestra that succeeded Duke Ellington's band at Harlem's Cotton Club in the 1930s. Calloway's trademark song was *Minnie the Moocher*, the story of a "low-down hootchy-kootcher." He later claimed that the chorus of "hi-de-hi-de-hi-de-ho" and other scat refrains were the product of a faulty memory.

John Candy, 43, comic actor. The deftest oversize comedian since Jackie Gleason, the Toronto-born star shared

The Invincible Man

RAISED THE PRECOCIOUS CHILD of doting parents in Oklahoma City, **Ralph Ellison** won a scholarship to Booker T. Washington's Tuskegee Institute, then published several short stories while in the merchant marine in World War II. One day, just after the war, he found himself typing, "I am an invisible man." Ellison spent seven years developing that sentence into the work that established him in the permanent firmament of American writers: *Invisible Man*. This groundbreaking novel, in which a young black man relates the surreal events leading to his ultimate isolation, earned best-novel-of-its-time raves from the college of critics. But *Invisible Man* was more than a gorgeously written piece of fiction. Because its phantasmagoric satire of mid-century life in Harlem and the American South proved prophetic, the book became a blueprint for inner-city discontent. Still, the unfashionable fact is that Ellison's writing was too refined, too elaborate, to be spray-painted on a tenement wall. He was a celebrator as much as a denouncer of the nation that bred him. In his

multicolored vision, America was not just a violent jungle but a vibrant jumble of many cultures and temperaments. Though he compiled two volumes of trenchant essays on racial identity and other matters, he never finished his second novel, on which he worked for four decades, before his death at 80.

his predecessor's gift for both broad, punchy sketches and more subtle and sustained comedy of character. Candy, who began his career with the Second City improvisational troupes in Toronto and Chicago, first received wide attention as a co-star of *SCTV*, a satirical comedy show. His successful movies included *Splash* (1984), *Uncle Buck* (1989), *Planes, Trains and Automobiles* (1987) and *Cool Runnings* (1993).

Amy Clampitt, 74, poet. A beacon to aspiring literati, Clampitt was 63 when she published her first major collection of poems, *The Kingfisher*, vaulting her to the forefront of American poetry despite an unfashionably enthusiastic embrace of rich, heightened language and density of thought and allusions.

James Clavell, 69, best-selling author of *Tai-Pan*, *Shogun*, *Noble House* and other lushly detailed adventure epics set in Asia. Born in Australia to a British military family, Clavell was captured by the Japanese during World War II and interned in the notorious Changi prison in Singapore. In the 1950s and '60s he became a Hollywood scriptwriter; his eclectic credits included *The Fly, The*

Great Escape and *To Sir, With Love. King Rat*, based on his experiences at Changi, was the first of his hugely successful Asian saga novels.

Joseph Cotten, 88, tall, elegant, popular and critically acclaimed leading man of stage and screen classics. Cotten got his first big break when he joined Orson Welles' Federal Theater and Mercury Theater in the 1930s. His Broadway debut in *The Philadelphia Story* (1939) and his Hollywood premiere in Welles' *Citizen Kane* (1941) propelled him to 40 years of stardom. Among his many films: *Shadow of a Doubt, Gaslight, Duel in the Sun, The Farmer's Daughter, The Third Man* and *Touch of Evil*.

John Curry, 44, figure skater. Curry brought a revolutionary level of artistic sophistication to his sport, becoming known to his admirers as "Nureyev on ice." His performances owed as much to ballet as to acrobatics. His golden year was 1976, when he captured top honors at the European and World championships and at the Winter Olympics in Innsbruck.

Jeffrey Dahmer, 34, serial killer. Dahmer died from a beating, apparently by another lifer at the Columbia Correctional Institution in Wisconsin. Dahmer had admitted killing 17 young men and boys and cannibalizing some of them.

Robert Doisneau, 81, photographer. The postwar Paris caught by the lens of Doisneau's camera was the Paris of one's dreams, rendered with both satire and great affection. Doisneau sought to capture the "little drama in everyday life," yet there was some stagecraft behind those supposedly candid moments: in a legal dispute in 1993, Doisneau acknowledged that he had paid two models to pose for his famous *The Kiss at the Hôtel de Ville.*

Erik Erikson, 91, psychoanalyst and author. Erikson was a disciple of Sigmund Freud's—but whereas Freud emphasized sex as a shaper of personality, Erikson focused on social interactions. Such writings as his 1950 classic *Childhood and Society* identified discrete psychological stages in a human life. His concept of the "identity crisis," a key problem of adolescence, entered the popular vocabulary.

Orval Faubus, 84, former six-term Governor of Arkansas who defied a federal order in 1957 to desegregate Little Rock's public schools. The Little Rock crisis bloomed when Faubus dispatched the Arkansas National Guard to prevent nine black students from entering Central High School. A federal judge ordered Faubus to stop interfering—an edict that was finally enforced by federal troops.

John Wayne Gacy, 52, serial killer; executed by lethal injection. Fourteen years after his conviction for the torture-slayings of 33 young men and boys, Gacy went to his death proclaiming his innocence.

Henry Geldzahler, 59, art curator and critic. As a curator of recent American art for the Metropolitan Museum of Art for 17 years, Geldzahler was in the thick of the culture wars, backing such trends as Pop, Op, Conceptual and Minimalist art.

Vitas Gerulaitis, 40, former tennis star. Deadly fumes from a defective heater brought an abrupt end to the life of the Brooklyn-born court star, once ranked No. 3 in the world. The golden-maned Gerulaitis based his game on court-sweeping speed and the sniper-like accuracy of his shots, an arsenal that earned him a Top 10 ranking from 1977 to 1982.

Elizabeth Glaser, 47, tireless activist for pediatric AIDS. The wife of actor Paul Michael Glaser, she was infected by the virus in 1981 after receiving a blood transfusion during pregnancy. Her daughter Ariel died of AIDS in 1988; her son Jake, 10, has tested positive for the virus. At the 1992 Democratic Convention, Glaser was a poignant symbol of the struggle against the plague. "I am here tonight," she said from the podium, "because my son and I may not survive another four years of leaders who say they care—but do nothing."

Clement Greenberg, 85, art critic and promoter of Abstract Expressionism.

zard's best-known works sum up his puckered view of the world: *Elvis Is Dead and I Don't Feel So Good Myself* and *My Daddy Was a Pistol and I'm a Son of a Gun.*

Raul Julia, 54, actor. Born in Puerto Rico, Julia moved to Manhattan in 1964 and began appearing in Shakespearean roles, creating a deliciously conniving Edmund in *King Lear* in 1973 and a smoldering Othello in 1979. Julia's stage successes led to Hollywood stardom in *Kiss of the Spider Woman* and two *Addams Family* movies.

Connie Kay, 67, Modern Jazz Quartet drummer whose command of chimes, finger cymbals, triangle and tympani, as well as the standard drum kit, lent a signature sound to the MJQ.

Virginia Dared

SHE WAS MORE THAN the mother of President Bill Clinton; **Virginia Kelley,** 70, was a survivor. She buried three husbands, one a sweet-talking salesman who died before her son was born and another with a weakness for bourbon and beating her up. She was a working mother before it became fashionable, and she led a life that would never please the life-style police: she liked to take a drink, eat red meat, stay up too late and exercise too little. Her famous fondness for playing the horses made her a refreshingly unpretentious First Mom.

Like her son, Virginia Kelley preferred to win, but she was never discouraged by defeat. It was his mother's indomitable ways, her ledger that listed credits and not debits, her capacity for friendship that exceeded even his own—all these that accounted for Bill Clinton's ability to get up off the mat just as the count was about to reach 10.

Almost as central to the development of the New York School he loved as the artists he critiqued, Greenberg argued that the proper subject of art was art itself, from the interplay of color and form to the flatness of the canvas and the physical properties of the paint. Among others, Greenberg championed Helen Frankenthaler, Mark Rothko and, most famously, Jackson Pollock.

Lewis Grizzard, 47, humorist. A "Faulkner for just plain folks" was how one newspaper publisher characterized Grizzard, who made hay of everyday angst in a syndicated column and 14 books as well as on speaking tours and sundry media gigs. The titles of Griz-

Walter Lantz, 93, animator. "Ha-ha-ha-*HA*-ha! Ha-ha-ha-*HA*-ha!" The maniacal cackle of Lantz's Woody Woodpecker is probably the most universally recognized laugh since Santa Claus first ho-ho-hoed—an enduring, if somewhat annoying, piece of Americana. Lantz produced the first Technicolor cartoon and a host of characters like Andy Panda and Oswald the Lucky Rabbit.

Christopher Lasch, 61, social critic and historian. A lucid, penetrating writer, Lasch dissected postwar American society in his best-known work, *The Culture of Narcissism* (1979). He contended that his fellow citizens had become self-absorbed and materialistic, losing faith

The Last Hard-Liner

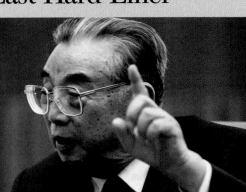

BORN KIM SONG JU in Mangyondae, a spot North Koreans now call the cradle of the revolution, North Korean leader **Kim Il Sung** outlasted such totalitarian contemporaries as Stalin and Mao—both of whom had been his protectors and his dupes—before dying at 82. With the apparent accession of his son and heir Kim Jong Il to top posts in the government after his death, Kim also became the first communist leader to pass on his authority dynastically. As absolute master of his impoverished half of the Korean peninsula for 46 years, he ignited one war, threatened the same again and again, and finally caused a flurry of global nervousness as he flouted the rules of nuclear nonproliferation.

Kim's family moved to Manchuria, then occupied by Japan, when he was in his late teens; he fought as a guerrilla against the invaders. He then fled to the Soviet Union in 1939 or 1940 and was given command of the Soviet-led ethnic Korean battalion. After the war he was named by local Soviet commanders as Moscow's choice to become Korean leader. With the tacit support of Stalin and a promise of aid

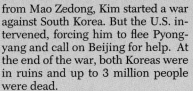

from Mao Zedong, Kim started a war against South Korea. But the U.S. intervened, forcing him to flee Pyongyang and call on Beijing for help. At the end of the war, both Koreas were in ruins and up to 3 million people were dead.

Kim survived to purge his government of his enemies and establish the strict totalitarianism and isolation from the world community that still hold sway in North Korea. Though his nation outraced rival South Korea economically in the 1960s, it ran out of steam in the '70s, the victim of inefficient Stalinist state planning and heavy defense spending. Meanwhile, Kim developed the personality cult into a virtual assumption of divinity. In his later years, he and Kim Jong Il went about the country building monuments to each other.

in the power of community to make life better. His prescription for combatting America's crisis of spirit, outlined in such works as *The Minimal Self* and *The True and Only Heaven,* involved a progressive philosophy that placed great importance on family and self-discipline. Said Lasch: "Today's culture has ceased to stand for the values that many people continue to believe in."

Fred Lebow, 62, marathon organizer. Beginning in 1970, Lebow built the New York City Marathon into the premier event of its kind, boasting the greatest long-distance runners on the planet. Born Fischl Lebowitz into a Romanian-Jewish family that was subsequently ravaged by the Holocaust, Lebow came to America in the '60s. Bitten by the running bug, he financed the first race with his own $300, beginning a nonstop devotion to the marathon. Lebow ran the marathon himself in 1992 while battling cancer.

Leo Lerman, 80, author, editor and cultural éminence grise. After years in the theater as an actor, stage manager and set designer, Lerman launched a prolific and learned career writing on fashion and the arts. In a half-century association with Condé Nast magazines, he wrote and edited at *Mademoiselle, Vogue* and *Vanity Fair,* where in 1983 he served briefly as editor in chief.

William Levitt, 86, pioneer suburban developer. In the years following World War II when returning veterans armed with federal assistance created a major demand for housing, Levitt erected thousands of affordable suburban homes in the Northeast, most famously in the instant Long Island village that carried his name: Levittown. In the space of four years, it went from a onetime potato field to a community of 17,500 one-family homes, along with schools and other public spaces. Levitt faced criticism for the numbing simi-

larity of his houses and the exclusion of blacks from his communities.

Giulietta Masina, 73, international film star. The wife of Federico Fellini, the round-faced, expressive-eyed actress starred in a string of Fellini masterpieces—most famously in *La Strada* (1954) and *Nights of Cabiria* (1957). Other works with her husband included the eponymous *Juliet of the Spirits* (1965) and her 1985 cinema swan song *Ginger and Fred,* which co-starred Marcello Mastroianni.

Ulrike Maier, 26, Austria's two-time world-champion skier. Maier broke her neck in a fall while going 60 m.p.h. downhill during the women's World Cup shortly before the Olympics.

Henry Mancini, 70, Grammy- and Oscar-winning composer for film and television. The son of a Pennsylvania steelworker, Mancini became a staff composer at Universal-International in 1952, scoring more than 100 films. The rest of his life was one long hit parade, from the driving urban insistence of the *Peter Gunn* theme to the romance of *Moon River* and *The Days of Wine and Roses* to the quirky novelty of the *Pink Panther* theme. Mancini's scores of scores included *Breakfast at Tiffany's* and *Victor/Victoria,* which he was adapting for the stage at his death.

Jose Francisco Ruiz Massieu, 48, Secretary-General of Mexico's ruling Institutional Revolutionary Party (P.R.I.). A single assassin's bullet pierced the neck of Mexico's second most powerful man as he was leaving a party function in Mexico City—only six months after the P.R.I.'s presidential candidate Luis Donaldo Colosio was gunned down while campaigning in Tijuana. His assassination renewed speculation that the P.R.I.'s internal battles may have been at the root of both deaths.

Rollo May, 85, humanist, psychologist and author. A founder of existential psychotherapy, May declared in his seminal *The Meaning of Anxiety* (1950) that personal anxiousness is not merely psychological but actually quite natural in an age marked by the death of reassuring cultural myths and the reality of H-bombs. Through such later works as *Love and Will* (1969), May's layman-friendly ideas were embraced by a generation.

Frank McGuire, 80, college basketball coach. The dapper son of a New York City cop, Frank McGuire did more than bring a new game to the South when he became coach at the University of North Carolina in 1952—he brought a whole new culture, via his own street-smart style of basketball and the brace of inner-city phenoms fresh from Gotham schoolyards, whom he transplanted to the Tar Heels on his "underground railroad." During a later stint with South Carolina's Gamecocks, he became the winningest coach in the state's history.

Melina Mercouri, 70-ish, actress and activist. Mercouri became an instant international star in 1960 with her Cannes-winning, Oscar-nominated portrait of a life-embracing prostitute who observed a scrupulous professional moratorium: *Never on Sunday.* An ardent foe of the right-wing junta that ruled her country from 1967 to 1974, Mercouri was named Culture Minister in 1981 when her friend Andreas Papandreou took the reins of government.

Henry Morgan, 79, radio satirist. In the polite world of early radio broadcasting—where he began announcing at age 18—Morgan became known for aggressively impertinent, ad-libbed satire that led to his own network program by the '40s. Unrestrained irreverence led to his blacklisting by red hunters during the '50s, but Morgan eventually returned to television, contributing withering irreverence and witty wordplay as a regular guest on such urbane game shows as *What's My Line?* and *I've Got a Secret.*

William Morgan, 88, astronomer. One of the most accomplished U.S. scientists of this century, he was a co-developer of the Morgan Keenan system for determining the luminosity of stars and hence their distance from earth—an invention he used as the foundation for his greatest discovery: the spiral structure of the Milky Way.

Harriet Nelson, 85, former Big Band singer, radio and TV actress. *The Adventures of Ozzie and Harriet,* which ran on radio and television from 1944 to 1966, starred the entire Nelson family. Harriet as Harriet was the sane center between increasingly restive sons Ricky and David and amiable but decidedly fumbling husband Ozzie (in real life the tireless creator and overseer of the series). But off-camera, the idyll was colored by tragedy: the 1975 death of Ozzie—Harriet's companion since he hired her as a singer for his band in 1932—and the plane-crash death of rock star Rick in 1985.

Louis Nizer, 92, trial lawyer and author. During six decades of wooing the press while mostly giving clients their money's worth, Nizer was one of the century's premier celebrity lawyers. The Brooklyn-bred son of a dry cleaner, Nizer had a client list top heavy with the famous: Salvador Dalí, Mae West and Julius Erving. A painter, composer and author of 10 books, Nizer published his autobiography in 1962; *My Life in Court* stayed on the New York *Times'* Best Seller list for a lengthy run of 72 weeks.

Allan Gilbert Odell, 90, former advertising manager and president of Burma-Vita. In 1926, Odell created one of the oddest and most memorable gimmicks in the history of American advertising—a series of six roadside signs, five containing portions of a whimsical couplet and the last providing the punctuation of the brand name: GRANDPA'S ... OUT WITH ... JUNIOR'S DATE ... OLD TECHNIQUE ... WITH BRAND-NEW BAIT ... BURMA SHAVE. The poems eventually sprang up at 7,000 locations in 45 states, becoming an essential part of the popular culture of their day.

John Osborne, 65, playwright/author. On May 8, 1956, John Osborne's play *Look Back in Anger* had its premiere—a seismic shock that seemed to signal the birth of a new urgency and the death of the reigning theatrical gentility. With his first play, the 26-year-old actor-author, who never went to university, forever changed the face of theater. This was drama as rant, an explosion of bad manners, a declaration of war against an empire in twilight. The acid tone, at once comic and desperate, sustained Osborne through a volatile career as playwright (*The Entertainer, Inadmissible Evidence*), film writer (*Tom Jones*) and memoirist (*A Better Class of Person*). Married five times, he inflicted pain on those close to him, perhaps himself most of all. He spoke, eloquently, to the worst in ourselves.

Joe Pass, 65, jazz guitarist. Joseph Anthony Jacobi Passalaqua was nine when his working-class father presented him with a $17 guitar. By his mid-teens, Pass was already playing with band leaders such as Charlie Barnet. Pass's fluid fingering, warm tone and improvisatory

"All Politics is Local"

H AS ANY POLITI-cian ever looked more the part, or seemed to revel more in his profession, than **Thomas** ("Tip") **O'Neill**? Yet there was nothing of the central-casting phony about the former Speaker of the House of Representatives, who died early in 1994 at 81. O'Neill's undiluted New Deal liberalism and Boston-Irish gregariousness marked him as a rare artifact of a bygone political era. He credited his famous axiom, "All politics is local," to his bricklayer father, and he lived by it from his very first race for the Massachusetts state legislature in 1936. In 1952 he handily won the House seat being vacated by Senate candidate John F. Kennedy—and he easily won the 16 races that followed.

O'Neill rose in influence on the Hill despite his courageous public opposition in 1967 to fellow Democrat Lyndon Johnson's Vietnam War. He was 65 when he became Speaker in 1977, bursting into national prominence as Mr. Insider just as fellow

Democrat Jimmy Carter, Mr. Outsider, was arriving in Washington. When Ronald Reagan came to the White House, O'Neill became the capital's most powerful Democrat, his belief in the power and duty of government to right social wrongs colliding head on with Reagan's assault on the apparatus of paleoliberalism. He left Congress in 1987 with a remarkably modest bank balance, but parlayed his fame into a best-selling book and endorsement gigs. At his death, Mr. Insider was finally a good guy.

skills drew him to the high-wire act of his profession—unaccompanied solo guitar.

Linus Pauling, 93, Nobel-prizewinning chemist. Son of an Oregon druggist, Pauling made hundreds of contributions to chemistry, publishing 50 research papers by the time he was 30. In 1954 he was awarded the Nobel Prize for Chemistry for his work on the nature of the chemical bond that holds molecules together, research that led to the discovery of the structure of DNA. He became a tireless campaigner against nuclear testing and in 1963 was awarded a second Nobel—for Peace. In the '70s he advocated large doses of vitamin C to guard against many ills, from colds to cancer, a treatment that is still controversial. DNA researcher Francis Crick once said that the core of Pauling's genius was "boldness in theory making— boldness as an aspect of rigor."

George Peppard, 65, actor. He first attracted attention as Audrey Hepburn's love interest in the 1961 film *Breakfast at Tiffany's,* but Peppard reached his widest audience on TV, first as the sleuthing insurance investigator *Banacek,* then as the cigar-smoking leader of the cartoonish *A-Team.*

Roy Plunkett, 83, DuPont chemist credited with discovering polytetrafluoroethylene resin, better known as Teflon.

Sir Karl Popper, 92, philosopher. Although he was best known for his criticisms of Marxism and communism, Popper established one of the most important principles of the philosophy of science. In his first book, *The Logic of Scientific Discovery,* published in 1934, Popper argued that what makes science scientific lies not in the fact that its basic tenets can be proved but rather that the arguments against them can be disproved. Born in Vienna, Popper left Austria in the late 1930s and eventually settled in England, where he was a professor at the London School of Economics until his retirement in 1969.

Lewis B. ("Chesty") Puller Jr., 48, soldier and author. The son of the most decorated member of the Marine Corps in its history, Puller served in Vietnam as a Marine combat leader. Both his legs and part of his hands were blown off when he stepped on a booby trap. He lived, tried to come to terms with his diminished physical self and became an attorney at the Pentagon

and a respected veterans' activist. In 1978 he ran for Congress in Virginia; his defeat depressed him. The following year his first attempt at suicide failed. Then, in 1992, he won a Pulitzer Prize for his autobiography, *Fortunate Son.* Yet his life had recently come to seem barren. His marriage of 26 years was dissolving, and he suffered a serious relapse in his battle against alcoholism. Despondent beyond consolation, he picked up a gun and extinguished a life that had given hope to so many others.

Martha Raye, 78, singer-comedian. Raye's calling card was her famous mouth, an impossibly broad swath of lips and pearly teeth. Debuting in vaudeville at three, Raye was performing opposite Bing Crosby in *Rhythm on the Range* (1936) at 20. The films that followed were enormously popular and just as forgettable, with one stunning exception—Charles Chaplin's grim comedy *Monsieur Verdoux* (1947). Raye's performance as Chaplin's hilariously indestructible wife suggested the possibilities of an entirely different career had Hollywood heeded her desire to be cast for comedy instead of glamour.

Fernando Rey, 76, sleekly handsome, soulful-eyed Spanish character actor best known for his portrayal of the drug baron who outfoxed Gene Hackman in *The French Connection.* Rey starred in such Luis Buñuel classics as *Tristana* (1969) and *The Discreet Charm of the Bourgeoisie* (1972).

Allie Reynolds, 79, ex-pitcher for the New York Yankees. Dubbed "Super Chief" for his Creek Indian ancestry, Reynolds hurled the Bronx Bombers to six straight World Series titles from 1947 to 1953. The right-hander with a warp-speed fast ball racked up 182 wins and 49 saves in a 13-year career that began with the Cleveland Indians and included a rare two no-hitters in a single season.

Stuart Roosa, 61, astronaut who flew the Apollo 14 command module *Kitty Hawk* during the third lunar-landing mission in 1971. Roosa orbited the moon in solitude, and often out of radio contact, while his fellow astronauts explored the surface. Despite his historic flight, he told a writer, "Space changes nobody. You bring back from space what you bring into space." On Earth, Roosa owned a Mississippi beer distributorship.

Jerry Rubin, 56, 1960s activist turned businessman. The erstwhile Yippie created some of the era's classic antiwar performance art—nominating a pig for

President; appearing before Congress dressed in Revolutionary War garb; sending stockbrokers diving for dollars by dumping bills on the floor of the New York Stock Exchange. Rubin and the other Chicago Eight activists stood trial for their roles in the "police riot" outside the 1968 Democratic National Convention; his conviction on riot charges was eventually tossed out. In the 1980s, the Yippie turned Yuppie without apology, sponsoring a series of "networking" functions at New York night spots. At his death, Rubin was a prosperous distributor of nutritional drinks.

Wilma Rudolph, 54, Olympic track star. Seriously ill as a child, Rudolph endured girlhood bouts of scarlet fever and polio that left doctors fearing she would lose the use of her legs. Not only did she overcome her illnesses; she also became a world-class athlete, one who would command the international stage at the 1960 Rome Olympics as the first American woman to win three gold medals in track and field.

Dean Rusk, 85, former U.S. Secretary of State. Rusk was second only to Lyndon Johnson as an architect of the divisive, ultimately fruitless war in Vietnam. Born to desperate poverty in Georgia, Rusk rose to graduate from Davidson College in North Carolina and win a Rhodes scholarship. His service during World War II in the Southeast Asian theater led to a career at the State Department where, as a deputy undersecretary, he played a pivotal role in Harry Truman's decision to send U.S. troops to Korea. As John Kennedy's Secretary of State, he advocated an aggressive response to the Soviet Union during the Cuban Missile Crisis. Retained by Johnson following J.F.K.'s assassination, Rusk became an increasingly controversial figure for his advocacy of unyielding military pressure on the North. It would be years before he acknowledged underestimating the staying power of Hanoi and the extent of war-weariness at home in America.

Telly Savalas, 70, hawk-nosed, bald-pated actor whose role as the gruff, lollipop-licking Lieutenant Theo Kojak became a prototype for two decades of gritty TV police dramas. Born Aristoteles Savalas, the actor first shaved his head in 1965 for the part of Pontius Pilate in *The Greatest Story Ever Told.* Nominated for a Best Supporting Actor Oscar for *Birdman of Alcatraz* (1962), he finally won immense

A Brittle Elegance

THE DEATH AT 85 of **Jessica Tandy,** the award-winning doyenne of Broadway and Hollywood, marked the end of a grand procession of characters she created by inhabiting them. The London-born actress arrived in the U.S. in 1940 and married the smart, craggy Canadian Hume Cronyn in 1942. Tandy's signature roles, as Blanche du Bois in the original 1947 production of Tennessee Williams' *A Streetcar Named Desire* and as Daisy Werthan in the 1989 film *Driving Miss Daisy,* were both mid-century Southern belles. They were also polar opposites: a woman plummeting from nymphomania into dementia; a lady struggling to balance propriety and humanity.

For *Streetcar* Tandy won the first of three Tonys (the others were for two collaborations with Cronyn, *The Gin Game* in 1978 and *Foxfire* in 1982); for *Miss Daisy* she earned an Oscar as Best Actress in 1990. Two years later, she received a Best Supporting Actress nomination for *Fried Green Tomatoes.* By then Tandy was more than an actress; she was a living monument to the old-fashioned belief in survival of the flintiest.

popularity with the TV series *Kojak,* which ran from 1973 to 1978. He took an Emmy for the role in 1974, becoming, in spite of his hairlessness, a sex symbol, greeted everywhere by fans with Kojak's signature line, "Who loves ya, baby?"

Rabbi Menachem Mendel Schneerson, 92, leader of the ultra-Orthodox Lubavitch Hasidim sect of Judaism. While shielding his followers from the modern world, Schneerson employed the most up-to-date technologies—including telethons and mobile "mitzvah tanks"—to reach out to secular Jews. The results of this proselytizing were 200,000 fervent acolytes worldwide and a powerful, right-wing influence over politics in New York and Israel. Some of Schneerson's followers expect the Ukrainian-born rebbe to reappear as the Messiah.

Randy Shilts, 42, journalist and author of a ground-breaking book about the AIDS epidemic. Shilts, one of the country's first openly gay reporters, joined the San Francisco *Chronicle* in 1981. Soon after, word spread of mysterious outbreaks of rare types of skin cancer and pneumonia among gay men. At the time, Shilts was one of the few journalists who took the disease—AIDS—seriously. He recounted his investigation in the 1987 best seller *And the Band Played On,* a blistering attack on the failure of governments and the medical establishment to recognize the epidemic.

Dinah Shore, 76, entertainer. Born Frances Rose Shore into one of the handful of Jewish families in Winchester, Tennessee, Shore first gained fame in the '40s as a singer with hits like her hugely popular 1947 cover of *The Anniversary Song.* She enjoyed phenomenal success on television with *The Dinah Shore Chevy Show* (1956-63), famous for Shore's closing warble of "See the U.S.A. in your Chevrolet" and an exuberantly tossed kiss. In the '70s Shore helped pioneer the now inescapable daytime talk-show format—and earned the admiration of some middle-aged women for her highly public relationship with Burt Reynolds, 19 years her junior.

John Smith, 55, Britain's Labour Party leader. In two years, the soft-spoken Smith brought his party, once battered by losses to the governing Conservatives, to a position of such national strength it was prepared to mount its strongest bid for the country's leadership in 15 years.

Jule Styne, 88, Broadway and pop composer. Styne's career peaked during the Golden Age of the American musical, and small wonder—his own music was much of what made those years golden. Working with lyricist Sammy Cahn, Styne brought forth his first Broadway hit in 1947, *High Button Shoes.* The 19 musicals that followed—including *Bells Are Ringing* (1956), *Gypsy* (1959) and *Funny Girl* (1964)—confirmed his instinct for the concise but indelible musical phrase as well as his chameleon-like gift for adapting to the sensibilities of his lyricists and stars.

Colin Turnbull, 69, anthropologist and author. At various times in his life a British navy man, a Buddhist monk and a museum curator, Turnbull found fame with two books: *The Forest People,* his 1961 study of the Pygmies in Zaïre, whom he admired for their profoundly just society; and the grimly contrasting *The Mountain People* (1972), which portrayed Uganda's hunger-plagued Ik tribe, driven to abandon the most basic social virtues, even the protection of their own children.

Jersey Joe Walcott, 80, heavyweight boxing champ. Born with the not very pugilistic-sounding name of Arnold Raymond Cream, Walcott—his ring name—owned the rare distinction of having knocked down Joe Louis three times over the course of two fights, both of which Walcott went on to lose. He finally won the heavyweight championship in 1951 at the age of 37—until George Foreman in 1994, the oldest man ever to attain the title. A year later, he lost his belt to Rocky Marciano.

Bud Wilkinson, 77, winning University of Oklahoma football coach and sports broadcaster. Wilkinson coached the Oklahoma Sooners to three national championships during the 1950s and 47 straight wins between 1953 and 1957, an N.C.A.A. record that still stands.

Marion Williams, 66, influential gospel singer. Williams was the greatest gospel singer of her generation and a performer who crossed over to a worldwide audience by sheer dint of her gifts as a vocalist and innovator. Born in Miami, Williams began singing when she was three. In 1947 she joined the Clara Ward Singers and swiftly became the group's star. In 1959 she formed the Stars of Faith before going solo in the '60s. Known for vocal pyrotechnics, including octave-spanning leaps into falsetto that inspired rocker Little Richard, Williams was an eclectic and canny stylist whose influences ranged from blues to folk to calypso music. ■

Nobel Prizes

Peace
YASSER ARAFAT, *PLO chairman*

YITZHAK RABIN AND SHIMON PERES
*Prime Minister and Foreign Minister
of Israel*

Literature
KENZABURO OE, *Japan*

Physics
CLIFFORD G. SHULL, *U.S.A.*

BERTRAM N. BROCKHOUSE,
*Canada for the development of
neutron scattering.*

Chemistry
GEORGE A. OLAH, *U.S.A.*
for advances in hydrocarbon research

Medicine
ALFRED G. GILMAN, *U.S.A.*

MARTIN RODBELL, *U.S.A*
*for their discovery of G-proteins,
molecules that help carry messages
between cells*

Economics
JOHN F. NASH, *U.S.A.*

JOHN C. HARSANYI, *U.S.A.*

REINHARD SELTEN, *Germany
for their work in the field of game
theory and decision-making.*

Academy Awards

Best Picture
SCHINDLER'S LIST

Best Director
STEPHEN SPIELBERG, *Schindler's List*

Best Actor
TOM HANKS, *Philadelphia*

Best Actress
HOLLY HUNTER, *The Piano*

Best Supporting Actor
TOMMY LEE JONES, *The Fugitive*

Best Supporting Actress
ANNA PAQUIN, *The Piano*

Tony Awards

Best Play
ANGELS IN AMERICA: PERESTROIKA

Best Musical
PASSION

Best Play Revival
AN INSPECTOR CALLS

Best Musical Revival
CAROUSEL

Best Actress, Play
DIANA RIGG, *Medea*

Best Actor, Play
STEPHEN SPINELLA,
Angels in America: Perestroika

Best Actress, Musical
DONNA MURPHY, *Passion*

Best Actor, Musical
BOYD GAINES, *She Loves Me*

Grammy Awards

Record of the Year
I WILL ALWAYS LOVE YOU
Whitney Houston

Song of the Year
A WHOLE NEW WORLD
(ALADDIN'S THEME)
Alan Menken and Tim Rice

Album of the Year
THE BODYGUARD
Whitney Houston

New Artist
TONI BRAXTON

Female Pop Vocal
I WILL ALWAYS LOVE YOU
Whitney Houston

Male Pop Vocal
IF I EVER LOSE MY FAITH IN YOU
Sting

Television

Favorite Programs
1. HOME IMPROVEMENT
2. GRACE UNDER FIRE
3. SEINFELD
4. E.R.
5. NFL MONDAY NIGHT FOOTBALL
6. 60 MINUTES
7. NYPD BLUE
8. ROSEANNE
9. MURDER, SHE WROTE
10. ELLEN

Hollywood Box Office

Domestic (in millions)
1. THE LION KING, *$300*
2. FORREST GUMP, *$299*
3. MRS. DOUBTFIRE, *$148*
4. TRUE LIES, *$146*
5. THE SANTA CLAUSE, *$138*
6. THE FLINTSTONES, *$130*
7. CLEAR AND
   PRESENT DANGER, *$122*
8. SPEED, *$121*
9. THE MASK, *$119*
10. MAVERICK, *$102*

Home Videos Rentals
1. MRS. DOUBTFIRE
2. THE FUGITIVE
3. ACE VENTURA: PET DETECTIVE
4. IN THE LINE OF FIRE
5. JURASSIC PARK

Home Video Sales
1. SNOW WHITE AND THE SEVEN
   DWARFS
2. JURASSIC PARK
3. MRS. DOUBTFIRE
4. THE RETURN OF JAFAR
5. SPEED

Books

Fiction

THE BRIDGES OF MADISON COUNTY
Robert James Waller

THE CELESTINE PROPHECY
James Redfield

POLITICALLY CORRECT BEDTIME
STORIES
James Finn Garner

THE CHAMBER
John Grisham

LIKE WATER FOR CHOCOLATE
Laura Esquivel

THE ALIENIST
Caleb Carr

DISCLOSURE
Michael Crichton

THE GIFT
Danielle Steel

SLOW WALTZ IN CEDAR BEND
Robert James Waller

DEBT OF HONOR
Tom Clancy

Non-Fiction

THE BOOK OF VIRTUES
William J. Bennett

EMBRACED BY THE LIGHT
Betty J. Eadie

MIDNIGHT IN THE GARDEN OF GOOD
AND EVIL
John Berendt

SOUL MATES
Thomas Moore

HAVING OUR SAY
Sarah and A. Elizabeth Delany

WOMEN WHO RUN WITH THE
WOLVES
Clarissa Estes

WOULDN'T TAKE NOTHING FOR MY
JOURNEY
Maya Angelou

THE HIDDEN LIFE OF DOGS
Elizabeth Thomas

SAVED BY THE LIGHT
Robert Brinkley

HOW WE DIE
Sherwin B. Nuland

Sports

Baseball
NO WORLD SERIES

Basketball
NBA CHAMPIONSHIP
*Houston Rockets over New York
Knicks*

NCAA MEN'S CHAMPIONSHIP
Arkansas over Duke

NCAA WOMEN'S CHAMPIONSHIP
North Carolina over Louisiana Tech

Football
SUPER BOWL XXVIII
Dallas Cowboys over Buffalo Bills

NCAA NO.1 RATED TEAM
Nebraska

Hockey
NHL STANLEY CUP
*New York. Rangers over Vancouver
Canucks*

Boxing
HEAVYWEIGHT
George Foreman over Michael Moorer

Horse Racing
KENTUCKY DERBY
Go For Gin

PREAKNESS
Tabasco Cat

BELMONT STAKES
Tabasco Cat

HORSE OF THE YEAR
Holy Bull

Golf
MASTERS
Jose Maria Olazabal

U.S. MEN'S OPEN
Ernie Els

U.S. WOMEN'S OPEN
Patty Sheehan

PGA CHAMPIONSHIP
Nick Price

LPGA
Laura Davis

BRITISH OPEN
Nick Price

Tennis
AUSTRALIA OPEN
Pete Sampras, Steffi Graf

FRENCH OPEN
*Sergi Bruguera,
Arantxa Sanchez Vicario*

WIMBLEDON
Pete Sampras, Conchita Martinez

U.S. OPEN
*Andre Agassi,
Arantxa Sanchez Vicario*

Motor Sports
DAYTONA 500
Sterling Marlin

INDY 500
Al Unser Jr.

LE MANS
*Hurley Haywood, Yannick Dalmas,
Marco Baldi*

World Cup Soccer
BRAZIL OVER ITALY

SOURCES: Films: *Variety;*
Television: *Nielsen Media Research;*
Books: *SIMBA Information, Inc.;*
Videos: *Video Business.*

INDEX

CREDITS

Credits listed clockwise from top left of page.

The Year in Review: ii Steve Liss for TIME
iv Terry Ashe for TIME, Louis Gubb—JB
Pictures, Steve Liss for TIME, Richard Hartog—
Outlook **v** Barbara Nessim for TIME (art)
Philip Caruso—Paramount, Molly Thayer
Collection—Magnum Photos, Nancy Kedersha—
Immunogen/SPL/Custom Medical Stock
1 Gianni Giansanti—Sygma, Ted Soqui—Sygma
for TIME, no credit, Jose Azel—Aurora for TIME

Images: 2-3 Terry Ashe for TIME
4-5 Louise Gubb—JB Pictures for TIME
6-7 Michael Lawton, William R. Sollaz—
Duomo **8-9** Christopher Morris—Black Star
for TIME **10-11** James Nachtwey—Magnum
for TIME **12-13** Jack Smith—AP, Internsport
Television **14** Pensacola Police Dept.,
Jonathan Tedder—The Rock Hill *Herald*/
Sygma **15** Steve Liss for TIME **16** (left to
right) Steve Brodner, Tim O'Brien, Greg
Spalenka, Robert Grossman, Joo Chung, John
Blackford/Reuter (photo), Eric White, Eric
White , Alan E. Cober **17** Mark Fredrickson,
C.F. Payne, Kinuko Y. Craft, John S. Dykes,
Glynis Sweeney, C.F. Payne, John S. Dykes,
C.F. Payne, Istvan Banyai—all for TIME.
18-19 Mark Alan Stamaty (art) **20** David
Levenson, Diana Walker for TIME,
Marimoto—Gamma Liaison **21** Yevgeny
Yevtushenko, Diana Walker for TIME, AP.

Nation: 22 Robb Nelson—Black Star for
TIME **23** Cynthia Johnson for TIME **24** Paula
Scully—Gamma Liaison, Michael Schuman—
Saba, Shelly Katz—Gamma Liaison for TIME
25 Diana Walker for TIME, Steve Schneider—
SIPA, Robert Trippett—SIPA **27** Robb Nelson—
Black Star for TIME **30-31** Cynthia Johnson
for TIME **32-33** Dirck Halstead for TIME
34-35 Luke Frazza—AFP (2), Terry Ashe for
TIME **36-37** Tomas Muscionico—Contact
38-39 Mark Ludak—Impact Visuals, Ted Soqui—
Sygma for TIME, Les Stone—Sygma for TIME
40-41 courtesy KCAL, no credit **42** Victor
Malafronte—Celebrity Photo, AP **43** AP (2)
44 Scott Downie—Celebrity Photo **45** Ted
Soqui—Sygma, Roger Sandler, Pool, David
Taylor—SIPA, Sygma **46-47** David Burnett—Con-
tact for TIME **48** U.S. Coast Guard—National
Archives **49** U.S. Army **50-51** Howard
Sochurek—Life, George Silk, International News
Photo, Bill Pierce for TIME, Chuck Nacke—
Woodfin Camp, Black Star, Henry Groskinsky—
Life **52** Bruce Chambers—Orange County *Regis-
ter*/Saba **53** Dirck Halstead for TIME **54** no
credit, Vincent Laforet—Reuter, Jeff Mar-
kowitz—Sygma, Mark Sofia—SIPA **55** Todd
Bigelow—Black Star, Bernie Sampo—Outline,
David Leeson—Dallas *Morning News*/JB
Pictures, Beth Bergman—*Virginian Pilot*/SIPA

World: 56-57 Denis Fairel—AP **58** Louise
Gubb—JB Pictures for TIME **59** Tomas Mus-
cionico—Contact **60** Louise Gubb—JB Pictures
for TIME **61** Sergei Guneyev for TIME, Paul
Lowe—Magnum for TIME **62-63** Christopher
Morris for TIME (2) **64** Ron Haviv—Saba for
TIME **65** Monique Stauber for TIME
66-67 Alfred—SIPA **68-69** Yaacov Saar—

G.P.O., Heidi Levine/Media/SIPA **70** Mary Ann
DeLeo—SIPA **70-71** Rickard Larma—AP
72 Robin Moyer for TIME (background),
Massimo Sambucetti—AP, **73** Diana Walker for
TIME **74** Hiroji Kubota—Magnum **75** Mariella
Furrer—SABA **76** Mariella Furrer—Saba,
Roger Job—Gamma Liaison **77** Luc Delahaye—
Magnum for TIME **78** Ettiore Malanca—SIPA
79 AP, Otto Pohl—Gamma Liaison, Pica Press—
SIPA, Varkonyi—Photo Plus/Sygma

Business: 80 Will Crockett for TIME
81 Duane Burleson—Sygma **83** Will
McIntyre for TIME **84** Ted Thai for TIME
86-87 Steve Liss for TIME **90** Dirck Halstead
for TIME **91** Steven Starr—Saba, Alan
Levenson—LGI, Alex Quesada—Matrix for
TIME, Glen Mitsui—Studio M.D. for TIME (art),
Brian Smith—Outline

Society: 92-93 Barbara Nessim for TIME (art)
96 Roberto Brosan for TIME **97-99** Gary
Baseman for TIME (art) **100-101** Jean Tuttle
for TIME (art) **102-103** Giraudon—Art
Resource, N.Y. (art), AP—Pool, Saba—Pool
(photos) **104** Giraudon—Art Resource, N.Y. (art),
Brad Markel—Gamma Liaison (photo), Scala—
Art Resource, N.Y. (art), Sygma (photo)
105 Granger Collection (art), Outline (photo),
Granger Collection (art), Outline (photo)
106 Barthelmy—SIPA, Gerardo Somoza—
Outline, Simons—Gamma Liaison **107** Gerardo
Somoza—Outline, C. Lecca, Gerardo Somoza—
Outline, Barthelmy—SIPA **108** Spartanburg
Herald-Tribune Journal/Sygma, American Fast
Photo—Saba **109** Barry Talesnick—Retna,
Steve Liss for TIME, Dayton *Daily News*/
Sygma, no credit.

Man of the Year: 110-117 Gianni
Giansanti—Sygma

Science: 118-119 Peter McGregor,
Australian National University, provided by
NASA/Goddard Space Flight Center **120** John
Spencer—Lowell Observatory, Darren Depoy,
Jay Fogel—Ohio State University, Nick
Schneider—CU/LASP, provided by NASA/God-
dard **123** NIC/NIH—Photo Take **124** Robert
Holmgren for TIME, Los Alamos National
Laboratory (background) **125** George Frey for
TIME, Nancy Kedersha—Immunogen/SPL/Cus-
tom Medical Stock **126** ©Jay H. Matternes,
Michele Burgess (background) **127** Mark
Richards—DOT for TIME **130** Stock Market, no
credit, Dan McCoy—Rainbow, Schleichkorn—
Custom Medical Stock, no credit (center)
131 Daniel J. Cox—Gamma Liaison, Nick
Ellison—American Museum of Natural History,
Robert Goldstrum for TIME (art) Research by
Karen Phillips, NASA/AP.

Olympics: 132-133 Clive Brunskill—All
Sport for TIME **134** Mike Powell—All Sport for
TIME, Richard Martin-Vandystadt—All Sport
for TIME, Clive Brunskill—All Sport for TIME
135 E. Sampers—Gamma Liaison **136** Jose
Azel—Aurora for TIME, Mike Powell—All Sport
for TIME Clive Brunskill—All Sport for TIME
137 John Biever—Sports Illustrated, Richard
Martin-Vandystadt—All Sport, Tom Lynn—

CBS/Sports Illustrated **138** Jose Azel—Aurora
for TIME, Mike Powell—All Sport for TIME,
Chris Cole—All Sport for TIME **139** Bob
Martin—All Sport for TIME, Pascal Rondeau—
All Sport for TIME (inset), Jose Azel—Aurora
for TIME (2) **140** Doug Bechtel—The *Orego-
nian*/Sygma, Brent Mojahn—The *Oregonian*/
Sygma, Joel Davis—The *Oregonian*/Sygma,
Scott Troyanos—AP, Pascal Rondeau—All
Sport for TIME

The Arts & Media: 142-143 Josh Gosfeld
for TIME (art) **144** Aaron Rapaport—Onyx for
TIME **145** Joan Marcus (2) **147** Ken
Regan—Camera 5 **148-49** Ben Radford—All
Sport, C. S. Botterill—All Sport, PhotoNews—
Gamma Liaison, David Cannon, All Sport (2),
Texeira-Giavelli—Zeta—SIPA, Rick Stewart—All
Sport, David Cannon—All Sport (2)
150 Bernie Sampo—Outline, Alex Bailey—
Sygma **151** Paul Harris—Outline, Lee
Crum—Outline **152-53** Mark Kaufman—
Sports Illustrated, National Baseball Library,
Cooperstown, N.Y. (3), Richard Schultz for
TIME, Bettmann Archive **154** Salvador Dali
Museum **155** Metropolitan Museum
156 Collection David Geffen **157** Richard
Schultz for TIME, no credit **158** Miramax
Films (2) Walt Disney Pictures, Miramax,
Fineline, Castle Rock **159** no credit,
Nannarello—Shooting Star, Steve Double—
Retna, Silvia Lelli—DGG, Brian Smith—Outline
(center) **160** Frank Griffin—SIPA, ©1994
Farworks, Inc., Paul Drinkwater, Sven
Arnstein **161** Carol Rosegg, William Mercer
McLeod for TIME, Andrew Leynse, Dan Rest

People: 162 Martin Keene—Press
Association **163** Alpha/Globe Photos
164 Hartley/Beirne/Rex, Rex Features
165 Dick Zimmerman—Shooting Star,
Deborah Feingold—Outline, Holly Stern—All
Sport, Richard Foreman—Sygma, Kathy
Banks—Sygma **166** Alan Levenson for TIME,
Wilfredo Lee—AP, Simon Bruty—All Sport,
Jonathan Daniel—All Sport, Vladimir Sichov—
SIPA for TIME **167** (top) Wayne Stambler—
Onyx, Harry Benson, Danny Clinch—Outline,
Marowitz—Sygma (couples) Steve Sand—
Outline, Kelly Jordan—Celebrity Photo, All
Action—Retna, Kelly Jordan—Celebrity
Photo—Mark Deville—Gamma Liaison—
Michael Ferguson—Globe

Milestones: 168 Molly Thayer Collection—
Magnum Photos **169** Mark Shaw—Photo
Researchers **170-71** Molly Thayer Col-
lection—Magnum Photos, Paul Schutzer—Life,
Ken Heyman—Woodfin Camp **172** Frank
Micelotta—Outline **173** Sharland—Life,
174 Ben Martin for TIME, **175** Mike
Stewart—Sygma **176** Victoria Yakota—
Washington *Times*/Sygma, **177** Dennis
Brack—Black Star **178** Larry Barns—Black
Star **180** Russel Wong—Outline, Walt Disney
Productions, Globe Photos, Exley—Gamma
Liaison, Deville-Merillon—Gamma Liaison,
Rangefinders **181** Ken Regan—TriStar, Ivan
Kyncl, Doug Pensinger—All Sport, Exley—
Gamma Liaison, Lisa Rose—Globe Photos,
Bernard Fallon—Outline